# elusive justice

The *Teaching/Learning Social Justice* Series
Edited by Lee Anne Bell, Barnard College, Columbia University

*Critical Race Counterstories along the Chicana/Chicano Educational Pipeline*
Tara J. Yosso

*Understanding White Privilege: Creating Pathways to Authentic Relationships Across Race*
Frances E. Kendall

*Elusive Justice: Wrestling with Difference and Educational Equity in Everyday Practice*
Thea Renda Abu El-Haj

# elusive justice

Wrestling

with Difference

and Educational Equity

in Everyday Practice

# thea renda abu el-haj

### foreword by michelle fine

Routledge
Taylor & Francis Group
New York   London

Routledge is an imprint of the
Taylor & Francis Group, an informa business

Routledge
Taylor & Francis Group
270 Madison Avenue
New York, NY 10016

Routledge
Taylor & Francis Group
2 Park Square
Milton Park, Abingdon
Oxon OX14 4RN

© 2006 by Taylor & Francis Group, LLC
Routledge is an imprint of Taylor & Francis Group, an Informa business

Printed in the United States of America on acid-free paper
10 9 8 7 6 5 4 3 2 1

International Standard Book Number-10: 0-415-95366-9 (Softcover) 0-415-95365-0 (Hardcover)
International Standard Book Number-13: 978-0-415-95366-5 (Softcover) 978-0-415-95365-8 (Hardcover)

---

**Library of Congress Cataloging-in-Publication Data**

---

Abu El-Haj, Thea Renda.
  Elusive justice : wrestling with difference and educational equity in everyday practice / Thea Renda Abu El-Haj.
       p. cm. -- (Teaching/learning social justice)
   Includes bibliographical references and index.
   ISBN 0-415-95365-0 (hb : alk. paper) -- ISBN 0-415-95366-9 (pb : alk. paper)
   1. Educational equalization--United States. 2. Discrimination in education--United States. I. Title. II. Series.

LC213.2.A25 2006
379.2'6--dc22                                                                 2006004864

**Visit the Taylor & Francis Web site at**
**http://www.taylorandfrancis.com**

**and the Routledge Web site at**
**http://www.routledge-ny.com**

## Dedication

*In memory of my father, Ribhi Ali Abu El-Haj, who learned early in life the injustices wrought by war and displacement, and shaped a life dedicated to creating conditions of greater economic equity in the Middle East*

*and*

*To my mother, Sandra Lee Abu El-Haj, who has modeled a steady commitment in her life and devoted her work to reaching across the differences that too often divide us*

# Contents

# Series Editor's Introduction

The Teaching/Learning Social Justice Series concentrates on issues of social justice—diversity, equality, democracy, and justice—in classrooms and communities. "Teaching/learning" connotes the vital connections between theory and practice that books in this series seek to illuminate. Central are the stories and lived experiences of people who strive both to critically analyze and challenge oppressive relationships and institutions, and to imagine and create more just and inclusive alternatives. My goal is for the series to balance critical analysis with images of hope and possibility in ways that are accessible and inspiring to a broad range of educators and activists. I want the series to resonate for those who believe in the potential for social change through education and who seek stories and examples of practice, as well as honest discussion of the ever-present obstacles to dismantling oppressive ideas and institutions.

*Elusive Justice: Wrestling with Difference and Educational Equity in Everyday Practice* by Thea Abu El-Haj realizes these goals so impressively and with such elegance that, in many ways, she provides the grounding philosophical frame for the work of this series. She considers essential questions about how we define justice that shape decisions about practice: How can we build just school communities, truly inclusive of diverse constituents, without forcing conformity to a dominant norm that privileges some over others? What are the limitations of the ideal of integration as a justice claim? Is it fair to hold students to the same standards when the conditions for meeting them are so grossly unequal? For whose benefit have reigning standards been constructed in the first place? How do we attend to difference, when the power and inequalities that construct difference are not themselves interrogated and so easily elide into deficit thinking?

Insisting on the possibility of a theory/practice of educational justice that can live up to the needs of an active democracy in which human diversity is truly recognized and valued, Abu El-Haj opts for a relational view of difference. Such a view requires us first to scrutinize and ultimately dismantle the unequal relationships and distribution of resources from which difference is currently constructed, ceding a "normalcy" that disadvantages and excludes those considered "different." From such newly prepared ground, we might then cultivate a process of social imagination that creates and recreates inclusive educational community from and for the needs and contributions of all. This is certainly fertile ground for teaching/learning social justice, and I am eager to see this articulate and insightful book enter educational debates about equity and justice that are so crucial to the realization of democratic aims for schooling.

**Lee Anne Bell**

# Foreword

In schools where inequities are naturalized, taken for granted, or assumed immutable, few speak about injustice. Dead air circulates and conversations-never-had occupy the teachers' lounge. Everyone coughs from the stale air, but most children of poverty and color choke—or they leave, with mind if not body.

In *Elusive Justice: Wrestling with Difference and Educational Equity in Everyday Practice*, Thea Abu El-Haj offers a rich analytic portrait of what relational justice sounds like in conversations held deliberately in schools situated at both ends of the American dream/nightmare. Her ethnography escorts us into two educational spaces explicitly committed to discourses of difference and justice: City Friends, a Quaker K–12 school dedicated at once to an elite legacy and to diversity, and Parks, a public middle school inspired by the Coalition of Essential Schools, crushed by paltry resources. Both schools are perched on a shared contradiction, the desire to educate for justice in a profoundly unjust world.

*Elusive Justice* makes visible the taken-for-granted assumptions that organize the accepted coexistence of well-resourced and under-resourced education. Navigating between these two very distinct schools, we confront the cruel deceit of the American dream. While a teacher at City Friends confides that a relative has offered a million-dollar contribution to the school, teachers from Parks routinely buy paper and resources with their own money. By examining the "ideas that animate action" in these settings marked sharply by wealth and poverty, Abu El-Haj insists that we see how "differences" of capital, racism, gender and disability politics, high-stakes testing, and the thickening walls that separate public from private mark the bodies, conversations, and possibilities of schools.

A brilliant ethnographer of educational policy and practice, Abu El-Haj helps us see when "difference" signifies a human right to access and recognition, and when it degenerates into a trope for deficit; where "difference" swells as a source of strength and where it shrinks to shame; and for whom "difference" embodies a mark of recognition and for whom it coagulates as a tattoo of disposability.

In this intellectual journey, Abu El-Haj delicately pries open a thick understanding of three educational "justice claims," interrogating how difference matters in "everyday practice." The first justice claim she considers is integration, at once advancing and troubling the notion. Rather than forwarding a simple version of placing "different" bodies into the same room or school, she argues for substantive inclusion, whereby all learners are considered "morally equivalent," with explicit consideration of their many delicious differences. We witness how this claim for integration was deliberated by examining how educators at Parks work with a broad range of academic biographies/learning differences, in the midst of a 30% budget cut that squeezed resources dry. As we realize the historic layering of disadvantages imposed on the bodies of these young people, we grow suspicious of the origin of their now embodied "disabilities."

To get inside the second justice claim of recognition, Abu El-Haj offers up complex examples of a school working to re-center and respect those who have been pushed to the periphery. Tracking the history and practice of the Gender Audit at City Friends, we can see that just beneath the spoken issue lay a series of highly inflammatory concerns left unattended. With Abu El-Haj's careful guidance, we witness how hard conversations about gender and race are launched, and then occluded, or sideswiped, when faculty discomfort prevails. "Although the Gender Audit Committee eventually opened the door for new conversations about both race and gender ... the Gender Audit lived constantly under the necessity of appearing to have no political agenda." Ultimately, the practitioner inquiry into race and gender opened up conversations that helped sponsor a performance of *For Colored Girls* to feature the contributions of African-American girls to the school.

The third justice claim that Abu El-Haj unpacks involves the highly contentious claim of equal standards. She argues convincingly that all learners deserve high-quality educators and rigorous curriculum, but reveals how simple-minded policies and practices undertaken in the name of equality often produce highly inequitable outcomes.

As I read her writings on the perverse consequences of the equal standards argument, I tripped upon a memory of my son's third grade classroom where I watched "difference-as-deficit" produced in the dangerous waters of public elementary school, where high-stakes testing is colonizing the developmental diversities of childhood in the name of equality.

"OK," the test prep monitor explains to a classroom rich in race, ethnic, and class diversity. "We're going to have timed multiplication practice tests. You'll have three minutes, and then the test will be over. At that point, you can multiply the number you got right by two to determine the percent correct. Remember, speed and accuracy count."

I glanced quickly at Caleb, my son. He was done way too early.

In what seemed like three hours, the three minutes passed.

"Who got 100?" She asked the dreaded question.

Caleb threw me a look, not sure if I would approve of his responding in the affirmative. We exchanged a knowing smile of pride, ambivalence, and warning. He knows he dare not perform that flailing-arm-in-the-air-to-prove-I-got-100-white-boy-routine.

Six arms shoot up: two white boys, two black boys, a black girl. Can't attach the sixth arm to a body.

Scanning the room, I see that tears slowly fall from Tashana's and Lavone's eyes.

Tashana, usually bold, sassy, in your face, running to me for a hug; Lavone, quiet, to herself, usually begging to read with me.

They got 72 and 80.

I wander over, to comfort and whisper, "Who cares about speed?" As an elementary school "slow reader," the echoes of "failing" are full-body for me.

Tracy, the light-skinned Jamaican-American girl, smiles hesitantly, "Michelle, I got 100!"

Lavone—sitting across from Tracy—snapped: "I hate this." She then refocused her eyes squarely on Tracy and said, "Shut up. You make me feel bad."

Tashana (fighting her own tears, protecting Lavone): "She cryin'. Stop showing off."

Tracy looked at me, so sweetly, as if to ask in a very quiet silence, "Can't I be proud?"

Teacher: "So, today we have six perfect scores; last time we had three. See, you're all getting better."

Two heads down, falling heavier and more publicly than the tears.

"If you got 100, you can play any of the games. If you got below 80, please do the multiplication games" (which, in fairness, looked like fun).

"That ain't fair."

"I hate math."

"I don't wanna do multiplication."

Comments of defeat popcorn through the room.

Amanda, a white girl with pigtails and a pink boa, asks: "Does this go on our permanent record?"

Now I have joined Tashana and Lavone. I too am crying. The tears, of course, do go on their permanent records. No one stands comfortably in the room. And difference—as deficit—is drip-fed into the soul. The tyrannies of time, sameness, and testing prevail, as inquiry, curiosity, and childhood passions drain.

Challenging the discourse of equal standards, Abu El-Haj takes the position that "for students to experience fully the power of academic achievement and be truly included in the educational community, we must interrogate the values, norms and assumptions embedded in the academic standards and pedagogical approaches themselves. As a justice claim, recognition offers a much stronger foundation for substantive inclusion. Acknowledging multiple perspectives, knowledge, values, and norms represented in the community allows people to participate in substantive, meaningful ways—to be full members of the community."

In this volume, Abu El-Haj at once enumerates the grotesque differences between Parks and City Friends, and she theorizes these schools as allies in the struggle for educational justice. By documenting how both schools wrestle with "what's fair," she signals a desire to stretch the moral community of education to include a broad, multicultural, cross-class landscape of public and private schooling in America. She crafts a cross-site community of educators working through differences across zip codes, toward substantive inclusion. Because Abu El-Haj is such a talented writer, you'll be seduced by the passionate commitments that drive educators' justice claims, and you'll understand that schools need hard, dissentful conversations to thrive. You may even hear Hannah Arendt's words from *The Origins of Totalitarianism*:

> Total loyalty is possible only when fidelity is emptied of all concrete content, from which changes of mind might naturally arise.

As if in conversation with Arendt, Thea Abu El-Haj makes it clear that critical talk about difference and justice nourishes schools, freedom, and democracy. When such talk stops, institutions ossify and democracy weakens. As Franz Fanon tells us, there is nothing as dangerous as an ossified society, where no new thoughts are possible.

Give this book as a gift to your child's teacher, your students, your colleagues, and then go out for coffee or ice cream or wine and talk about the small moves that make, and unmake, just educational communities. And then press on to ask about the big difference that too few are willing to discuss: not the "differences" within these schools, but the enormous difference between. In the first major text of what promises to be a rich and provocative scholarly career, Thea Abu El-Haj invites us into conversations never had.

## Further Reading

Arendt, H. (1973). *The Origins of Totalitarianism*. New York: Harvest Publishers.

Fanon, F. (1967). *Black Skin, White Masks*. New York: Grove Press.

Griffin, A. G., and Parkerson, M. (1995). *A Litany for Survival: The Life and Work of Audre Lorde*. New York: Third World Newsreel.

**Michelle Fine**

# Acknowledgments

I have always begun books by reading the author's acknowledgments because I am curious to get a glimpse of the community within which the work took shape. I have long looked forward to acknowledging the many colleagues, friends, and family members who have nurtured this work.

The practitioners at Parks Middle School and City Friends deserve my greatest thanks for their generosity in opening their school communities to me, offering their ideas and perspectives, and being supportive of this project. For their willingness to let me journey alongside them for awhile as they engage the brave, difficult, and imperfect work of making schools more responsive and caring places for all children, I am deeply appreciative.

Many people supported this work long before the book took shape in its current form. Bryan Brayboy, Caroline Brayer-Ebby, Jody Cohen, Ellen Foley, Alice Ginsberg, Peter Kuriloff, Alice Lesnick, Cathy Luna, Dirck Roosevelt, and Paul Skilton-Sylvester were all critical readers of my work well before the idea of justice claims organized my thinking. Patricia Carini, Frederick Erickson, and Michelle Fine have been true intellectual mentors. My very first year of teaching, Pat taught me to see *and* practice what many years later I have come to call "a relational stance toward difference." Her unwavering commitment to putting children's strengths, passions, and interests at the heart of teaching has offered a constant reminder of what might and should be at the center of schools. Michelle Fine's sparkling intellect, boundless passion, and political commitment to shaping a better world have been an inspiration for many years. Her work exploring the ways that institutions structure inequity, examining possibilities for social transformation and theorizing research methodology for and with communities has influenced, in uncountable ways, my own. Fred Erickson, through his own work on the politics of cultural differences, his ethical commitments to children and teachers, and his profound faith in human agency, has fundamentally shaped how I think about how differences come to make the differences they do in schools. He is truly one of the few "Renaissance" men I know, and I have delighted in the surprising paths, across history and societies, upon which our conversations have roamed—conversations that broadened the scope of this work and helped me see how we, as educators, might make a real difference through the school communities we build.

I could not have written this book without the many years of constant support from my writing group. Janine Remillard, Kathy Schultz, and Ellen Skilton-Sylvester saw this project through more drafts than I can count. At every point, they encouraged me and were the best "critical friends" a writer could want. In addition, Kathy and Ellen have proved the most constant of friends, contributing to this book in so many different ways. They have written side by side with me in libraries and coffee shops, and provided steadiness, moral and intellectual support, and much good humor over so many years. Kathy read the manuscript from beginning to end in its final stages, and her close reading and intellectual insights helped sharpen the argument in important ways. Ellen read and reread multiple versions of the final draft of this book up to the very last minute. She helped me organize, edit, and clarify my writing and my arguments, and held out the promise of play as a reward when I was all done.

Cheryl Stayton has been the best of friends from start to finish. I also owe many thanks to her for spending a week in Vermont with me, helping me stay focused during long days of writing, and preparing wonderful meals to share each evening.

Dana Barron, Demi Kurz, and Luz Marin, of the Alice Paul Center for Research on Women and Gender at the University of Pennsylvania, deserve many thanks for providing support and a quiet place to work and write for two years. The Spencer Foundation helped support this work at different stages. A Dissertation Fellowship for Research Related to Education offered me protected time to write up my first study of Parks and City Friends. A School Reform Planning Grant allowed me to return to Parks for a second round of data collection. My colleagues Jolley Bruce Christman, Ellen Foley, and Rosalie Rolón-Dow took that journey back to Parks with me, and I am grateful for the many insights they offered about systemic reform.

The central ideas in this book have benefited from the feedback of many generous colleagues. Chapter 1 benefited from Jim Giarelli's philosopher-perspective. Bill Ayers, Bryan Brayboy, Rosalie Rolón-Dow, and Jacob Hodes all offered invaluable insights about Chapter 3. (Rosalie is also due thanks for her constant presence, wise reminders of what is really important in life, and many days of writing alongside me throughout this process.) An important conversation with my philosopher friends Meira Levinson and Rob Reich pushed me to think about and articulate the argument I am making about why integration is a justice claim. Liz Blair, Caroline Brayer-Ebby, Amy Rhodes, Beth Rubin, and Paul Skilton-Sylvester have all helped me think through Chapter 4. Sukey Blanc, Rosalie Rolon-Dow, Caroline Brayer-Ebby, Alice Ginsberg, and Peter Kuriloff offered important insights on parts of Chapter 5. Thanks also to *Curriculum Inquiry* for permission to reprint, with revisions, my work on gender that is now part of Chapter 5.

Lee Anne Bell encouraged me to believe in this project and gave me valuable feedback on the arguments; I feel honored to have this book in her Teaching/Learning for Social Justice Series. Catherine Bernard and Brook Cosby, my editors at Routledge, were attentive to argument and detail. Three anonymous reviewers offered careful critiques and helped me sharpen my language and my argument. My thanks also go to Alison Anderson who was a wonderful copyeditor. Carla Shalaby provided amazing assistance in so many ways, attending to everything from the small, tedious details of reference lists to critical feedback on my writing with great suggestions for revisions. She met impossible deadlines that I gave her, and for that I am truly grateful.

Above all others, my family has provided the love and care necessary for this work to emerge. My mother, Sandra Abu El-Haj, has modeled the importance of and capacity for reaching across differences through her cultural travels. She has been a steadfast and reliable presence, and she spent many weekends visiting me and caring for my children while I worked. Sadly, my father, Ribhi Abu El-Haj, did not live to see this book published; however, his constant faith that his three daughters would find their own paths to contribute in some way to building a better world has never left me. My passion for justice has its roots in his life commitments to creating conditions for economic equity in developing countries. My sister Nadia Abu El-Haj has given much wise council about how to go about writing a book and has helped me understand questions of culture and power more deeply. My sister Tabatha Abu El-Haj has influenced me greatly with her deeply philosophical approaches to the dilemmas of everyday living and her strong commitments to social justice; a careful listener and subtle thinker, she has shaped this text in ways she probably cannot imagine. My mother-in-law, Mildred Rosenzweig, and late father-in-law, Benjamin Rosenzweig, have been a tremendous source of support and love in more ways than they know.

Steve Rosenzweig, my husband, has maintained faith and commitment to my work and to the possibility of building relationship across differences, without which I would have quit many times. He has also supported this work in many important tangible (food, outings with our girls, and more) ways. Steve demonstrates every day that intellectual and spiritual commitments need not be mutually exclusive, and that it is possible to deconstruct dominant paradigms with heart as well as mind. His steady love, humor, and belief that there is purpose in all we do and face in our lives teaches me much about living in this world. Reem and Saria Rosen-Haj, my daughters, have patiently shared their mother with this book for many years. Reem's constancy of purpose and vision, passionate stance for everyday justice, and her amazing skills as a budding novelist amaze and inspire me constantly. Saria's lightness of spirit, compassion, and grace in meeting the challenges and joys of her life awe me. Reem and Saria remind me that children make their worlds with passion and commitment every day, and in that, I hold hope for our future.

# Introduction

On January 18, 2006, *The Philadelphia Inquirer* ran a front-page article on the controversial move to open several new single-sex public schools in the local school district (Woodall, 1/18/06). The article described a growing movement, across the nation's cities, to offer single-sex public schools as one more remedy for the persistent educational inequalities that students of color and students from low-income families endure. According to the article, advocates argue that single-sex schools benefit both boys and girls, and focus on research that purports to show that girls and boys learn differently. Opponents worry that these schools violate antidiscrimination statutes and tend to reinforce rather than debunk race and gender stereotypes. I offer this story as one example of powerful, and ongoing, public debates about education that, as I argue in this book, entail conflicting notions of justice and contentious beliefs about difference. At the heart of this disagreement, for example, rests a debate about whether educational equity is served by treating boys and girls the same or differently. Equally important, as I explore in this book, this debate about educational equity is intertwined with our understanding of difference. The question of whether single-sex public city schools serve to promote or detract from equity turns, in part, on our conflicting ideas about why and how the differences of race and gender come to make the differences they do in educational settings.

This book addresses how we, not only as individuals, but as a society, think about and act upon the differences that make a difference in education. Looking inside local schools, I examine how discourse and practice about difference inside these institutions are intimately bound up with a set

1

of contending claims about educational justice. In focusing on discourse about difference and justice, I am explicitly working against the recurring tendency of legislators, policy makers, and many educational reformers to move directly to practice-based remedies for educational inequality, bypassing critical, contentious dialogue about the sources of this inequality and about various definitions of equity. I argue that by uncovering the multiple, conflicting notions of justice and difference that operate inside schools, we can better understand why the search for educational equity remains elusive, and we can engage in dialogue about the broad aims of equitable education in a democratic society.

As an educational anthropologist, I am advocating for a view of justice firmly grounded in the complexity and contradictions of everyday practice. In 1995, I began a longitudinal ethnographic study of two schools in which educators were investigating, challenging, and renegotiating their assumptions and practices in relationship to particular dimensions of difference. At Parks Middle School,[1] a small public school that was part of a large Northern U.S. city's desegregation program, practitioners were engaged in rethinking their practices in relationship to learning diversity. City Friends, a K–12 independent Quaker school in the same city, had undertaken a study of gender and was simultaneously investigating questions about race and ethnicity. In my initial research, I was interested in tracking the range of discourse about difference in the midst of self-conscious efforts at social change. As I listened to the various frameworks within which educators understood the meaning and significance of difference in their schools, what I heard was an intertwining set of claims about justice. Discourse about difference was always intimately bound up with complex, puzzling, and often-contentious ideas about what constitutes a fair and just educational community.

In their work to create more equitable practices, these educators were wrestling with fundamental questions about justice and its relationship to the differences that make a difference in education. The feminist political philosopher Iris Young argues that thinking about difference challenges our basic ideas about justice. She urges that, rather than building theories about justice based on abstract universal principles, we must pay attention to justice claims in particular local contexts, for it is only in the specifics that justice can be conceptualized and pursued (1990). In this book, I offer an account of how various justice claims animate the work of educators struggling to build more equitable educational institutions across the lines of race/ethnicity, gender, and disability. I ask how ideas about justice and difference, implicit within educational discourses and practices, facilitate and limit the elusive strivings to build just, inclusive schools.

This book has three broad arguments. First, I focus on key claims about justice—manifested in the two schools—that implicitly organize various approaches to redressing educational inequality. I connect these local justice claims to broader public discourse about the interaction between difference and justice in a democratic society. Although this public discourse about justice and difference resonates with contemporary debates in political philosophy, I approach this book not as a philosopher but from the position of an anthropologist of education concerned with how difference and inequality are produced and resisted within particular institutional contexts. I trust that political philosophers will forgive me for borrowing various threads of their disciplinary conversations as they inform the central arguments of this book; however, I hope to illuminate the gritty, everyday dilemmas that arise out of these competing claims about educational justice to inform our thinking about policy and practice.

Second, through an examination of discourse about difference (specifically race/ethnicity, gender, and disability), I explore how our ways of thinking about difference often structure possibilities for action. Ultimately, I argue for a relational view of difference that focuses on how differences are produced in specific contexts by virtue of reigning institutional norms and assumptions. These norms and assumptions must be made visible to create more inclusive, just educational environments (see especially, Minow, 1990; Varenne and McDermott, 1998; Young, 1990).

Third, in focusing on ideas that animate action, this book seeks to illuminate the relationship between discourse, practice, and power. Rather than searching for specific policies or practices that aim to solve the problem of educational inequality, I argue for the power of discourse as a key site for social action and change. Interpretation matters. It propels what we can and cannot imagine and, as such, it creates and limits possibilities for action. Those of us who work in the field of education constantly face the push for reliable remedies and guaranteed solutions to the seemingly intractable problem of educational inequality; however, I suggest that this press to action too often fails to interrogate our fundamental assumptions about difference and justice—assumptions that are critical to the solutions we devise.

This, then, is a book about the relationship between ideas and practice. I seek, from a perspective grounded in the everyday work of schools, to open up to scrutiny and dialogue the range of ways we conceptualize difference and justice. Ethnography makes vivid the everyday dilemmas of practice that arise from the conflicting ideas about difference and justice embedded in policy, curriculum, and pedagogy. In the midst of the cacophony of recurrent educational debates about which specific policies and practices will realize educational equity, I listen instead for the ideas—manifested in talk and practice—that power educators' work. Through an exploration of these ideas in action, I hope to offer a picture of the complex and uneven nature of teaching for equity in contexts deeply saturated with inequality. It is only, I believe, by accounting for this complexity that we can generate possibilities for action that might truly make all the difference in particular schools and classrooms.

## Studying Discourses of Difference in Everyday Practice

Parks Middle School and City Friends are, in most ways, very different from each other. The contrasts are plentiful. Parks is a public school, part of the city desegregation program; City Friends is an independent Quaker school. Parks's students are majority African-American; City Friends's students are majority white. Parks struggled to maintain its level of programming because, every year, it saw its finances reduced by an underfunded school district; City Friends had a large endowment that allowed it, in the late 1990s, to undertake a major new building project and to expand programs. Although the contrasting contexts of the schools had a deep impact on the questions I address in this book, it was not for comparative reasons that I chose these research sites. Rather, I chose City Friends and Parks because of their similarity: Practitioners at both schools were committed to examining their practices in relationship to some dimension of difference to build more equitable educational environments.

I began this study as an exploration of how these educators thought about difference in the midst of self-conscious efforts to address and redress educational inequalities. By perching inside the various sites in which these educators were investigating questions about race, gender, disability, and learning diversity, I sought to understand how discourse about difference framed the practice-based approaches that educators took to create more equitable schools. Looking inside these transformative projects, I wanted to investigate how undergirding discourses about difference created or limited possibilities for educational change. Wishing to take what McCarthy (1990) has called a nonsynchronous approach to difference—one that accounts for the intersection and relationship between race, class, gender, sexuality, and disability—I chose schools that had very different social ecologies (particularly along the lines of race and class) as a way of highlighting particular dynamics that might take different courses in each setting.

What began as a study of the discourses about difference that were articulated in contexts of educational inquiry and reform ended up revealing a set of justice claims that implicitly structured these local efforts. Through my analysis of the data, I came to hear, echoed within everyday discourses and practices, ideas about justice (or justice claims) that reverberate through public discourses about education. By public discourse, I mean all the ways that we, as educators, parents, policy makers, and legislators—as a nation—deliberate about educational equity. These justice claims are not the same as those debated by political philosophers. They are ideas afloat in the public imagination that take shape in the everyday practices of schools, and engender queries and struggles for educators.

## Justice Claims: Public Deliberation in Practice

This book explores how powerful public arguments about justice and difference play out within local school contexts. The educators with whom I worked, similar to their counterparts elsewhere, were wrestling with the messy, contradictory nature of ideas in practice. Woven through the practitioners' inquiries into difference and their efforts to create more inclusive schools were critical justice claims. I use this term "justice claim" to suggest frameworks within which ideas about equity are organized in everyday discourse and practice. Young (1990) argues for the importance of developing situated analyses of justice. She writes:

> While everyday discourse about justice certainly makes claims, these are not theorems to be demonstrated in a self-enclosed system. They are instead calls, pleas, claims *upon* some people by others. Rational reflection on justice begins in a hearing, in heeding a call, rather than in asserting and mastering a state of affairs, however, ideal. The call to "be just" is always situated in concrete social and political practices that precede and exceed the philosopher. ... Reflective discourse about justice makes arguments, but these are not intended as definitive demonstrations. They are addressed to others and await their response, in a situated political dialogue. (1990, p. 5)

I understand each school's grounded struggles about how best to address difference to reflect "a situated political dialogue" in which educators were making and responding to claims about what constitutes just practice. The educators with whom I worked would not describe themselves as explicitly engaged in political dialogue about justice. At the heart of their struggles to improve educational practice for their students, however, rested the questions: What is fair? How can we make this a more inclusive community? How can we make this a place where all students are successful? I suggest that these questions—and the disagreements they engendered—reflected an ongoing, grounded dialogue about what educational justice looks like in practice. Through my analysis, I came to see that this dialogue was organized around three central justice claims that invoked integration, equal standards, and recognition of difference as organizing principles for thinking about building just educational communities.

Through a close examination of these three claims, I want to draw our attention to the fact that, in relationship to difference, multiple important justice claims are being debated inside schools. Since the 1980s, public debates about educational justice and the policies that ensue have focused primarily on economic productivity and the "achievement gap," and have seriously narrowed the scope of our imagination for what educational justice might entail. Elaborating the three justice claims—integration, equal standards, and recognition—makes visible a range of important goals to which truly democratic schools must aspire. The two schools are rich sites from which we can hear echoed the broader public debates about justice and its relationship to difference in a democracy. The problem of educational justice is a problem of our society. Schools are important sites for change, hope, and possibility, but they do not float free of the broad inequalities embedded in our larger society. Through this ethnographic account, we can see these deliberations about justice and difference unfold within the complexity of practice.

## Integration

One enduring outcome of the Civil Rights Movement is that the ideal of integration is bound up with our notions of educational justice. This is the case, even though the racial integration of schools (and the educational equality it was intended to effect) has faced strong opposition from white communities and has never been realized on a national scale. The persistent erosion of desegregation orders across the country may soon relegate the aspiration for racially integrated schools to the annals of history (Orfield and Eaton, 1996; Orfield and Yun, 1999; Frankenberg and Lee, 2002). Moreover, some critics looking back on the *Brown v. Board of Education* decision have argued astutely that integration has often served to perpetuate the educational inequalities that it aimed to redress because it has been primarily an assimilationist strategy (Bell, 1987, 1995, 2004: Powell, 2005). Education that is assimilationist—that aims to fit students from racially oppressed communities into the dominant schools without a transformation of those institutions and the larger society within which they operate—has been shown to further educational inequalities in contradictory ways. For some students from subordinated communities, assimilation leads to alienation and disengagement from schooling; for others, molding to the dominant society comes at the cost of alienation from families and communities (see for a few examples, Fordham, 1996; Ladson-Billings, 1994; Valenzuela, 1999).

Despite the overall trends toward resegregation and these insightful critiques, inside many educational institutions the ideal of integration (particularly across the boundaries of race, ethnicity, and disability) is tenaciously intertwined with notions of educational justice. The argument I am making—that integration is a justice claim at work in local schools—may not be immediately obvious. *Integration* is almost a historical word, surely one rarely used by practitioners speaking about their schools and classrooms. *Diversity* is a more contemporary term guiding educational discourse. However, I have chosen to talk about integration and diversity under the same discursive umbrella because of the historical trajectory that I trace from the *Brown* decision to the more recent *Grutter v. Bollinger* (2003). When the U.S. Supreme Court declared in *Brown v. the Board of Education* (1954) that "in the field of public education, 'separate but equal' has no place," it inscribed an idea that would compel activist educators in many different contexts to wrestle with what it means to create diverse, integrated, *and equitable* schools and classrooms.

I trace this ideal of integration at Parks and City Friends and illuminate how it guided each school's work, albeit in very different ways. City Friends, a predominantly white, Quaker, independent school, felt directly compelled by the demands of the Civil Rights Movement in the United States to reconsider its admissions policies, which were exclusionary in effect, if not explicitly in intent. The Society of Friends's (Quaker) history of struggle for racial justice deeply influenced the practices of the school. Thus, although *Brown* did not address private education or segregation that was de facto, as a Quaker school, City Friends began to interrogate the contradiction between its commitments to the goals of the Civil Rights Movement and its own practices as an exclusionary institution. Beginning in the 1960s, City Friends wrestled with how to create a more racially and economically integrated school. Holding integration to be one principle of a just community generated difficult questions about the dominant institutional practices of the school. The ideal of integration led to critical dialogue about shaping equitable practices in the context of elite, independent school education. What constitutes a "diverse" community? Is access a sufficient condition for equity? What were the school's goals and purposes in increasing racial/ethnic diversity? Looking at the justice claim for integration, I show how City Friends was slowly forced to confront its tendency to focus on individuals and view its system as meritocratic, thus ignoring the critical ways these practices reproduced white power and privilege, making it difficult for students of color to be fully engaged and valued members of the community.

Parks Middle School, a public institution that was part of a city desegregation program, struggled to implement a different kind of integration: inclusion of children labeled with disabilities[2] into all classrooms. The ethical rationale behind the inclusion movement draws upon the central premise of *Brown v. Board of Education* that separate education is inherently unequal. Importantly, however, the inclusion movement envisions integration of children labeled with disabilities to require transformative rather than assimilative educational practices, and this provides an important contrast from City Friends (Dyson, 1999; Lipsky and Gartner, 1999; Rizvi and Lingard, 1996). Educators at Parks framed their support for inclusive education on integrationist grounds; segregation of children labeled with disabilities was inherently stigmatizing and had proven to offer them an academically inferior education. However, as teachers implemented inclusive education, they struggled with the decision for material and ideological reasons. As a city school that had adopted full inclusion in response to a budget cut, teachers did not have the resources (personnel, professional development opportunities, and so forth) to develop new approaches to teaching in these integrated classrooms. At the ideological level, educators wrestled with the very question that justified segregated education in the first place: Are students labeled with disabilities fundamentally different kinds of learners from their peers? If so, do they indeed need a different kind of education? Although the material conditions of Parks demonstrate the critical import of treating full inclusion as more than a placement decision (Rizvi and Lingard, 1996), I suggest the discursive questions—how we think about the difference of disability—must be interrogated if justice is to be served.

Situating struggles over integration within two particular school contexts, I then show how the tendency for integration to collapse into assimilation turns, to a significant degree, on the particular discourses through which we think about and address difference. I investigate the material and discursive pathways through which the justice claim for integration often elides into assimilation, with the hope that this understanding can help educators create schools that are diverse *and* equitable. The struggles of practice and the rich debates with which educators at both schools wrestled show how starting with integration as an ideal can engender new questions that challenge the limitations of assimilationist approaches. Looking deeply into practice serves to keep alive the democratic vision that we can and must learn in communities that are integrated by race, ethnicity, disability, and so forth, even as it challenges us to think about how we must transform the shape of those communities for justice to be achieved.

## Equal Standards

A second justice claim has reverberated throughout public discourse about education in recent years and aims to have a direct impact on the quality of education delivered to students. This justice claim insists that equal standards should form the basis upon which a challenging, meaningful curriculum is developed for all students. This claim was embodied in the standards-based reform[3] efforts undertaken by Parks and its larger school district; it reflects the national discourse about educational standards and equity. It rests on the premise that educational inequality derives from the unequal academic treatment of students. This unequal educational treatment tracks, uncomfortably, along the lines of class, race, ethnicity, disability, and gender. The argument holds that the academic underachievement of some groups of students results from low expectations within the curriculum and from an impoverished view of pedagogy (see for examples, Anyon, 1980; Gartner and Lipsky, 1987; Haberman, 1991; Lipman, 1998; Oakes, 1985). Ideally then, the justice claim for equal standards aims to interrupt the inequality of educational outcomes by ensuring that all students receive the same excellent educational program. Moreover, equal standards also focus attention on students' educational outcomes. This justice claim proposes that looking to student outcomes offers an important measure of equity. It is not enough to say that all students have access to an equal education; schools must also be responsible for helping students attain the standards.

Examining how this justice claim played out at Parks illustrates a recurring dilemma of practice that emerges when equal standards serve as the foundation for educational equity. Educators at Parks were chagrined by the low expectations and standards that had characterized most of their students' earlier school experiences. They saw these as reflective of the patterns of racial and economic discrimination throughout our society. The practitioners felt ethically compelled to prepare students for high academic achievement in the future, and they developed a set of rigorous educational standards to guide the education of all their students. However, as they implemented their educational plan, they found that many students still could not demonstrate mastery of these new standards. Teachers struggled with a troubling dilemma of practice in the face of students' widely variable academic performance. Should all students be expected to meet the same standards? Should they be expected to do so within a specific timetable? If so, should students who did not demonstrate mastery of the standards fail? Or, should teachers take into account students' differences (their knowledge, skills, learning strengths, and development over time) and, consequently, assess them differently? At the heart of this debate lay questions about whether equal standards demanded the same or differential treatment for students in relation to the standards. If students needed differential treatment, did that mean teachers would "lower" standards for some students? Did differential treatment, in fact, indicate inequitable education? Alternately, did equity demand acknowledging students' differences and thus engaging in differential treatment (e.g., different pedagogy, timetables, or assessments) to get them to those standards?

This dilemma about whether students should be treated the same or differently has a long history in education and is central to debates about justice in a democracy (Minow, 1990). Teachers are truly caught in an everyday dilemma. Treating students differently can lead back into an impoverished vision of education for students marked as "different." Ignoring differences and treating all students the same in the face of equal standards, however, slides inexorably into failure for some. In teasing apart this dilemma of everyday practice, I focus my analysis on discourse. I argue that this dilemma is connected to tenacious and contradictory beliefs about difference, learning, and human capacity—beliefs about whether learning is a matter of individual choice or is limited by each individual's intrinsic abilities. Moreover, I look at the failure of most discourse about standards to investigate the structural inequalities through which these standards are generated. Once again, looking closely at competing ideas about justice and difference that rest implicitly underneath practice helps us think our way out of the dilemma of practice by forcing us to reexamine the reigning norms, assumptions, and values embedded in the contexts in which difference and inequalities are produced.

## Recognition

A third justice claim proposes that a fair and equitable educational community is one that reflects the values and knowledge of its constituent groups: "recognition" is an important principle of equity (Taylor, 1992; see also Bingham, 2001). This is the core argument underpinning multicultural education. Multicultural education is, of course, a broad movement that encompasses a range of educational practices (see for overviews, Banks, 1997, 2004b; Gay, 2004; McCarthy, 1990; Nieto, 1996; Sleeter and Grant, 1993). However, even widely disparate approaches to multicultural education share a commitment to broadening our educational perspectives to be inclusive of groups that traditionally have been marginalized in schools. Justice is served not by ignoring difference but by recognizing and focusing on it. Multicultural education calls to task the idea that any curriculum or pedagogical approach can be neutral. It demands that we understand all educational practices to be grounded in particular values, knowledge, and assumptions.

Multicultural education is situated within broader critiques of liberal democratic states reflected in what has been called the "politics of recognition" (Taylor, 1992). It is one outgrowth of diverse contemporary social movements that argue that institutions (for example, schools and government) must acknowledge group differences and organize in ways that recognize, and are inclusive of, multiple identities, cultural values, and knowledge bases. These social movements point to the ways that liberal democratic institutions focus rights around individuals rather than groups, and mask interests of particular groups behind a façade of neutrality. In doing so, these institutions fail to attend to the power and privilege that accrue to dominant social groups (males, whites, heterosexuals, etc.) and the consequent silencing and marginalization of people who do not belong to such groups.

At City Friends, students and faculty critiqued aspects of pedagogy and of the curriculum on the premise that justice demanded recognition of group differences. One group of high school girls asked the math department to reconsider the pedagogical approach of their calculus class in light of what they perceived to be differences in girls' and boys' dominant learning styles. At the same time, some faculty members and students challenged the dominant narrative embedded in the school's curriculum—one that excluded or marginalized the voices and experiences of communities of color and white women, and focused almost exclusively on Europe and North America.

Examining how discourse about recognition unfolded at City Friends makes visible the exciting possibilities, as well as the limitations, of organizing ideas about justice around group differences. As teachers and students framed their critiques around the need for recognition, they raised up for public consideration the ways that all pedagogy and curriculum represent partial and particular perspectives. They focused attention on the ways that the normative practices of the school were not neutral, but served to privilege certain groups while excluding and marginalizing other members of the community.

Even as I examine the real potential that recognition holds to build more equitable educational practices, the contentious struggles at City Friends allow me to illuminate some of the thorny questions that arise in everyday practice in relation to this justice claim. What are the implications of adding history and English classes that focus on traditionally marginalized groups without reconstructing the school's entire curriculum? Should the school adopt single-sex math classes to address girls' needs and values? Do all boys and all girls learn in the same way? For whose benefit is multicultural education? Moreover, looking at recognition from a practice perspective puts flesh to theoretical concerns about approaches to equity that focus on difference (see Appiah, 1996; Benhabib, 2002; Minow, 1990). Justice claims based around recognition tend to rest on a discourse that treats differences as the property and responsibility of particular groups, those that have been marginalized by the existing social order. This focus on groups oppressed by the social order often fails to reveal the dominant relationships of power against which certain "differences" stand out.

## Toward a Relational Model of Difference

Discourse about difference is at the heart of all these deliberations about justice. As I track the three justice claims across the two school contexts, I explore the implicit discourses that undergirded these claims and critically shaped the parameters within which justice was defined and contested. These discourses about difference also implicated various approaches for redressing educational inequalities.

Two dominant approaches to difference frame the remedies for educational inequalities. These frameworks, which I call a sameness approach and a difference approach, emphasize, respectively, the fundamental similarities or differences between groups (Minow, 1990; Scott, 1988). Exploring these two approaches through the everyday practices of two schools, I argue that neither of them adequately addresses the knotty and tenacious "problem of difference"—the persistent tendency for educational inequality to coincide with the oppressions of race/ethnicity, class, gender, disability, and so forth. I advocate for a third approach to difference—a relational view—that understands inequality to be an outcome that is produced continually in the relationship between dominant and subordinated groups (McCarthy and Crichlow, 1993; Minow, 1990; Young, 1990).

The first two justice claims (integration and equal standards) rest firmly on a framework that emphasizes fundamental similarities between all human beings as the foundation from which to develop equitable educational practices. Focusing on the shared capacities of all children as learners, this approach suggests that when difference is the criterion for structuring participation in educational environments, inequality ensues. Differences that do exist (for example, in the academic achievement of children from various class or racial/ethnic backgrounds) are viewed as deriving from treating children differently in the first place. Justice claims for integration and equal standards are largely premised on the idea that it is our fundamental similarities that matter. Equity demands that all children have the same educational access and opportunities.

This focus on sameness is based on a universalist stance toward difference: "We are all human" is the message. This critical reformulation of the "problem of difference" attempts to interrupt biologically or culturally based explanations that justify hierarchical differentiations between social groups and strives to reassert the equality of all persons. It disrupts justifications for inequality that are based on presumptions about differences between males and females, white people and people of color, and people identified with disabilities and those who are not—differences that have condoned discriminatory social, political, economic and cultural practices. Refusing, for example, to view some groups of people as less capable (for example, less rational, less intelligent) than their counterparts, means there can be no justification for social practices that deny each and every human being the right to participate in the same environments and opportunities (Jaggar, 1983; Minow, 1990).

In education, policies as different as desegregation, full inclusion of students labeled with disabilities, and standards-based reforms share—at least in the ideal—a commitment to the same treatment of all students, regardless of race, ethnicity, gender, disability, or class. This commitment to equal treatment is a powerful and important claim that resonates with the fight for justice in a democracy. It is one that directed the work of both Parks and City Friends to build more equitable communities. The commitment to create a more racially and economically diverse community (City Friends) and to build classrooms inclusive of children labeled with disabilities (Parks) signaled a decision to focus on students' commonalities as the basis from which to develop more equitable practices. At Parks, the new reform efforts were premised on a commitment to offer each and every student an education based on equal standards that represented rigorous, rich curriculum and practices. This approach to difference importantly challenged a range of practices that, in treating groups of students differently, had served to exclude them from educational access and opportunities. Looking closely at how this approach to difference unfolded in practice at City Friends and Parks, however, also points to the limitations of this approach. These limitations rest in its tendency, in focusing on the fundamental similarities between groups of students, to ignore how power structures inequalities across dimensions of difference.

A second approach to difference exists in constant dialogue with the first. The claim that justice is served by recognition—by focusing on, rather than ignoring, differences—draws attention to the ways invisible norms and assumptions uphold the power of dominant groups. This paradigm for understanding difference suggests that, although we are all human, we find ourselves located in different cultural spaces. These differences are generally viewed as outcomes of specific sociohistorical circumstances.[4] This difference approach disrupts the invisibility of the dominant norms, exposing cultural practices that, while appearing to be neutral, in fact reflect the values and qualities of particular groups.

Bringing into focus differences between social groups, this approach proposes that fairness can be achieved by recognizing and acknowledging these differences (see for discussion, Bingham, 2001; Gutmann, 1992, 2003; Minow, 1990; Taylor, 1992). This difference approach argues that equal treatment does not constitute an appropriate response to difference because, in presuming universality, it fails to recognize different needs and values of various groups. Equity requires that educational institutions attend to the different values, cultures, and learning styles of different groups of students. The question for schools—one that was alive in different ways at both Parks and City Friends—becomes how curriculum, pedagogy, and structural organization can accommodate students' differences along the lines of race/ethnicity, gender, and (dis)ability.

Across the nation, this approach to difference is represented through various educational programs created for particular groups of students. Some schools and programs are designed for students from oppressed racial/ethnic groups, with the aim of creating environments that reflect the histories, knowledge, values, and commitments of these communities (see for a few examples, Hale, 2001; Murrell, 1993; Ramos-Zayas, 1998). Single-sex schools and classrooms aim to support the academic achievement of girls, especially in the areas of math and science (see American Association of University Women, 1992; Datnow and Hubbard, 2002; Phillips, 1998). In recent years, some educational reformers have advocated in favor of single-sex schools in the public sphere as a remedy for racial and gender inequalities for both boys and girls (Riordan, 2002; Salamone, 2002). The assumption in all these examples is that educational equity requires recognizing, rather than ignoring, difference.

At City Friends, this difference approach offered practitioners and students a powerful tool with which to advocate for recognition as an important component of a just educational community. Advocates of this approach pushed the school, with varying degrees of success, to develop curriculum and pedagogy that acknowledged the different values, histories, knowledge, and experiences of people of color and women. Through their stories, I argue that the difference approach holds greater potential than the sameness approach for redressing educational inequalities, precisely because it exposes dominant norms and values as particular and not neutral. Once again, however, through a careful examination of practice, the problematic nature of this difference discourse also becomes evident.

One major limitation of this approach is that in focusing on differences, difference is viewed as the property of particular individuals or groups (Hare-Mustin and Maracek, 1990; McCarthy and Crichlow, 1993; Minow, 1990; Rhode, 1990; Unger, 1990). Differences are located within the bodies of particular students (for example, students labeled with disabilities) or identified as generalized qualities of specific groups of children (for example, racial/ethnic groups or female students). This problem is illustrated most starkly by the dominant discourse through which we tend to describe the variable ways that children learn, and here, Parks provides a vivid example. Paying attention to the discourse about disability and learning diversity at Parks demonstrates how the variability in the ways children learn is translated into the language of identifiable "disabilities" or "ability levels," which are then described as qualities that are located inside individual bodies and brains, rather than in the institutional contexts that make these differences stand out (Carrier, 1986; Christensen, 1996; Gartner and Lipsky, 1987; Lipsky and Gartner, 1996; Mehan, Hertweck, and Meihls, 1986; Slee, 1999; Varenne and McDermott, 1998).

The view that disability is a difference located within the bodies and brains of particular people saturates educational discourse and practice with, I argue, serious consequences for our ability to redress the inequalities that accrue around disabilities. Challenging this way of thinking about disability is not to deny differences in the ways children learn. Ignoring differences that exist will not help us create inclusive and equitable educational environments. What I am, however, attempting to illustrate in this book is how framing disabilities as qualities of particular individuals does not help practitioners call into question the ways that educational practices make certain differences—for example, the approach and rate at which a child comes to reading—matter, and matter in particular ways (Varenne and McDermott, 1998).

City Friends offers an illustration of a difference approach organized around group rather than individual differences. Through a close examination of the arguments in favor of pedagogy and curriculum that attend to, rather than gloss over, group differences—specifically, gender, race, and ethnicity—I offer a grounded account of theoretical critiques of this difference approach to equity (see McCarthy, 1990; Minow, 1990). Focusing on group differences tends to leave in place existing power structures (embodied in curricular narratives and pedagogical practices) because this approach does not focus on the relationship between dominant and subordinate groups. For example, it is not simply that a school's curriculum needs to reflect the experiences of groups that are too often invisible. It is that those narratives must be understood in relationship to European-American conquest, colonization, and supremacy. Teaching the history of American Indian nations, African-Americans, Mexican-Americans, Chinese-Americans, and Japanese-Americans, and so forth, without unteaching the dominant narrative about European-Americans masks the deeply entwined trajectories and permeable boundaries of all these histories. Moreover, focusing on differences between groups glosses within-group variability. It is not that all boys are competitive and all girls are cooperative. It is that competition is valued over cooperation, and that schools are organized to accrue privilege around competition and individualism (Abu El-Haj, 2003a).

Focusing on differences between groups can hide from view the way that difference is a "statement of relationship" (Minow, 1990). Joan Scott (1988) writes:

> Fixed oppositions conceal the extent to which things presented as oppositional are, in fact, interdependent—that is, they derive their meaning from a particularly established contrast rather than from some inherent or pure antithesis. Furthermore, according to Jacques Derrida, the interdependence is hierarchical with one term dominant or prior, the opposite term subordinate and secondary. (p. 37)

Recognizing this hierarchical relationality is fundamental to our ability to redress the "problem of difference" in schools—the fact that differences continue to make a difference in academic and social opportunities and outcomes. Failure to pay attention to the *relationship between* the terms along which difference is organized (for example, male/female, ability/ (dis)ability) leads us to scrutinize the bodies that occupy the subordinated positions, without paying attention to the norms and assumptions that privilege the dominant term and simultaneously shield it from our view.

Thus, in this book, I argue for developing a relational view of difference in our work in schools. This relational approach focuses on the ways that differences are deeply embedded in relationships and mark the axes along which power is organized in society (Hare-Mustin and Maracek, 1990; McCarthy, 1990; McCarthy and Crichlow, 1993; Minow, 1990; Scott, 1988; Young, 1990). In this model, differences such as gender, race, or disability are not viewed as the property of individuals or groups; rather, they indicate relationships that are constructed and reconstructed in specific institutional contexts. These relationships are intimately bound up with domination and subordination. Race, gender, (dis)ability, and sexuality do not reference inherent biological, or social determinants that divide the world easily into different groups. Moreover, these differences are continually made, remade, and challenged through institutional processes, such as those of schooling.

By locating the "problem of difference" as deeply embedded within institutional relationships, we shift away from focusing our attention on people defined as "different." Gender is no longer simply a code word for women; race does not only reference people of color. This relational approach to difference demands confrontation with "whiteness," "maleness," "able-ness," and so forth. The relational approach suggests that, as educators, we must examine not only how certain practices result in inequalities for particular children and groups, but we must also attend to the ways that these practices simultaneously privilege others (Fine, 1997; Minow, 1990; Varenne and McDermott, 1998). It is the relationship between marginalization and power that must be scrutinized. This theme is one to which I return again and again throughout the book.

## Practicing for Justice in the Face of Power

The conflicting, if interwoven, ideas about difference and justice that I investigate in this book implicitly drive policies and practices at the macro level of educational legislation, litigation, and systemic reforms as well as within the local sphere of school and classroom decisions. This is a critical time to investigate the interpretive frameworks individuals hold and the discourses institutions deploy, which sustain and constrain the work of building just, inclusive school communities. Conflict over how to address difference and equity has been a recurring theme in the history of education in the United States (see Reich, 2002; Spring, 2004; Tyack, 1974). Over the past five decades, civil, feminist, and disability rights groups have succeeded to varying degrees in creating wider educational access and opportunities for traditionally marginalized constituencies. Despite the victories activists have won, the burden of discrimination in schools remains high for students from subordinated social groups. Across the country, desegregation orders are being dismantled, bilingual education is under serious attack, and the rights of students labeled with disabilities to be served in all classrooms continue to be limited (see Lipsky and Gartner, 1996; Orfield and Eaton, 1996; Staff, *Rethinking Schools*, 1998). Educational achievement continues to track all too predictably along the well-worn lines of race/ethnicity, gender, class, and disability.

As educators, we are called upon to address an ongoing ethical crisis facing our nation, one reflected in our schools but not limited to them: How can we imagine and build more inclusive *and* just communities? I do not offer this book as another remedy for educational inequality. In truth, I would argue that remedies for inequality are hard to come by, given the deeply inequitable society to which our schools (as well as our institutions of higher education) are bound. I am convinced, however, that this is no reason for despair. Our capacity for transforming schools may be limited by the broad inequalities of our society, but the actions we take in our everyday practices, small and large, can serve to create what Myles Horton (1990) dubbed so beautifully: "islands of decency." In focusing on discourse about difference and justice, and attending to the processes of inquiry in which practitioners at City Friends and Parks were engaged, I am arguing that working for justice with difference in mind is an ongoing endeavor that demands constant wrestling with our most basic assumptions and values, as well as systematic inquiry into our everyday, taken-for-granted educational practices.

## On Language

As a book that is centrally concerned with the analysis of discourse, I think it is important to address how I am using several key terms: difference, diversity, justice, and discourse. These terms, I argue, are used in complex and contradictory ways. These complexities and contradictions are precisely the subject of this book; therefore, my efforts here to capture "what I mean" by these terms are not definitive, but a starting point for reading the book.

### Difference and Diversity

I use the terms "difference" and "diversity" very differently. I employ the term "diversity" with the intention of invoking basic human variability that, at least in our imaginations, need not be organized into hierarchical relationships (see, for example, Erickson, 1987). In this sense, diversity reflects the rich variety of human societies and the range of cognitive and emotional sensibilities that individuals manifest. In this book, "diversity" is most often used in reference to the variability in children's ways of knowing and expressing themselves in the world.

However, I invoke the term "diversity" at the risk of slipping into two related pitfalls. The first is the danger of naiveté. In the world in which we live, "diversity" rarely signifies simple human variability, and where it does, we often do not notice or name it. For example, while humans vary greatly in their shapes of noses and foot sizes, we do not commonly invoke the term "diversity" to reference those aspects of our variability. Thus, diversity usually refers to significant variability among human beings, and significance most often relates to hierarchically organized differences. This point brings me to the second pitfall of using the term "diversity": It often glosses relationships of power and privilege. Thus, talk about "diversity" often serves to invoke categories such as race and gender, with a word that connotes benign variability instead of deeply structured relations of power and this usage of the word is a subject of concern in this book.

I use the term "difference" to refer purposefully to the dimensions along which power is organized in our schools and society. Race/ethnicity, gender, class, disability, and sexuality[5] are all significant categories that structure relations of power and privilege in our society. A central assumption I hold is that "difference" references a socially constructed relationship, instead of essentialized qualities that belong to one group of people or another.

However, one of the challenges of writing this book has been that the practitioners with whom I worked do not necessarily share my definitions and assumptions about the meanings of "diversity" and "difference." The conflicting uses of these terms reflect the deeply contested terrain across which this study traverses. Thus, readers must be prepared to wrestle with the necessary messiness of these central terms, for we have, as yet, no better language.

*Discourse*

Because "discourse" is a term used liberally in contemporary academic literature, I want to be explicit about what I mean by it and why I chose to focus my analysis around it. Because this book is about how we think about difference and justice, I am fundamentally interested in questions of what Hirshman (2003) calls "the discursive construction of social meaning" (p. 81). That is, I am concerned with the ways that our interpretive frameworks shape our realities, setting the boundaries for what we imagine to be possible. I employ "discourse" to follow the use of many social theorists, most notably Foucault, to refer to social practices of talk and action that constitute objects that bring into being what we can know and not know (see Erickson, 1996a; Fairclough, 1995; Foucault, 1972; Gee, 1999; Hirshman, 2003; Scott, 1988; Weedon, 1987). Discourse refers to sets of undergirding values, beliefs, relationships, and assumptions that are manifest across institutions and individuals. Weedon writes:

> Meanings do not exist prior to their articulation in language and language is not an abstract system, but is always socially and historically located in discourses. Discourses represent political interests and in consequence are constantly vying for status and power. The site of this battle for power is the subjectivity of the individual and it is a battle in which the individual is an active but not sovereign protagonist. (p. 41)

The concept of discourse pierces the apparent transparency of difference: that differences (race, gender, class, disability, and sexuality) exist before the social practices that constitute them. It allows us to understand that difference is constituted continually through power relationships, and that the multiple meanings assigned to difference and justice are embattled territory. This theory of discourse helps explain the multiple shifting assumptions about difference and justice in local settings and grounds the battle over the meaning of difference and justice in the two schools to the deeply entrenched, powerful interests in our society at large. Thus, discourse offers a framework for connecting individual interpretation to broader social and institutional practices (Fairclough, 1995; Gee, 1999). It also allows for the possibility that the same person may hold multiple interpretive frameworks: that the contradictions of discourse speak through all of us.

However, to use the concept of discourse in this sense is not to imply that individuals are simply the mouthpieces for power relations, that they have little or no agency. I do not wish to suggest that the struggles inside schools represent ideological battles in which there are no actors. Teachers are not puppets through which discourses ventriloquize (Erickson, 1996a). Moreover, as Erickson (2004) points out, it is hard to know for sure when and if, at a local level, we are seeing those larger social discourses. Instead, it is more fruitful to think of practitioners, like the rest of us, as both adopting and adapting the available ways of conceptualizing difference and justice (Alcoff, 1988; Erickson, 2004; Fairclough, 1995; Gee, 1999; Hirshman, 2003). Educators at City Friends and Parks were, as we all are, mucking about in the complex, contradictory, and multiple discourses about difference and justice, and in the process, were both shaped by and gave shape to them in various ways in their everyday practices.

## Justice

Because the point of this book is to explore a variety of justice claims at work in the public imagination and the everyday practices of schools, I do not offer a definition of justice. I must, however, offer two clarifications.

The first involves my use of language. I use justice and equity (or educational justice and educational equity) interchangeably in this book. I do so because my "read" of educational talk and literature suggests an overlap of meanings. These meanings, as this book suggests, are indefinite and contested. I purposely do not use equity and equal/equality interchangeably. Equal and equality, here, are meant to indicate sameness.

Even as I argue that the concepts of justice and equity have multiple meanings, I do hold to an expansive and encompassing sense of educational justice, one that I develop in the final chapter. Suffice it to say here that I believe educational justice entails much more than equitable academic outcomes for students. For me, justice is intimately entwined with a vision of education as enabling of the transformation of conditions of oppression.

## Organization of the Book

Chapter 2 offers a case study overview of both schools that traces how educators came to be concerned with particular aspects of difference in their settings. Parks had changed from its configuration as a magnet alternative program for 50 students to a desegregation school serving 250 students from all over the city. That change and a fiscal crisis in the district, which pushed the school to adopt a full-inclusion policy for children labeled with disabilities, had focused educators' attention on the diversity of learners in their classrooms. The school's involvement with the Coalition of Essential Schools led the school to think about its academic program in new ways, building a curriculum based around equal standards for all students.

The concern about race/ethnicity at City Friends emerged from its contradictory status as an elite, independent school with Quaker roots that kept issues of social justice on the institutional agenda. The school's commitment to a curriculum firmly grounded in the traditional Western canon and a Greek and Latin Classics program, and an orientation toward preparing its students to matriculate in the most elite colleges and universities, worked against its stated goals of creating an inclusive, multiracial community. By the early 1990s, some practitioners were determined to engage this tension. At the same time, the popularity of research on the benefits of girls' schools led the school to undertake a study of gender. This chapter narrates the school's rocky journey as it used inquiry to open up, in fits and starts, important conversations about race and gender. Importantly, because my analysis in this book is focused primarily on discourse, this chapter also offers a perspective on the constraints that each school faced because of their very different positions in the tangled web of the racial and socioeconomic order of our society.

With an understanding of how each school came to focus on different aspects of difference, Chapter 3 takes a journey through both schools, exploring two different articulations of the justice claim for integration. I begin this chapter by considering the ideal of integration as it has lived and evolved in the public imagination over the past 50 years. Looking to the 1954 *Brown v. Board of Education* decision as a public symbol of the justice claim for integration, I examine the implicit assumptions of this decision—assumptions that echoed, often in problematic ways, inside the two schools. The moral imperatives of the Civil Rights Movement challenged City Friends to become a more racially and economically integrated school. In the early years, the school's approach to integration focused on increasing access to the school for students of color, particularly those from low-income families. The school intended to increase the racial diversity of its student body without rethinking its curriculum, pedagogy, or practices in significant ways. Examining discourses that evolved around diversity makes visible the ways that City Friends's deeply held commitments to individualism, excellence, and a belief in meritocracy yielded an approach to integration that proved painful, often harmful, to its students and faculty of color. Examining these discourses over time, faculty of color and their white allies challenged the school's approach to integration. Chapter 3 describes these critiques, which are explored in greater detail in Chapter 5.

Parks's full-inclusion policy offers a contrasting angle from which to explore the everyday practice of integration. Full-inclusion policies are ideally conceived to integrate children labeled with disabilities into all classrooms, while simultaneously challenging those classrooms to change in ways that make it possible for all students to participate fully in the educational processes. This approach to integration should offer a challenge to the kinds of assimilationist strategies that we see at City Friends in relation to race. However, looking inside Parks illustrates the dangers of implementing full inclusion without the resources to support significant changes in classroom practices. Integration is reduced to a placement decision, instead of a truly educational one. As critical as the lack of resources was to the struggles of full inclusion, I argue that discourse about disability also limited, in critical ways, educators' stated commitments to integration. Without denying the import of resources, I explore, in each school, the ways that particular discourses about difference constrained the power of integration to effect educational equity.

If integration made its demands primarily in terms of students' access to schools and classrooms, equal standards aimed to affect what actually happened inside classrooms and focused practitioners' attention squarely on student outcomes. The justice claim taken up in Chapter 4 is equal standards. I play out this justice claim in relationship to Parks's standards-based reforms. The national debates about standards offer the framework within which I examine shared assumptions about educational equity embedded in the disparate top-down and bottom-up approaches to standards-based reforms. Parks grounds the national debates in the dilemmas that emerge as standards are adopted in everyday practice. Parks implemented a set of equal standards for curriculum and performance that aimed to ensure that all students' education was characterized by a rigorous approach to disciplinary knowledge that taught them to demonstrate their skills and competencies through meaningful application. In practice, however, this approach was complicated by the diversity of knowledge, skills, experiences, and learning styles of the students. In the face of equal standards, a painful dilemma emerged: Does treating students the same by holding them to the same expectations for performance, or treating them differently, constitute educational equity? Again, I look to discourse to explore the contradictory beliefs about learners and undergirding assumptions about standards that lead teachers, in practice, to this perpetual dilemma.

Chapter 5 returns us to City Friends to explore the idea that it is not sameness but difference that must serve as the foundation for practicing for justice. The justice claim for recognition demands that educational institutions acknowledge and respond to group differences. The field of multicultural education, diverse as it is, represents this call for recognition as a key component of educational equity. This chapter opens with an examination of the assumptions about equity that undergird the arguments, in the field of education and the public sphere, in favor of multicultural education. These assumptions are taken up inside City Friends in relation to two very different stories in which members of the school community called for recognition. The first story explores the evolution of arguments to support the development of a curriculum that would include, in meaningful ways, the knowledge, histories, and experiences of communities of color. As a justice claim, recognition offered a powerful framework within which to challenge the school's historic commitment to a curriculum based on a traditional Western canon. At the same time, this attention to historically marginalized groups, without a concomitant focus on the relationship between dominant and subordinated groups, did not create a new narrative in which everyone in the community felt implicated.

The second instance of recognition that I explore in this chapter arose in the context of student activism. A small group of high school girls charged that the pedagogy of their math class, in ignoring the particular ways that females learn, constituted a hostile and inequitable learning environment. Their story allows me to examine the ways that focusing on difference, rather than on the relationships that lead to difference, risks either essentializing or denying the salience of, in this case, gender. It is only, I suggest, by looking at difference as a relationship of power produced within and through particular everyday practices that it is possible to make significant moves toward equity.

The concluding chapter builds on the themes that cut across this book, to develop four key observations about educational equity as it relates to the differences that make a difference in education. I suggest particular ways we might think about inclusion, equality, and difference and create an expansive, encompassing, and transformative view of education that is equitable. At the heart of this view of educational justice rests a relational understanding of difference, one that we must adopt if we have any hope of making all the difference in education.

# CHAPTER 1

# Justice Claims and Everyday Practice: Portraits of Two Schools

The three justice claims—integration, equal standards, and recognition—emerged from the everyday practices of teaching in two very different local contexts. In offering brief case studies of these schools, this Chapter portrays key contextual factors that shaped the everyday discourse and practices about justice and difference that are the subject of Chapters 3–5. The aim of this chapter is not a comparative one. In proposing that we, as educators, must attend to local contexts and struggles to unknot thorny questions about difference and educational justice, I am more interested in narrating how teachers at each school came to be concerned with particular differences, and how specific justice claims emerged in relation to those differences. A historical perspective frames the development, over time, of particular ways of thinking about, and acting upon, the differences that educators found salient in their settings.

Importantly, in a book that focuses its analysis primarily on the discursive realm—on how our thinking about difference shapes our practices for educational equity—these case studies offer a view of each school that is deeply located within the race and class divisions of our society. Researching across these two very different schools, I attended to the ways that the politics and economics of race and class in the urban United States wove insidiously into the local fabric of each school, fundamentally shaping the paths that educators could take in their quest to build more equitable school environments. The process of social change may, as I propose in this book, turn on how we understand the "problem of difference"; however, it would be naïve, at best, to suggest that our work inside local schools is not also fundamentally constrained by the vested interests of the existing, inequitable social structure.

## Parks Middle School

Parks serves approximately 240 children in grades 6–8 who come from all over the city. Parks was an ideal site for this research for several reasons. First, in recent years, inquiry and innovation had been central to the school's practices. Parks had joined a national reform movement, the Coalition of Essential Schools, and was known in the district as a place where educators were routinely involved in the reexamination of their educational practices. A team of practitioners, parents, and outside researchers had recently engaged in a multiyear ethnographic project to document how well the school was meeting its academic goals and preparing students for high school. Furthermore, the spring before I was to begin my fieldwork, Parks received a grant from Brown University and the Annenberg Institute on School Reform to fund teacher inquiry groups to promote the further development of innovative pedagogy and curriculum.

For practitioners at Parks, it was learning diversity that raised the most pressing questions about educational equity. I employ the term "learning diversity" to capture a range of expressions practitioners used in describing the difference that they found most salient in their school context: "learning diversity," "intellectual levels," "disability," "ability levels," and, occasionally, "learning styles." Learning diversity encompassed, but was not limited to, children who were labeled with disabilities; it was at the forefront of practitioners' concerns for different reasons. The school had recently moved to a full-inclusion program, whereby students labeled with disabilities were no longer served in separate special education classes for any part of the day. A majority of the teachers philosophically supported the full-inclusion program, drawing on the justice claim of *integration*; however, teachers struggled with *how* to integrate children labeled with disabilities in ways that served their particular learning needs.

Practitioners were also deeply concerned that a majority of their students entered sixth grade with underdeveloped literacy and numeracy skills, and without a good foundation of knowledge in the various disciplines. Teachers believed that students' weak preparation and academic underachievement were due to the inequitable, impoverished educational opportunities (curriculum, pedagogy, expectations, and so forth) they had experienced in their elementary schools. Teachers sought to remedy these inequalities by creating a program based on a set of equal standards intended to engender a rich, challenging curriculum for *all* students. This approach to school reform reflected the justice claim for equal standards that is explored in Chapter 4.

Practitioner inquiry groups and a team approach to teaching offered opportunities to investigate, deliberate about, and experiment with various pedagogies and curricula that could address the diverse needs of the students. Integration and equal standards were the different, albeit interrelated, justice claims through which practitioners explored the relationship between learning diversity and educational equity. In what follows, I tease out contextual strands that contributed to the two primary justice claims that were in play.

### First Impressions: A Vital Community Buffeted by Change

Turning off a busy thoroughfare and entering the lush, expansive grounds of a former community college, the first time I visited Parks, I was struck by the sharp contrast between the physical environment of most city schools and the feeling on this campus of a calm retreat from the bustle of urban life. It was easy, however, to identify the school. Parks is housed in a squat, two-story modern structure surrounded by imposing Victorian-era stone buildings. As I opened the front glass doors and stepped into a large entrance hall, a buzzer alerted the office to my arrival. To the right of the door, a commercial poster featured caricatures of children from different ethnic backgrounds calling out greetings in various languages. On the wall directly across from the door, a collage of multihued tracings of children's hands surrounded the word "Parks." Linoleum floors and cinder block walls gave a clean but definitely institutional feel, softened by displays of students' projects that lined the hallways: watercolors and pencil drawings of nature that were the fruits of recent elective courses.

A large poster opposite the front entrance detailed the nine common principles of the Coalition of Essential Schools. Next to it, newspaper articles about recent accomplishments of Parks's students were displayed. A line of print extending the entire length of the hall hailed the central importance of being a lifelong reader. Parks's entrance visibly conveyed several of its core values and assumptions: a respect for students' work and accomplishments, a philosophy of education emphasizing community and students as active participants in the learning process, and a commitment to diversity that, in practice, went well beyond the stock symbols on the entrance display boards.[1]

Parks is located in a middle-class neighborhood, Old Town, which through the ongoing work of local social activists had achieved a degree of racial integration unusual in the larger metropolitan area. The school rented its space from the current owners of the former community college. The middle-class, almost suburban ambiance of the campus provided a contrast to the neighborhoods of most students, who commuted from many areas of the city. The majority were members of low-income families. According to figures from the school district Office of Accountability and Assessment, in 1995, the year I began my fieldwork, 68.3% of the students were members of families qualifying for free or reduced-price lunches, and 30.9% of the families received Aid to Families with Dependent Children funds (AFDC). Unlike many of the district's neighborhood schools, Parks was racially integrated, a part of the city's desegregation program. In 1995, district statistics reported Parks's student population as 62.3% African-American, 3.2 % Asian-American, 1.6% Hispanic, and 32.8% white.

At Parks, collaboration was the norm. In classrooms, students were usually working on projects in small groups. Often, chairs would be pulled into a large circle as students and teachers engaged in lively, respectful discussions and debates. The library, which doubled as a cafeteria for breakfast and lunch, was, in many ways, the heart of the school. The librarian was usually huddled with small groups of students, helping them to conduct research or to choose books she thought they would enjoy. A large, soft couch outside the main office provided a place for students to lounge while seeking help or awaiting discipline from the school's counselor, vice principal, or principal. Ease, familiarity, and ownership characterized students' interactions in the hallways and classrooms. Many teachers began class periods with a time for students to share news, a favorite song, a burning concern, and other topics with their peers. Students, teachers, and staff mostly knew each other by name. On my initial visit to the school, the principal walked me around and introduced me to everyone we met, child and adult alike. Students often took me under their wings, guiding me through the day and eagerly sharing their expertise and opinions on life in school.

Two years after I began my fieldwork, I was again reminded of the close attention students received from adults. I arrived for a meeting to find the principal, Melanie Post (a white[2] woman who is well-known and respected as a leader in the school district) at her computer working with an eighth grader on her high school entrance essay. Apologizing that our meeting would be slightly delayed, she drew me instantly into the process. She explained that the student, Anne, had an interview the next day at the magnet high school for the performing arts, for which she had to prepare a journalistic piece of writing. Melanie had spent most of that day helping Anne write an essay about the funeral of a friend's mother. As I helped Melanie and Anne change the font size on the computer and proofread the essay, I thought of the many times I had been drawn into similar interactions as adults extended themselves to support students in need. At Parks, relationships between adults and children were characterized by mutual respect and a commitment on the part of practitioners to create a community in which all children might see themselves as talented and capable students.

As I entered more deeply into school life, I came to understand that the easy, respectful, and affable atmosphere that greeted visitors rested in uneasy proximity to one of crisis and deprivation. The quiet, removed quality of the campus and the relaxed atmosphere inside the school walls provided a vivid contrast to the pressured, unsettling circumstances under which teachers and administrators constantly worked.

*A Brief History: Building an Alternative School in the Midst of Flux*

Parks was 18 years old at the time I began fieldwork. From the perspectives of faculty and staff,[3] these years had been characterized by a sense of uncertainty, change, and lack of control over their budget and program. This was a school in which practitioner-led reform was the norm, yet their efforts were often thwarted by the will of the school district.

Parks was founded in the late 1970s as a community school with an alternative program for middle school students. In its early years, it functioned as a magnet school, drawing what one administrator described as "an elite group—really top kids." As Melanie recalled, the initial program was targeted at students who were labeled "gifted." The former principal had been allowed to develop interview procedures and admissions tests for both students and faculty, thus establishing a community he had chosen.

By the time Melanie arrived as principal six years later, the school had become a more democratic institution, part of the district's voluntary desegregation program. It had grown from its initial 50 neighborhood students to approximately 250 students from all over the city. Admittance to the voluntary desegregation program was based on a lottery system where the one criterion was to balance the student body racially in proportion to the city population. Having once had complete control over the process, a few of the teachers and administrators resented the change, wishing that the school still had influence over student admissions. These teachers also lamented that they could no longer offer the type of program they once had: a program geared toward what they perceived as the "elite" students of the school's early years. However, a majority of teachers and administrators felt the changes in the student population had created new opportunities to explore how the rich, innovative education for which the school had gained a reputation could be reshaped to include a broader range of learners. Overall, educators at Parks were committed to fostering a school culture in which high standards were the norm for all students. They were keenly aware of the uneven and inequitable educational opportunities that characterized many of their students' earlier academic experiences, and their central concern was how to offer all students a creative and demanding education that addressed the broad range of learning styles, skills, knowledge, and experiences.

Although some district policy changes, such as incorporation into the city's voluntary desegregation program, furthered Parks's vitality as an innovative, reflective place, the faculty resented the myriad decisions that undermined their authority over the direction and shape of their program. Some faculty regretted that they were no longer allowed to interview prospective parents to ascertain whether the families would be active members of the program. The school wished to enroll families deeply committed to Parks's mission because parents were involved in vital school activities, such as action research and the governance council. In the early 1990s, Parks had moved to a school-based governance model in which an elected committee of administrators, teachers, and parents was given the power to make programmatic and budgetary decisions. By the time I began my research, five parents were active members of this governance council. In the years immediately preceding my arrival, four parents had been members of a team with teachers, students, and outsider ethnographers that engaged in a self-study. Faculty valued their collaborative relationships with parents; educators were committed to having parents be active, important decision makers in school policies and practices.

Beyond concerns that the district would and could override its local decision-making processes, a further source contributing to the school's sense of instability had been its frequent relocations. Over its 18 years, the school had been housed in a rented college building, the fourth floor of an otherwise deserted middle school, and a school building that eventually was condemned. In earlier locations, Parks had been in close proximity to several of the city's magnet high schools, affording students the option of enrolling in elective classes off campus. The school's current location had cut off these possibilities of cross-school enrollment. Furthermore, faculty, staff, and students expressed their frustration at the lack of facilities at the present site. There was no gym to which they had regular access, no large assembly place for community meetings, and no cafeteria; students ate lunch in the library. Despite the building's inadequacies, everyone feared yet another move if the district failed to come to a rental agreement with the current owners of the property. Faculty and staff were especially concerned that they might be forced to share space with another middle school—a change that would strain the distinctive cohesiveness of their small community.

All these changes contributed to a sense of instability, but the greatest source of strain was the shrinking school district budget. A series of budget cuts, discussed at length in the next section, strained educators' efforts to address their central concerns about learning diversity and implement practices that met the needs of all their students.

### The Current Context of School Reform: The Coalition of Essential Schools

Parks had long been involved with school reform efforts. Even in its early incarnation as a magnet school, inquiry and experimentation were the norm. The most recent reform wave arrived in the late 1980s, when Parks became a member of the Coalition of Essential Schools, a national network of schools committed to a set of principles to improve education (Sizer, 1992). Melanie Post, the principal, was the first member of the school community to be exposed to the Coalition philosophy. She learned of the Coalition after enrolling one of her children in an alternative independent school that was a member of the network. As a result of this exposure, Melanie went to hear Professor Theodore Sizer, the Coalition's founder, discuss the work of the group. Impressed with the principles he espoused, she found a resonance between the language Sizer was using and the philosophy the Parks faculty and staff had been developing over the years. Melanie invited others to join her in local Coalition events, and soon the teachers were reading the Coalition's philosophy and discussing its relationship to Parks's existing program. After much discussion, the faculty decided to seek Coalition membership.

Shortly after joining, the school faced the first in a series of significant budget cuts. Parks drew on the Coalition's "nine common principles" (see Sizer, 1992) to inform the shape its reorganization took to address these cuts. In a first round of budget cuts, the school had lost its art, music, foreign language, and physical education programs. Several teachers were forced to leave. Two teachers who had formerly taught Spanish and music were able to remain at the school by shifting to language arts and science, respectively. The Coalition's principle that teachers and administrators should view themselves as generalists and expect to play multiple roles led the faculty and administrators to consider alternative ways to maintain at least some of these programs. In addition to their regular classes, all teachers and staff members taught elective classes in areas of particular interest to them, such as the arts, sports, drama, musical appreciation, and so forth. Although practitioners agreed that these classes were no substitute for the fully developed arts, music, sports, and language programs the school had lost, the elective courses supported a broad range of important, expressive experiences for students. Moreover, through these courses, staff came to know a wider group of students, building a greater sense of community across the school.

Two years before the start of my fieldwork, another fiscal crisis led the school to adopt the full-inclusion program for students labeled with disabilities. In the face of this budget cut, the school again drew on the principles of the Coalition of Essential Schools and structured its program around three teams of teachers. Each team was responsible for approximately one-third of the students and was organized around disciplinary boundaries of language arts, social studies, math, and science. The school's designated reading specialist and three special education teachers became members of these teams, teaching language arts, social studies, civics, and expressive arts. Students were grouped into teams by age. Two teams, called Stage 1, served students in their first two years at the school. Graduating students were grouped together on one team known as Stage 2. The team structure had positive effects for teachers who were able to create closer working collaborations with their colleagues and their students, and for students who were able to build stable relationships with caring adults. Moreover, the school schedule was arranged to allow each team of teachers to meet one afternoon a week during school time for collaborative discussions and planning across traditional disciplinary boundaries. Parks's membership in the Coalition helped the school envision a structure that fostered the growth of community among and between children and adults.

### Analyzing Inequality, Devising Equitable Practices to Address Learning Diversity

Practitioners viewed learning diversity as the difference that was most important to address in relation to educational equity. What most educators meant by this was that only a few of their students appeared to possess the knowledge, experiences, and approaches to learning that would lead to successful academic achievement. The move to a full-inclusion program for children labeled with disabilities had only heightened teachers' ongoing concern with meeting the highly variable learning needs of their students. The diverse ways in which students were, in a sense, equipped to engage with the task of schooling created a "problem of difference" for practitioners. A few students were academically successful; many were not. This violated any sense of fairness.

Moreover, learning diversity appeared to the teachers to suggest broader structural inequalities because it coincided with the divisions of socioeconomic class. Students who were academically successful tended to have more of the markers of middle-class existence. Teachers described these students as "exposed" to certain types of opportunities (for example, travel and museum trips) that related to middle-class cultural capital (Bourdieu, 1984). Teachers also pointed to the role that racial oppression played in structuring educational inequalities; however, many noted that at Parks, where a majority of the white students came from working-class or low-income families, academic achievement was often differentiated along class rather than racial lines. Given the stratified academic achievement of students, practitioners' primary focus for their reform efforts was how to create a more successful learning environment that could address the diverse needs of all learners and bridge the academic divide between middle-class and working-class to low-income students.

In this struggle, practitioners were acutely aware of how critical a role education played in relation to class and race oppression in the larger society. One veteran African-American mathematics teacher, Mary Davis, speaking in an interview about what stood out to her in terms of student diversity, said:

> Ability levels, intellectual levels. And I'm less concerned with the issue of racial diversity than I am with the kind of intellectual mix that is present here because I kind of aggregate everyone under the banner urban. And to me, implicit within urban is the race, sex, ages, you know, cultural and all that other stuff. Within this setting, I'm concerned with who exhibits and who does not exhibit particular attitudes toward learning. Many of our youngsters who in this context have their diversity being defined by their being white, come into our midst with not a clue about how their world has changed from situations that, at one point, would have guaranteed them access to the job market. Their chances have been sliced down to where now the battlefield—the playing field is indeed equal. There is nothing out there for anybody, unless we can prepare them.

In a school serving a majority of low-income "urban" children, Mary proposed that the most salient difference—the difference that made a negative difference—was "ability/intellectual" levels and their relationship to educational achievement. As working-class jobs dried up in the city, Mary recognized that economic survival depended on adequate educational achievement. Like Mary, all of Parks's educators were especially attuned to the particular risks their students would face as they entered high school and, later, the work force without strong academic skills. When educators spoke about the problem of learning diversity, they were signifying their concern with vastly inequitable outcomes in academic achievement. Many young adolescents arrived at and left Parks without the resources they would need to succeed in school and beyond.

Most educators explicitly argued that the students' academic achievement patterns reflected, to a large extent, the types of educational practices offered to poor children, children of color, and children labeled with disabilities.

As Chapters 3 and 4 will show, this was not the only discursive framework through which educators explained learning diversity among students. In fact, in both of those chapters, I argue that other important conflicting discourses about disability and learning diversity often reinforced, rather than remedied, educational inequalities. However, the approach to curricular reform that Parks adopted—reform organized around inclusive, integrated classrooms for children labeled with disabilities and clearly delineated, challenging, equal standards for all students—emerged in response to educators' strong beliefs that their students had been subject to an educational system that did not prepare children identified with disabilities, children from low-income families, and children of color to be academically successful. Ann Page, an experienced African-American social studies teacher, explained:

> And so I think we have taken on, sometimes not realizing it, those stereotypes we have heard in the media, and it determines how we react or treat our students. I don't think we challenge them enough. I think we have bought into that inner city—characteristics of the inner city child, including whether they are a minority or they are just poor. In a way, we've just given up, and we just figure we're doing the best we can. And we really don't have high expectations of them. I think we're too lenient in terms of behavior and academics. And I don't like the message it sends.

In Ann's view, cultural expectations and stereotypes are filtered through teachers who communicate to students the message that they need not succeed. By attributing school disengagement to low educational expectations, Ann challenged deficit thinking that writes off entire populations of children under the racially (and, as she pointed out, economically) coded heading "inner city." Ann suggested that teachers must understand their complicity in creating and perpetuating educational inequalities. These inequalities, in her view, actually reflect the reality that teachers simply do not expect enough of particular groups of students, and the students perform accordingly.

Lisa Bird, a young African-American social studies teacher, also challenged educators to consider how schools produce inequalities, particularly in relationship to disability. Citing a well-known, exemplary urban educator, she said:

> Marva Collins disproved the theory of special ed. She took a bunch of special ed. inner city kids and educated them. She had like a 95% rate of college-educated kids who graduated from her school. So my thing is there is a gap somewhere, and I don't think it's with the mentality

of these children. I think it's somewhere between the family and the school system. We are making the mistake.

In pointing to the case of Marva Collins, Lisa implied that poor teaching, rather than a child's disability, is responsible for academic failure. She proposed that all children could be educated well, given a teacher committed to doing so. A majority of teachers at Parks argued that the academic underachievement of most of their students was a result of impoverished educational opportunities as well as the low expectations that schools and society in general held for their children.

This analysis of educational inequality engendered specific justice claims and directed the approaches Parks took to educational reform. Although it was a budget cut that instigated the full-inclusion policy, it was the conviction of the principal and some of the teachers that special education classes underserved students by providing a context of low expectations and skills that was inherently inequitable. The justice claim for integration embodied in the full-inclusion program rested on the observation that children labeled with disabilities deserved access to a different kind of education—one based on meaningful, challenging academic experiences.

Understanding that it was not only children labeled with disabilities but also a majority of low-income children and students of color whose educational underachievement was due to impoverished academic practices, Parks focused its reform efforts on developing an academically challenging program for all its students. Thus, the second justice claim for equal standards emerged in response to educators' analysis of inequality. Its work with the Coalition led Parks to adopt a common set of standards to guide the curriculum. The year before the start of my research, the faculty had worked intensively to define and delineate exactly what they wished students to know by the end of their tenure at Parks. They had focused on developing standards that would engage students in meaningful work related to real-world tasks. The new standards, which are discussed in Chapter 4, promoted a vision of education grounded in the development of disciplinary thinking and the meaningful application of disciplinary tools. Writing was central across the disciplines. Teachers viewed these new standards as an important tool for guaranteeing that all students had the opportunity to engage in the same high-quality curriculum and be held to equal (and challenging) standards.

In the first year of my research, Parks once again felt buffeted by district directives as a new superintendent launched a reform effort. The school's efforts to further refine its standards came to a halt as it awaited new directives from the central office. Ironically, although Parks served, in many ways, as a model for the kind of reform the school district wished to promote in all schools, the system-wide nature of the reforms soon undermined many of the specific decisions educators had made for their local school community. This contributed further to teachers' frustrations that their efforts to make a difference and interrupt the cycle of academic underachievement for many of their students were once again thwarted by the larger school system in which they worked. In the years subsequent to my initial fieldwork, Parks increasingly lost its autonomy to direct its own school-based curriculum and assessment. The school district's systemic reform effort quickly shifted away from an initial vision that supported decentralization, local control over curriculum development and instructional design, and support for multiple forms of assessment. More significantly, the district's new accountability system, with its emphasis on standardized testing, restricted Parks's capacities to refine its curriculum standards and performance-based assessments. In Chapter 4, I take up the implications that narrowing assessment measures have for educators' efforts to address learning diversity in relation to educational equity.

## Poverty and Its Discontents

Although I focus my analysis in this book primarily around everyday *discourse* about difference in relation to justice claims, I recognize the danger of implying that educators have the capacity to change conditions of inequality if only they would think and act differently in relation to difference. Teachers' questions about how to build equitable practices that would best serve children labeled with disabilities and support the learning diversity of the student population were bound up with the realities that the school had neither the personnel nor the resources to accomplish this mission. The broader political and economic contexts of race and class within which Parks orbited greatly circumscribed educators' capacities to address educational inequality at the local level.

That enormous inequalities exist in school budgets across the nation is a well-documented phenomenon (see Kozol, 1991, 2005); however, as reform efforts have been increasingly organized around strong accountability measures for schools, it is critical to unmask the impacts of these budget cuts inside particular urban schools—cuts that render disingenuous the political rhetoric about educational equity. Since the mid-1990s, educational reform has been adopting punitive approaches ostensibly aimed at effecting greater educational equity. Practitioners and schools are under ever more pressure to improve student performance or face disciplinary sanctions and budget cuts. High-stakes testing threatens more children with academic failure, retention, and dropping out (Hauser, 2001; McNeil, 2000; Natriello and Pallas, 2001). Given this scenario of educational reform, I want to focus briefly on the broader material contexts of inequality within which justice claims are being engaged, for these contexts profoundly constrain possibilities for action in local schools.

I initially chose Parks as a research site because of its recent move to full inclusion. I assumed, wrongly as it would turn out, that this decision was born out of the school's commitment to rethinking practices in relationship to democratic education. During the research process, as I reviewed interview transcripts, I was constantly puzzling over why many teachers appeared—to my mind—so resistant to the daily workings of full inclusion. Although practitioners drew on the language of the justice claim for integration to support the ideal of inclusion, repeatedly I heard the refrain "I guess the philosophy is good, but ..." I wondered: Why did teachers who spoke of the benefits of inclusion only point to social and never to academic benefits for children labeled with disabilities? Yet, despite these observations, for a long time I tenaciously clung to my presupposition that the impetus behind the full-inclusion model had been the school's philosophical and ethical commitments to educational equity. Six months into my fieldwork, I scheduled a meeting with the principal to discuss why she thought that so many teachers, despite clinging to the ideals of diverse classrooms integrated by disability, seemed to resist and even resent this full-inclusion program. Melanie Post looked puzzled and answered:

> What thrust us into the setup that we have is the cut of 30% of our staff allocation one year. So, I asked [the vice-principal] to make a contractually correct roster ... and it was an awful mess. ... It looked like the most traditional junior high school roster you could imagine. ... The other alternative I came up with was pretty simple. I just took the available number of teachers, which was 14; and I broke them into 3 teams and said, "Well, what if you took a third, you took a third and you took a third?" And that's basically the design that was chosen. I also opened it up and said, "If anybody else can see other ways to do this, I'm sure there are." I wish I could say it was out of this great, grand pedagogical vision. It's not true. Although I would say I had a lot of ideas that allowed me to imagine that kind of structure.

For half a year, I had refused to hear what I had been told repeatedly by numerous staff members in many different interviews and focus groups. The initial decision to move to a full-inclusion model was not driven by lofty democratic ideals. A fiscal crisis forced teachers to accept a structure that would distribute the number of children per classroom more equitably, but it left faculty and staff increasingly overwhelmed and feeling incapable of meeting the needs of their students. The full-inclusion policy was, in a sense, a Band-aid approach to the hemorrhaging of academic support services for children as the city and state cut back on educational spending.

Even though this fiscal crisis precipitated the adoption of a full-inclusion model, educators drew support for their decision from the ideal of integration—a just educational community is an integrated one. However, constructing a full-inclusion model in the context of severely limited resources and huge needs created a structure that often left teachers feeling overworked and defeated rather than capable of developing innovative pedagogical approaches that could meet the needs of children labeled with disabilities.

This feeling was perhaps exacerbated by the fact that the 30% cut in teaching staff had been part of a long series of cutbacks. Peter Elliot, the white school counselor, explained:

> We saw everything just fall to pieces in terms of any specialness about Parks. We began losing classroom aides. Extra personnel were slowly taken away. And over about a three-year period starting five years ago, we lost over 30% of our teaching staff. We've lost a tremendous number of people that were here that allowed us a lot more flexibility. Philosophically, I agree with inclusion in terms of special ed. kids, but we don't even have the option to do pull-out now for those that need extra support in a smaller setting because we've lost so many people.

Inclusion was the most recent of many budget cuts that left Parks's teachers with little capacity to support all students' learning needs.

Furthermore, these teachers related the lack of resources in their district to societal racism and classism. Noting the difference with programs in suburban communities, Martha Silverman, a white language arts teacher, and Lisa Bird, the social studies teacher quoted earlier, became animated and angry:

**Martha:**  I think it's one of the greatest underground conspiracies going. And all you have to do is listen to your politicians, and what they're supporting and where they're giving their money. When they say that we have a country of kids in trouble, illiterates, drugs—and they don't put a penny up for education. What are they saying? If that's not important, then what is important? And that's not important because the kids who are not succeeding are the throw-away kids in our society. They are the minorities; they're the kids that have been labeled; they're the kids we don't expect to rise to any power anyway. And I never believed that [conspiracy theory]; I thought that was somebody's garbage, propaganda. And I'm telling you every year that passes I believe it more and more.

**Lisa responded:**   People say that we're [African-Americans] just talking out of both sides of our faces. But it is so real. The expectation of failure for many minorities in this country is so real, and in a lot of cases, it's very blatant. … It's out front. It's in your face.

Many teachers shared Lisa's and Martha's recognition of, and anger about, the political and economic contexts that drove policy within school walls. The budget cuts reflected society's willingness to abandon certain groups of children and to limit the possibility of academic success for many students.

For Parks, as for schools across the city, budget cuts were a constant, not an occasional, threat to the program. The financial condition of the school reflected the larger struggles of an urban district in crisis. In 1995, the governor proposed a freeze on state funds for basic education. The city had recently lost about one-third of its Title I funding. In a city with a weak property tax base and no independent authority to tax residents further, the Board of Education and new superintendent of schools faced a serious budget shortfall. This crisis occurred just as the new superintendent was proposing his major systemic reform effort organized around standards as the means to raise student achievement across the city. He premised his reform efforts on finding additional funding sources to implement the plan. Five years into this reform, the superintendent quit, in part because of the state's failure to provide adequate resources to fund these reform efforts.

I offer here only one of many examples of how the school district's fiscal crisis affected educators' capacities to address the needs of diverse learners. In 1995, Parks had its first professional development day of the school year, on the Monday after spring break. Two earlier scheduled days had been canceled due to excessive snow during the winter. The agenda planned for this long-awaited day was focused on rethinking class and team structures for the following academic year. Concerned about what they perceived as the failure of their current organization to meet the range of students' diverse academic needs, teachers and administrators were seeking to learn about other possible grouping structures and new approaches to teaching and curriculum. Discussions about the various possibilities threatened to be controversial; the opportunity for a whole day of working discussion was welcomed.

The meeting was scheduled to begin at 8:45 a.m., and the staff gathered in the library as usual, chatting over coffee and breakfast snacks. All awaited the arrival of the principal, Melanie Post, who was usually quite prompt. On this day, however, she arrived at 9:35, agitated and apologetic. She had spent the previous hour on the phone to the central district office, discussing the budget for the following academic year, which she had received the Friday before spring break. The school was faced with a reduced budget that specifically targeted their reading specialist, Laura Glenn, cutting her full-time position back to three days a week. This cut not only threatened Laura's position but also placed the entire academic program—small classes and full inclusion—in jeopardy because Laura had been, for the past three years, functioning as a full-time language arts teacher. Eliminating her position would increase class sizes across her team and leave the team without a full-time language arts teacher. The agenda for the professional development day was derailed, as the staff faced the work of reimagining how they might allocate their resources to buy back the two days scheduled to be eliminated.[4]

The meeting brought into stark relief the school's embattled position. The tone was alternately angry and depressed as the staff discussed possible solutions. The teachers knew that any service they decided to cut would never be restored, and that every decision would leave them feeling even more overworked and stretched. Previous experience had taught them that agreeing to give anything up was permanent because once they had done without a service, the district assumed they could always do without it. Teachers scrutinized the schedule to see if they could redistribute class time and give up prep time to buy back the reading specialist's lost days. This possible solution not only violated the teachers' contract (they had previously given up all the prep time they could), but it made several teachers balk at the thought of losing more precious time to meet together and plan curriculum. Several suggestions were ruled out, again on contractual grounds, even when the suggestions were to give up money that the school was allocated but could not use. (For example, an allocation for 100 hours of safety patrol was untouchable, although they did not need or use it.) The staff made a list titled "Lenses for prioritizing cuts" that included three items:

1. Least direct impact on kids
2. What we don't have already: "our entitlements"
3. Something we're willing to give up forever and ever

In the end, the decision was made to buy back the reading specialist's time by relinquishing the one-day-a-week allocation for a "mentally gifted" teacher and two lunchtime aides.

In this case, practitioners found a solution that did not pit core staff members against each other, but just barely. Instead, and with great reservation, they eliminated the jobs of employees who were not part of the decision-making process. Moreover, the staff devised a means by which they did not have to further reduce support for the most basic of all academic skills:

reading. The budgetary maneuvers that allowed Parks to keep its reading specialist represented yet another chapter in the school's ongoing struggle to support literacy education for its students.

During my time at Parks, a majority of faculty meetings were devoted to imagining creative solutions for improving student literacy without additional resources. Proposals included asking all administrators to devote significant time to teaching reading and attempting to cultivate a cadre of volunteers who would teach children to read. These proposals often pitted members of the community against each other. For example, administrators resented the implication that their work was not as important as teaching children to read. Teachers questioned the wisdom of having nonprofessional volunteers teach middle school children to read. It was a further twist of the system that, as faculty argued about which jobs to cut or what new programs to cobble together, they were unable to spend their professional development time engaged in substantive philosophical and practical discussions about educational practices that might better serve the diverse needs of their students. Practitioners were incensed by the brazen injustice of a school system that could not provide even the most basic education: adequate reading instruction and support.

The lack of resources to support reading represented only one of many areas of need at Parks. Inadequate fiscal capital had a direct impact on practitioners' abilities to engage students more deeply in their schooling and to support students' capacities to meet the new academic standards that were being developed. Scarce economic resources had easily visible material effects. Students frequently cited the absence of the art, music, and athletics programs as evidence that "this is not a real school." Emphatically stating that she would not recommend Parks to her friends, Jamila's response was representative of many students' feelings:

> In my other school, we used to have gym, art class, and everything. Only most of the boys get to go into fall sports. We don't got no girls' basketball team, no softball team, nothing. So, I wouldn't really recommend this school for nobody else.

Jamila was pointing to these missed opportunities as important components of a good school experience. The absence of these programs in art, music, and athletics signaled a lost chance for drawing students more deeply into an engagement with schooling. Imagining her ideal school, Jamila stressed the central importance of these programs:

> If I had my own school, I would name it after a famous person, like I would name it after a famous ballet teacher. And in my school, I would have more than one teacher. And in my school, I have music,

so like everybody's going to have an interest in college and stuff. We'd have a music section and a dance section. But you'd still have— say like Catherine, she wants to be a doctor. I would have a medical helper program, but they would still learn math, science everything. In the dance program, one-half of your classes you'd learn dance, but then you'd have to learn math, everything, your basics, and music and stuff. My school would be different. You'd go on a lot of trips. You won't have to pay for stupid things. Like you won't have to pay to go into the gym for a school dance. And have to raise the money. Like we had to raise money to get our snack machine.

Jamila articulated a longing felt by many students—a desire for a school not characterized by lack and the inability to provide a range of modalities through which students could pursue their studies. In a school that was deeply interested in supporting learning diversity, there was a visible absence of expressive media through which students could demonstrate their strengths and knowledge.

In addition to the lack of specialist teachers, the dearth of material resources in the school was constantly evident. In May, the school district ran out of the most basic of school supplies: paper. With no discretionary funds to buy paper, teachers had to ask students to buy their own. Eighth graders in the midst of the rush to complete final projects for graduation read this as evidence that, as one student put it, "This school is cheap; they have no more paper!" Teachers repeatedly reminded students that they had to bring supplies from home to complete the visual component for their final projects; poster board, markers, note cards, and other art supplies were nonexistent. Eighth graders expressed their frustration with the limited number of computers as they competed with others for work time. Students and teachers commented on the fact that the few students who had computers or art supplies at home were at a great advantage compared with their peers.

For anyone who has spent significant time in urban schools, these scenes should be remarkably familiar. They may even appear to be unworthy of mention, given the fact that Parks had significantly more resources than many urban schools, such as well-equipped science labs and a library staffed by a full-time librarian. As Chapters 3 and 4 will demonstrate, however, the lack of materials and personnel profoundly shaped and limited the possibilities for redressing educational inequality.

Parks's teachers were infuriated by the audacity of local and national reforms that increasingly held teachers accountable for student outcomes without providing additional resources needed to implement programs and practices that would adequately address the academic (let alone social) needs of their students. As the school district's systemic reform initiative took hold in the years following my initial fieldwork, Parks was subject to curricular directives and accountability measures that impinged on its autonomy. Students faced new sanctions with high-stakes testing and promotion requirements that threatened them with grade retention. Parks was expected to raise academic standards without a large infusion of resources to offer academic support to a student population that, for the most part, arrived in middle school underprepared for grade-level work. In the following chapters, I continue to explore the ways discourse about difference and justice must be understood to be connected with the material contexts of structural inequalities. As teachers struggled with two key questions related to educational equity—how to integrate children labeled with disabilities into mainstream classrooms and how to implement equal standards for all students—they often felt thwarted by insufficient material and human resources.

## City Friends

City Friends is a K–12 Quaker school serving approximately 900 students. Through an admissions policy that actively seeks students from different ethnic and racial backgrounds, as well as a large endowment to financially support students from working-class backgrounds, the student body is unusually diverse for an elite independent school. As a Quaker institution, a commitment to justice anchored the school's mission to some degree. The Society of Friends's (Quaker) core spiritual belief that "there is that of God in everyone" engendered a commitment to nonviolence and a history of involvement with social justice causes, such as abolition and civil rights. I chose City Friends as one site for this research because, drawing on the rich tradition of Quaker commitments, there was a lively interest in questions about race and class, as well as an active practitioner inquiry committee that examined gender issues. In a school that had a strong tradition of teacher autonomy, a new director of curriculum was promoting an inquiry model for investigating issues of concern to the community. This climate of inquiry offered an ideal site for exploring everyday discourse about difference and its relationship to ideas about justice.

By the time I began my research, the school's commitment to recruit students from diverse racial, ethnic, and economic backgrounds had led many faculty, staff, parents, and trustees to confront troubling questions about the meaning of "diversity" in a majority white, upper-middle-class context. It was the Quaker involvement with the Civil Rights Movement that, in the 1960s, morally compelled the school to become a more racially and economically diverse institution. However, by the mid-1990s, activist practitioners were critical of the school's approach to integration—one they argued served to reinforce rather than remedy racial injustice. These critiques drew upon a different justice claim: recognition. Recognition argues for the importance of acknowledging and being responsive to groups' different cultures, values, knowledge, experiences, and so forth. One strand of my research at City Friends examined the two justice claims through which practitioners wrestled with racial and, to some degree, socioeconomic diversity.

The claim for recognition was also articulated in relation to gender. The growing literature about successful single-sex schools ignited an interest on the part of the governing board of City Friends, known as the School Committee,[5] to form a practitioner research group, the Gender Audit Committee, to investigate what a coeducational environment can offer boys and girls. At the same time that practitioners began this research project, a group of high school girls charged that their math education was inequitable because it was unresponsive to the particular ways that girls learn differently from boys. As I tracked the work of the Gender Audit Committee, I began to explore these girls' charges, paying particular attention to the claim for recognition that they invoked. In the next section, I draw a portrait of the school to set the background against which the justice claims—integration and recognition—that I explore in Chapters 3 and 5 come into focus.

### First Impressions: Cities and the Race/Class Divide

The City Friends campus occupies a square city block a short distance away from Parks. Although contiguous, the two neighborhoods in which the schools reside demonstrated significantly different urban trends over the past few decades. While Parks's environs had remained economically and racially integrated, City Friends was located in a neighborhood that, similar to neighborhoods in many other U.S. cities, had become increasingly economically strapped and racially isolated—a majority of the local residents were African-Americans (see, for example, Massey and Denton, 1993). Most of City Friends's students traveled to the campus from nearby neighborhoods, but some came from the suburbs. Although the majority of students did not travel great distances to get to City Friends, they arrived from worlds apart—being primarily middle and upper middle class and, at the start of my research, 80% white.

The main campus featured many buildings, both old and modern, in close proximity to each other. The Quaker influence was immediately visible through the central location of the large, simple meetinghouse, where once a week all students attended Meeting for Worship, the Society of Friends's worship ritual. When the weather was fair, small groups of middle and high school students spread out in every available outside space, lying about, playing catch, or studying. Larger groups of elementary age children often shuttled between their classrooms and the gym or meetinghouse. The campus had the feel of a college in miniature scale, one in which the grounds were considerably smaller and the students significantly younger.

My first impression upon entering the main building at City Friends was one of easy familiarity and high energy, under the watchful eyes of established tradition. Climbing up the front steps and passing through a columned porch, I walked inside to find a large central foyer strewn with students' backpacks and jackets. Here, I often saw high school students standing in groups, sprawling across the floor, and popping their heads into the office to ask if they might use the phone. Most students appeared comfortable and proprietary in relation to this space. Middle and high school students were on a first-name basis with their teachers and administrators. Teachers and students interacted, for the most part, in a casual and friendly manner in public spaces. A permanent collection of portraits of former headmasters, all of whom were white, lined the walls and hallways of the main building. Rotating displays of students' artwork in various media proclaimed the central importance of visual expression in the school.

The Quaker commitment to social justice was often in evidence through visual displays in hallways and classrooms. One spring, for example, a middle school history teacher arranged a loan from a local museum of a large exhibit about the Civil Rights Movement; it occupied one wall of this central foyer. There was nothing ostentatious about this space or that of any other building on campus. Yet, the abundance of resources the school had at its disposal was apparent everywhere: for example, a well-provisioned library and bookstore, posters announcing student performances, and the new construction of a large, multipurpose building. The school confidently communicated an air of understated wealth in its simplicity.

An edgy relationship existed between City Friends and its surrounding neighborhood, and security concerns set a tone of some distance between the two. The feeling on the perimeter of the campus was of a school lightly barricaded against the neighborhood. Although there was no central gate through which students, staff, faculty, and parents had to pass, and no process for screening and announcing visitors, most of the main campus was fenced off from the city streets. Several classroom and administrative buildings were just across the street from the central campus. The school's security personnel, who were mostly African-American men, were ever present with go-carts and walkie-talkies, watching over students as they moved from building to building and keeping their eye on some of the high school students who snuck off campus to smoke on a nearby street corner.

City Friends's handbook that was distributed to the school community asked "all members of the community to be part of our security effort by being vigilant and by reporting unusual or suspicious situations or incidents to the switchboard as soon as possible." While security concerns were warranted—for example, one educator's relative had recently been murdered near the school, and car and computer thefts occurred during my fieldwork—they often served as powerful symbolic reminders of the race and class divide between City Friends and the neighborhood. The uneasy distance between the school and community was reflected in the stories of some African-American male students who had found themselves "mistaken" for neighborhood adolescents; such incidents created real conflicts for these students regarding their ability to belong to the school community. Moreover, they reflected troubling assumptions about African-American males that exist within our school communities, and our society at large. Positioned at a nexus of economic and racial boundaries, City Friends had begun to engage in critical inquiry into the borders that divided members within the school community, as well as those that created distance between the school and the broader neighborhood community.

The scenes that greeted me immediately at City Friends offered powerful symbolic indicators of the unsettling tensions that were at work in the school. As practitioners struggled to make City Friends a more equitable, inclusive community, they were deeply influenced by Quaker commitments to social justice, particularly in relation to race and class equality; however, they wrestled with the contradictions between creating a more inclusive school and preparing students to be academically successful in the most elite colleges and universities.

### The Contradictions of Elite Education

Halfway through my first year of fieldwork, the relatively new head of school gave a speech to the faculty, in which he laid out his vision of the school's mission. In that speech, Tom Whitman, a white man, described first how he saw City Friends—as "[a] white [school] in a black community" and later how he defined the school's mission: "We're intellectual, we're spiritual, we're urban, we're multicultural. Those to me are the most important parts of our mission." With these two descriptions, Tom pointed to a critical dynamic that deeply affected the school's work around difference. City Friends had made an explicit and genuine commitment to be intellectual, spiritual, urban, *and multicultural*; however, the reality of Tom's first statement—that City Friends was a predominantly white school in a primarily African-American neighborhood—set a course that often worked at cross-purposes to the goal of building a more inclusive school. The landscape Tom described highlighted the contradictory forces braided into the everyday life of the school: tensions between City Friends's privileged status and its vision of building a more multiracial, multiethnic, inclusive environment.

In the same speech, Tom referenced the Quaker meeting's decision in 1957 to maintain the school on its urban campus rather than move to the suburbs. He explained the consequences of that decision in the following way:

> Our mission is urban. ... [In 1957] the Monthly Meeting had a series of choices to make. They could have moved to the suburbs. They chose not to do that. They could have said we're a school for [the local] community which would probably have made us bankrupt. Or they could choose to do both. To reach out and bring people back into the neighborhood. And that's what the Meeting decided to do. We are drawing people back in and frankly the way demographics are running, we may have to draw further and further to bring them in here. So we've got to be good. We've got to make it worth their while to get here.

Thus, City Friends sought to survive by reversing the trend of "white flight" to the suburbs, working actively to attract wealthy, primarily white families to send their children to school in a neighborhood that those same families saw increasingly only as a security risk. City Friends, to some degree, hinged its ability to "make it worth their while to get here" by carving out a special niche in the market of independent schools in the greater metropolitan area.

Seeking to distinguish itself, City Friends established a program of curricular and after school activities that reflected upper-class interests. The Classical Western canon reigned strong across the curriculum. In an interview, Tom described this emphasis on the Classical canon as that which differentiated City Friends from other local private schools, attracting a group of parents who might otherwise have preferred to send their children to their local public schools or private schools in other locations:

> We had to draw families back in. And we had to draw them in with an attractive program. And our attraction is that we offer something that is somewhat unique—our emphasis on Classics. I don't know that too many schools have it. That's our market niche. Is that a better program than somebody else's? Maybe not. But it is ours. ... And frankly, in terms of the Watertown [a nearby suburb] crowd, those are our margins. Those are the people who if we can get them in, those are the people who balance the budget. The last 90 families, that's a

million bucks. So they count very much. So it is economic to a certain degree to draw them. What we want from Watertown is somebody who is somewhat countercultural. They live in Watertown, but they don't really buy the Watertown stuff. They don't feel very connected to the community. So they go, "Oh that school across the river that's got that fancy college list and they teach Greek and Latin."

The school's emphasis on the Classical Western canon and its relatively small but important Classics program served, in Tom's eyes, as bait for an economically vital group of parents and students—a symbolic shibboleth, drawing the line separating ordinary independent schools from the most elite.

The first class I observed at City Friends was an eighth grade section of Latin. Students rambled into class, dropping book bags and settling themselves in a tight circle of individual desks. A teacher who was walking by the room quipped to a female student, imploring her to take her feet off her desk: "Try a little culture." Although this comment was clearly made in jest, it marked symbolically one larger mission of a school that sought to teach students, both implicitly and explicitly, the knowledge, tastes, and values of the dominant culture (Bourdieu, 1984).

At the end of a fast-paced lesson conjugating Latin verbs and checking homework problems, one girl lingered behind to talk with the teacher. She was visibly upset and concerned about a recent grade she had received in Latin, particularly with the impact the grade might have on her chances of getting into a competitive college. The Latin teacher, clearly cognizant of the girl's anxiety, reassured her that her grades would not have an impact on her college admissions until her ninth-grade year. I would come to find that, like this Latin teacher, many teachers worried about the intense academic pressure students felt.

The culture of City Friends communicated its college preparatory mission to students at a young age. For example, early in the spring, seventh grade students were assembled at a class meeting to discuss the academic choices they would need to make for the following year. Three decisions needed to be made: what sports they would engage in, whether they would take instrumental or choral music, and whether they would embark on a study of Latin. The last choice was discussed as the most critical because it signaled a demarcation between the more and less academically serious students. Students who chose Latin, subject to the approval of their parents and the middle school principal, would carry a heavier course load than their classmates. John Carroll, the white middle school principal, commented to me that Latin was one of the test courses that many students chose for its symbolic academic value. A psychologist himself and the leader of a new middle school division,[6] John was seeking to build a program that was responsive to the developmental needs of early adolescents. In this meeting with the entire seventh grade class, John implored students to think carefully about their decision about Latin because "there are ramifications from here on out. ... Every so often over the course of your lives, the dials get turned up. People are asking you to take on a little more responsibility for the direction of your lives. This is one of them."

Throughout this meeting, many students asked questions about their college futures, particularly how studying Latin might put them in a better position regarding admissions. John responded to this repeated question at different times in different ways. After first telling one student that "The further along you can push your course of study [i.e., taking Latin], the better off you'll be [in terms of college admissions]," he later responded to another, "In and of itself, no [Latin will not help you get into college]. You need to choose a course of study here that you can be committed to. What you really want to show to anyone is what you believe in." As John spoke with the students, it became obvious that many young adolescents regarded Latin as highly prestigious.

As the meeting progressed, the conversation about academic choices became increasingly difficult to hear over the din of young adolescents whispering secrets, flirting, and joking. A few students stayed intensely focused on the discussion of college preparation. Most, however, were quickly distracted. When the meeting finally ended, I overheard one girl comment as she was leaving, "I don't feel like making choices about the course of my life—not now."

By the mid-1990s, City Friends, like many other schools, found itself at a crossroads; deeply invested in a particular way of defining its "intellectual" mission, it was also seeking to address its stated commitment to be "multicultural." In its curriculum, the school was trying to hold on to the essence of this traditional canon, while simultaneously representing new voices in the curriculum. In the initial stages of transformation, the new curriculum most often reflected what Banks (1997) refers to as an additive approach: Multiracial, multiethnic, and female perspectives were, at first, added to the curriculum without significantly undermining the narrative, standards, and values of the traditional canon. Demands by some students and faculty for a more transformative approach to multicultural curriculum appeared to threaten the school's primary mission. Jim Baker, a white administrator, justified the school's ongoing commitment to a traditional canon:

> For example, Afrocentric courses, as important as they may be in making someone feel comfortable here, if they are too heavily weighted that way, it's going to sufficiently weaken the program on the standards by which kids get into the most selective colleges. ...

> We also have to be familiar to a certain clientele that says those [traditional Western canon] courses do symbolize—even if you discard what I just said and said, "That's bunk." That you can do it [i.e., get students into elite colleges] by having more Afrocentric literature, Asian literature, or whatever. If our parents don't believe it, that's a problem. They won't come here.

As City Friends sought to rethink its curriculum from the perspective of multiculturalism, one central struggle involved its view of academic "excellence," which was primarily defined in terms of the traditional Western canon. As Jim admitted, to some extent the school clung to this curriculum to guarantee the support of a particular group of white, upper-class parents. Moreover, in a school that highly prized teacher autonomy, it was often difficult to move practitioners to adopt new curricular initiatives, especially because many also held to this perspective on academic excellence.

The curriculum was not the only area of the school that strongly represented elite interests; the majority of City Friends's extracurricular activities also reflected the taste of the upper class. Several teachers described how the choice of sports—for example, soccer, field hockey, and tennis—represented specific class interests and ethnic cultures. Emily Franks, a white sixth grade teacher, asked:

> What do we offer? We offer, it's like the white bread and jelly or something. Hockey, basketball, lacrosse for girls. Well, right there you've narrowed down your culture. Who plays hockey, lacrosse outside of the private schools in this area? Basketball yes; hockey and lacrosse, not even.

Patricia Lewis, a white athletic coach, shared this perspective. She argued that the choice of sports—field hockey, tennis, and squash—were unfamiliar and held little appeal for many students of color.[7] Even in arenas such as the middle school student talent show, classical music and ballet were the preferred modes of expression. The deeply entrenched elite interests of the school rendered its stated commitments to multiculturalism complex and contradictory.

### Race, Quakerism, and Social Activism

Complex and contradictory as it might be, the school was also serious about its commitments to being a multicultural community. As a Quaker institution with deep roots in the movement for social justice, City Friends was actively engaged in the difficult work of reimagining itself in relation to racial/ethnic diversity. In the speech cited previously, in which he described the mission of the school, Tom argued that the hardest task facing the institution was how to *be* a multicultural community:

We are multicultural. We are not great at it, but I have yet to find a place that is. Multiculturalism is the most difficult challenge that we have. Look at the eclecticism of this group [the faculty], and we're just nothing compared to the 880 families we serve. Bringing our nested ethnicity, bringing our personal backgrounds. Many of us never saw the inside of an independent school before. …We have to bring that all together and work it into a community. It takes a lot of work and patience to make that all work.

The difficult work of re-forging the community in inclusive ways continually challenged the school to rethink its elite tradition.

This reimagining of the community had taken different shapes since 1948 when the school decided to admit its first students of color. Over the next six decades, City Friends's commitment to become a more racially/ethnically diverse school engendered two different justice claims that framed educators' approaches to educational equity. In the early years, *integration* drove the school's approach to racial/ethnic diversity. As I discuss in detail in Chapter 3, in the beginning, the justice claim for integration often collapsed into an effort to assimilate a small number of students of color into the dominant culture of the school. As the number of students and faculty of color increased over the decades, however, the teachers, the students, and their parents, along with white activist educators, insisted that City Friends rethink its assimilationist stance, and they challenged color-blind positions that rendered invisible white power and privilege. A new justice claim, *recognition*, emerged as activist educators articulated the need for a transformative approach to creating a diverse school community. This early history is described in more detail in Chapter 3, in reference to the justice claim for integration, whereas the push for a different stance toward justice—recognition—is the subject of Chapter 5.

Research conducted at the local school level was partly responsible for changing the discourse about racial diversity at City Friends. In the late 1980s, a new head of school arrived and was eager to put concerns about race at the forefront of the school's agenda. Specific events, such as a Writers' Assembly in which a high school student read a piece that was perceived by many to be racist, as well as the establishment of the school's first racial affinity groups, had catalyzed public conversations about race and racism. In an effort to address race and racism in a more systematic way, the school engaged in a multicultural assessment plan (MAP), a program offered by the National Association of Independent Schools. During the 1990s, the MAP was popular with independent schools interested in evaluating their institutions in relation to multicultural concerns. In the MAP process, school practitioners began by conducting a self-study to assess their institution's current program with regard to racial diversity. This self-study was followed by an evaluation conducted by an outside team. The MAP team read the school's self-study, visited the school to conduct its own research, and wrote a final report describing the state of the school in relation to race and multiculturalism. As part of the report, the MAP team made recommendations to the school about steps it might take to address multicultural issues.

In the MAP self-study, educators looked to "the Quaker commitment to unreserved respect for the individual" as providing a particular rationale for, and approach to, addressing differences within the school community. This commitment had led the school to focus its attention and efforts on building a climate of respect for each individual in the community. This attention to individuals, instead of groups, led to the belief—expressed in several places in the report—that the school should take a color-blind stance toward racial/ethnic diversity. In the early 1990s when the MAP was undertaken, the school primarily interpreted the spiritual commitments of the Society of Friends to suggest that individuals, not groups, should be the focus for concern and action. This focus on the individual had, as I argue in Chapter 3, a profound effect on how the school took up the call for integration.

At the same time, as the school sought to become a more racially/ethnically diverse community, it found itself confronted with the idea that respect for individuals required attending to their diverse cultures, values, perspectives, and experiences. Some educators began to argue that it was critical to represent the experiences of all members of the community in the life of the school (for example, in the curriculum, assemblies, and social clubs). Moreover, practitioners concerned with racial equity observed that members of racially oppressed groups often shared experiences of alienation and discrimination within the school that were reflective of racial oppression in our society.

The idea that addressing racial equity requires focusing not just on individuals but on shared group experiences was slow to take hold; however, by the early 1990s when the MAP was engaged, there were signs that the school was beginning to attend to race through a more structural framework. For example, in distinct contrast to the general lack of official policy to address systemic racism, two administrative positions were created to support the needs of students of color. A coordinator of multicultural services was responsible for advising the multicultural students' union and for bringing multicultural issues and events to the school community. The second position was created to provide specific support for students entering through the Community Scholars Program—a scholarship program for students of color from low-income families, which is discussed at length in Chapter 3. The growing realization that to work for racial equity required attention to collective experiences laid the foundation for the emergence of a new justice claim, which is explored in Chapter 5: A just community is one that recognizes *group* differences.

The report of the outside MAP evaluation team urged City Friends to take a more systemic approach to building antiracist practices. The MAP report suggested that the school needed to focus study on its normative culture, which represented white interests. The team argued that the school should consider the ways its core value of individualism affected the program with regard to multicultural issues. In particular, the team observed that the autonomy of teachers most often worked against the development of a comprehensive approach to multicultural education that would weave together the curriculum across the grades and disciplines. In addition, they noted that simply adding materials, such as books, and sponsoring events with a focus on traditionally marginalized groups did not constitute an adequate response to racial diversity, and proposed that the school adopt an antiracist or antibias curriculum committed to addressing fundamental questions of power and privilege (see, for example, Banks, 1997; Nieto, 1996, 1999).

The MAP represented a huge effort on the part of the school to address racial diversity. In its immediate aftermath, however, many white practitioners felt that the MAP had created a distrustful environment among faculty. Many white faculty members felt severely criticized by the evaluation team's report and became wary of both outside researchers and the possible political agendas of insiders advocating multiculturalism. An in-service day workshop on diversity conducted a few years later exacerbated the feelings of distrust of outsiders among many faculty members. Paul Weiss, a white teacher, felt angered and frustrated by these attempts to deal with race: "We did do that other racial thing [the MAP]. I was annoyed. It was extremist. It was painful. And the workshops we had to endure that were set up supposedly to help us, for lack of a better phrase, turned out to be very disappointing." Thus, for Paul and some faculty, the MAP process represented an "extremist" position on multicultural issues that left them hurt and disappointed.

Many faculty and administrators—supporters and detractors alike— attributed the climate surrounding the MAP to the particular personality of the former head of school who had initiated the effort. One administrator, for example, described the problem in the following way:

> The MAP came about at a time of difficult leadership. [The former head of school] came with his agenda—to make the school reflective of the community. Also, we did this early in the process of the

development of the MAP. [The former head's] management style took a new and unrefined instrument [the MAP] and made it explosive.

Some resented the MAP as a destructive, top-down initiative from a difficult head of school. It was viewed as a tool for implementing his and his supporters' ideological agenda. It rubbed strongly against the grain of teacher autonomy.

From a completely different perspective, some activist educators were disappointed by the MAP, ultimately viewing it as a harmless tool that was undermined by the silent resistance of many faculty. One white English teacher, Ruth Bliss, saw the MAP as ineffectual rather than explosive:

> The MAP is doing diddly. There's nothing that came out of the MAP that was in any way destructive, in any way invasive, in any way damaging. It was ineffective I guess if it was supposed to nudge us in the direction of making improvements or having rich dialogue around issues of diversity—if it was in any way supposed to spark, and then we, of our own momentum, would continue these lively and rich discussions of diversity. Issues of diversity, since the MAP, are either initiated by or facilitated by people of color. That proves to me the MAP was not effective. "It's not *our* issue." "We've already dealt with that issue." And I don't feel that that's true.

From the vantage point of Ruth and several of her colleagues, the MAP gave some white members of the school an excuse for abandoning necessary conversation and action about racial diversity, while placing primary responsibility for the issues on faculty and administrators of color.

Donald Powell, an African-American teacher, spoke of his feeling that many white faculty members had developed little, if any, sense of their racial identity through the process. Speaking of why most white teachers had not engaged further in professional development seminars around multiculturalism, Donald argued:

> It's indicative of the degree to which white adults are dealing with their racial identity. On the one hand, "City Friends has done it. We're diverse. We're enlightened." On the other hand, there may just be a handful of people who are comfortable talking about, or even exploring their own racial identity. What does it mean to be a white person in the world, let alone at City Friends, in the classroom, in the hallway, talking to a student of color, etc.? So that the likelihood of a very small, small number of white teachers broaching the topic of whiteness with students is, unfortunately, rare. Then it becomes easy to let Eugene [an African-American colleague] and them do it.

We've been saying white people have to put themselves in the place to fight racism.

Donald echoed Ruth's sense that the MAP process left many white practitioners with the idea that the school had "done" race and was ready to move on. Donald argued that many white adults did not have an awareness of, or language for, understanding their racial identity. As such, they rested responsibility for work around race and racism with faculty of color and had no sense of how they might engage students on these issues.

The MAP process highlights how critical it is for schools to take a long view as they work to address racial diversity. Despite the perception that the MAP had had a limited impact on the school, it represented one important step in the school's ongoing quest to address racial diversity. By the mid-1990s, when I began my fieldwork, City Friends was thinking about questions of race and ethnicity through both official and less formal venues. For example, the school had drafted a long-range plan that committed itself to increasing the presence of students and faculty of color on campus within five years, with specific targeted goals of 25–40% student enrollment and 25–33% of all new faculty hires. In some places, the MAP team's recommendation that teachers think collectively about curriculum had come to fruition; the seventh grade team had placed at the center, not the margins, of its English and history curriculum the experiences of people of color and white women in this country. Conversations and actions about race and ethnicity were, albeit often awkward and stumbling, very audible at City Friends. Questions about race and educational equity were at the forefront of the school's agenda. The imperative to build a more racially and economically integrated community led the school to wrestle with the tensions between integration and cultural recognition. Chapters 3 and 5 address the complex discourse about race and educational justice.

### The Gender Audit Committee: Reform from the Ground Up

Although race/ethnicity was one area of concern for City Friends, the school was also investigating gender equity. The MAP, contentious as it was, generated an interest in research as a means to investigate local school issues. However, the experience with outside researchers led the school to adopt a practitioner inquiry model to inform its work on gender. Interestingly, the results of this gender inquiry led the school to investigate questions of race once again.

The practitioner inquiry group, called the Gender Audit Committee, was born out of the Long Range Plan of the School Committee. The Gender Audit Committee was a faculty research group charged with the task of examining the health of the community for boys and girls. Marketing concerns were one explicit motivator for the gender inquiry process. The committee was to formulate a response to recent research that suggested single-sex schooling offered benefits that coeducation did not. Paul Weiss, a committee member, explained why the long-range planning committee saw the need for research on gender:

> I think, first off, it's trendy. I also think that the research being done by all-girls' institutions has been fairly persuasive, telling the public that if you want the best for your daughter, send your daughter to an all-girls' school. And it's important for us to point out the realities that this may not necessarily be the case. So, I think that the Gender Audit Committee comes from a good place because we're genuinely concerned about this issue. And it also comes from a place of cultural pressure and the reality of needing to market ourselves in a very competitive world.

In a competitive independent school market, City Friends sought clear evidence for the benefits of its coeducational program.

Although the marketing strategy was, in the eyes of many members of the committee, not insignificant, the prime impulse for the Gender Audit Committee grew from an honest query on the school's part into several specific questions about gender. At City Friends, gender was not simply a substitute term for girls; rather, several of the committee's questions were focused on the experiences of certain groups of boys at City Friends. The summer before I began my fieldwork, Mike Knight, a white man who was the director of studies, set up a meeting to introduce me to Tom Whitman and the middle school principal, John Carroll. Tom, Mike, and John told me that the Gender Audit Committee was created out of a concern for two groups of male students—African-American boys and athletic boys—who did not appear to be well served by the school. All three men shared the feeling that, in general, the school climate was a healthy one for girls. However, in the course of our meeting, it emerged that the previous year, a small group of girls in the junior class were upset about their upper-level math class, feeling that it did not accommodate their needs and learning styles. These girls became one focus for my research. As explored in Chapter 5, they drew upon the justice claim for recognition in arguing for a different kind of math education.

This early meeting alerted me to several critical issues in play surrounding inquiry into race and gender. Many practitioners at City Friends saw the gender problem in terms of boys who did not fit in. Athletic boys—those who one committee member called "the lost boys"—were perceived to be without a place in this highly verbal, college preparatory environment. African-American boys posed a puzzle because many transferred out during middle or high school, or seemed to lose voice in their adolescent years. It is to the school's credit that concerns about boys and their experiences were included in a study of gender—an inquiry that often focuses only on girls. However, the school's concern with African-American boys initially erased the struggles of African-American girls. When, early in the research process, I asked one administrator why the school named the plight of African-American boys a gender issue, he responded, "because African-American girls are doing fine." Focusing on the manifest differences between the academic outcomes of African-American boys and girls left unnamed and unexplored the crucial questions about other important issues of racial equity, such as the cost for African-American girls of belonging and succeeding in this community. Acknowledging the complexity of gender, however, the Gender Audit Committee used research to explore the intersection of race and gender, and in doing so, it uncovered some important patterns that affected male and female African-American students. As I would come to realize once I learned the history of the MAP, the Gender Audit Committee opened up another way for the school to investigate racial differences in student experiences from an angle that felt less confrontational to educators who were threatened by the subject.

Although the Gender Audit Committee eventually opened the door for new conversations about both race *and* gender, it was initially greeted with skepticism and distrust among the faculty at large—feelings that reflected broader political struggle about change. In November, Ruth Bliss, a member of the Gender Audit Committee, stood up at an upper school faculty meeting and requested that teachers think of alumni who might be interesting to interview regarding their experiences as boys or girls at City Friends. This plea provoked some faculty members to attack the committee as methodologically incompetent, seeking anecdotal rather than "hard" evidence. These critics wondered what the real goals of the Gender Audit Committee were, and whether it was simply promoting a particular political agenda. This attack reflected the climate of distrust and fear of change that many teachers blamed on the MAP process.

As a result of this attack the Gender Audit Committee wished to emphasize to the school community that it had no political agenda. Members of the group decided that they should introduce the committee and its purposes to the entire faculty. Mike Knight, the committee's chairperson, spoke at an all-school faculty meeting, delineating the Gender Audit's agenda in terms that initially stressed its attention to healthy aspects of coeducation:

> I just want to make some salient points. One is that we are affirming that this is a healthy school. The School Committee—one of the major legs of their work was to respond to the single-sex schools in

ascendance [the fact that single-sex schools were growing in appeal in the independent school market]. The research has been a boon to single-sex schools and rightly so; they have something to say. But we feel a need to explore coeducation. What is it in coeducation that is healthy? What are things that we need to look at in coeducation that we can learn from? The second point is that this is a faculty-led committee. This is not a team from the outside. I think we set an important precedent in doing our own work. It's important in our school to have a climate of inquiry in which we go after and ask our own questions. It's important that we trust each other enough that we can make that a healthy process. We welcome your feedback and your cooperation.

Mike told the faculty that this committee's main goal was to affirm the health of the school for boys and girls. In a competitive independent school climate in which single-sex schools were on the rise, coeducational institutions had to articulate a rationale for the value of educating boys and girls together. Mike emphasized that this faculty committee was developing a "climate of inquiry," one that invited others to join in the process.

Mike used this entree to subtly prepare the ground for more difficult questions, particularly about race and the use of qualitative research:

We're also interested in issues of race because there is strong suggestion, if not conclusions, in the gender research that race makes a big difference in the experience of gender. For instance, the Harvard Project for Girls and Women, which writes deeply and profoundly of the silencing of girls' voices as they enter adolescence, seems to find an odd echo in African-American boys' adolescent experiences as well. We need to attend to that in our work because we have in our school problems with success, retention, and feelings of belonging with our minority students as they move from lower grades to upper grades.

This passage signified the way that the Gender Audit Committee would use its research as a way to revitalize an investigation of race through an exploration of students' experiences. In a school in which public discussion of race was often difficult, the committee's research was one critical component for reopening these conversations. Mike also viewed the committee's work as a means to argue for the importance of hearing *all* students' voices:

There's one thing about this research; it's not a democracy. If the majority of students feel great about this school or feel ill about this school pertaining to issues of gender, that doesn't necessarily mean that there's nothing for us to look at or think about. It's not as if majority rules on this. There are individual stories, individual stories rooted in family background, class, and race that we need to listen to. The point is we are curious. We want to find out if there are questions that should be prompted by this research for us as a larger faculty. We will be looking for individual stories, for people who have something to say. And I feel that we have lots of context in which to put those individual stories.

Here, as in other talks he gave to the faculty, Mike carefully argued against the tendency to dismiss individual stories as anecdotal. He imagined practitioner inquiry as a site from which qualitative research focusing on the individuals' varied stories could become a powerful tool for reassessing educational practices. He was fully aware of the delicate political environment in the school; many teachers were quick to dismiss research and to discount the voices of students who felt marginalized. As an administrator new to the school, Mike saw the Gender Audit Committee as holding the potential to use insider research as a way to crack open necessary conversations about gender and race privilege. Given a faculty climate that was generally distrustful of educational research as a field and of outsiders suggesting directions for the school, the newly launched Gender Audit Committee introduced a novel way for educators to engage with questions of difference in relationship to institutional practices. Practitioner inquiry offered City Friends a space from which to pry open difficult questions about students' experiences across categories of gender and race.

Over the course of a year and a half, the Gender Audit Committee designed and conducted a survey of students' experiences across the three divisions of the school. The data from those surveys were analyzed by race and gender, offering a picture of the school from multiple perspectives. The results of the survey made visible the highly variable experiences of different constituents of the school. The survey indicated, for example, that students of color felt less connected to the school community in general, and less well known by their teachers. It demonstrated huge discrepancies in academic awards along racial lines. The report also challenged the faculty perception that girls and boys felt equally well served in their math and science classes, and showed that girls took significantly fewer AP (advanced placement) tests than their male counterparts. This survey supported the arguments of many activist educators that the school needed to attend more closely not only to the individual student, but also to patterns of marginalization and exclusion of certain members of the community. Over the next few years, it opened up new conversations about race and gender. It lent credence to the idea that, rather than maintaining a focus on individuals, justice may be served by the recognition of groups (the subject of Chapter 5).

## Justice Claims in Everyday Practice

As these portraits of City Friends and Parks suggest, justice claims about difference emerge from particular local struggles. Activist educators in each setting were, to a large extent, working with vastly different issues and constraints. The material interests of both schools—the profound poverty of Parks and the abundant wealth of City Friends—limited the scope of change that was possible at each school. As I shift focus, in the subsequent chapters, to explore how discourse about difference in relation to justice claims create but also limit possibilities for action, it is critical to remember the contexts within which educators work for social change.

CHAPTER 2

# Integration

City Friends was not intentionally a segregated school. However, by the late 1950s, even as many members of the Society of Friends were actively engaged in the Civil Rights Movement, it remained a racially isolated school, with students of color making up only 5% of the student body. From its inception, City Friends was guided by the core Quaker beliefs that "there is that of God in everyone" and that differences must be resolved without violence. The Quaker Monthly meeting responsible for the school's care had deep roots in the struggle for racial justice. It had a history of involvement with the abolitionist movement and the Underground Railroad. It was the Civil Rights Movement that compelled practitioners at City Friends to address a set of moral claims regarding the school's responsibility to become more racially and socioeconomically diverse. Beginning in the Civil Rights era, the claim that a just community is an integrated community would shape educational initiatives at City Friends for more than half a century.

Parks, a school that was part of the city's desegregation plan, was struggling with this justice claim from a different angle. Having recently adopted a full-inclusion program for students labeled with disabilities, its educators were wrestling with creating integrated classrooms that served all learners well. On the heels of a budget cut, teachers were struggling to maintain a commitment to an ideal of integrating classrooms by disability, while meeting the variable needs of all their students without the resources formerly allotted to special education.

Because integration is a word with an almost historic ring, my proposal that integration is an ideal that continues to serve as a justice claim that drives educators' practices must be explained. There are two reasons I have chosen to reference this justice claim in terms of integration and not, for example, in terms of equal opportunity (a much more familiar idea in the literature of education and political philosophy). First, I do so to highlight a historical trajectory, set in motion by the Civil Rights Movement, which continues to resonate at City Friends and Parks, as well as at educational institutions across the nation. The 1954 *Brown v. Board of Education* decision by the U.S. Supreme Court (*Brown v. Board of Education*, 1954) inscribed into law a specific vision that proclaimed de jure segregation as inherently unequal. Although the ruling explicitly addressed itself to intentional school segregation, it *implicitly* linked the ideals of democratic society with integrated schooling. Symbolically, *Brown* embodied one justice claim made by many civil rights activists: that creating diverse, racially integrated environments is a just aim of a democratic society—one that ideally transforms relations of racial inequality and promotes equality in schools and society (Balkin, 2001; King, 1986; Powell, 2005). Integration may be a more elusive ideal than ending legal segregation. Nevertheless, it is one that, for over half a century, has compelled and continues to compel many educational activists.

The dream of a nation of integrated schools appears to be fading into the annals of history, given the tenacity of segregated housing and the rescission of desegregation orders across the country (Frankenberg and Lee, 2002; Orfield 2005; Orfield and Eaton, 1996; Orfield and Yun, 1999). Even when schools' demographic data indicate they are integrated, they are often internally segregated through tracking and special education programs (Artiles, 2003; Donovan and Cross, 2002; Eitle, 2002; Lucas, 1999; Mickelson, 2005; Oakes, 1985). Moreover, from a contemporary vantage point, the deeply entrenched patterns of racial inequality and injustice in the United States render suspect the idea that building diverse schools and classrooms is a sufficient condition for bringing about educational equity (see, for example, Bell, 2004; Ladson-Billings, 1994). Education that is integrated *and* equitable requires much more than simply changing the student body composition (Fine, et al, 2005; Ladson-Billings, 2004; Powell, 2005). Despite this troubled history, the idea that a fair and just educational community is a diverse community now permeates the discourse of many K–12 schools and institutions of higher education. In 2003, the Supreme Court decreed that race-based admissions policies that aim to create and maintain a diverse student body serve a compelling government interest (*Grutter v. Bollinger*, 539 U.S. 306 2003). Sadly, the *Grutter* decision did not aim to remedy the tenacious legacy of racial inequality and transform society in the ways that *Brown* had intended. Nevertheless, it affirmed the importance to democratic society of educating all students in racially/ethnically diverse settings (Powell, 2005). *Integration* and *diversity* may be embattled terms, but—implicitly and explicitly—they drive educational policies and practices that aim to effect equity.

This, then, is my second reason for naming integration as a justice claim: It is an ideal that reverberated at both Parks and City Friends. In late 20th- and early 21st-century parlance, educators did not talk explicitly about a desire for an *integrated* community—they were more apt to speak of *diversity*—but the words integration and segregation do appear in institutional documents and teacher discourse. Moreover, educators expressed an almost taken-for-granted belief that a just community is one that is integrated across dimensions of social difference; heterogeneity is the explicit value. This notion of integration, while inclusive of the ideal of equal opportunity, represents a more encompassing claim for educational justice.

This chapter examines how the justice claim for integration drove educational practices at both City Friends and Parks, albeit in relation to different groups of students. Deeply aware of the problematic nature of integration as a justice claim in relation to City Friends—a school that is, by nature, exclusionary—I nevertheless show how the school felt directly challenged by the Civil Rights Movement and the ideal of integrated schooling to examine its exclusionary practices closely, particularly in relation to students of color. In the 1960s, the school embarked on a journey that continues to the present: to build a more racially and socioeconomically diverse community. Throughout this journey, educators have struggled over the goals and definition of a diverse community. By the mid-1990s, many were calling into question the school's assimilationist approach to what was, by that time, known as diversity; they argued that equity could not be served by simply inviting more people to participate in the community without examining and changing curriculum, pedagogy, and practices in fundamental ways.

Parks offers a very different vantage point from which to explore the justice claim for integration. I began my research shortly after Parks had moved to a full-inclusion model for students labeled with disabilities, in which those children were no longer served in special education classrooms. Full inclusion is an idea premised on an iteration of civil rights discourse that rejects the segregation of students labeled with disabilities. Students labeled with disabilities should be served in classrooms with their nonlabeled peers to the greatest extent possible. Disability-rights advocates argue that equitable inclusive education requires much more than simply placing students with and without disabilities in the same classrooms; it entails fundamental changes to educational practices (Lipsky and Gartner, 1999; Rizvi and Lingard, 1996). The argument for including students labeled with disabilities in mainstream classrooms expands the justice claim for integration beyond an assimilationist stance. Parks's experience with full inclusion, however, reflects the difficulty of implementing this more encompassing vision of integration, given both the inequalities of resources in urban schools and a pervasive and dominant medical discourse that views disability as a problem located in the body of particular individuals.

In proposing that integration is a justice claim that frames educators' work, I am not arguing that, *in practice,* it always serves the goals of equity. In fact, what I show in this chapter is that, in practice, integration can fatally collapse equity with assimilationist treatment of all students, and that in doing so it becomes an inequitable strategy. Through an analysis of these two very different manifestations of justice claims based around notions of integration and diversity, I raise up for consideration the normative goals of many integrationist approaches. Examining the practices at both schools makes visible how the justice claim for integration, working in relation to particular discourses about difference, can reinforce and reinscribe, rather than challenge, dominant educational practices.

In what follows, before turning to how the idea of integration structured practices at City Friends and Parks, I briefly consider the ideal of integration in the public imagination, particularly as expressed in the Supreme Court's *Brown* decision. I do so, despite the exhaustive existing discussions of *Brown*, because it continues to represent a strong symbol of educational equity in our public consciousness.

### *Brown v. Board of Education: Integration and Educational Equity*

*Brown* has been enshrined in public consciousness as an icon of American democracy at its best; however, given a historic vantage point, it has also been soundly critiqued for its limitations in effecting educational equity (Balkin, 2001; Bell, 2004; Ladson-Billings, 2004). Nevertheless, despite its limitations, *Brown* has strongly influenced public discourse about race, education, and equity, and its logic has been extended to support gender equity and disability rights. The decision continues to offer a critical challenge to educational institutions: If separate is inherently unequal, what does a just educational community look like?

*Brown* proclaimed the inextricable link between full citizenship and the need for equal education for all. Delivering the opinion for the court, Chief Justice Warren argued that public education plays a central role in contemporary democratic society and, therefore, must be afforded to all children on equal terms:

> Today, education is perhaps the most important function of state and local governments. Compulsory school attendance laws and the great

expenditures for education both demonstrate our recognition of the importance of education to our democratic society. It is required in the performance of our most basic public responsibilities, even service in the armed forces. It is the very foundation of good citizenship. Today, it is a principal instrument in awakening the child to cultural values, in preparing him for later professional training, and in helping him to adjust normally to his environment. In these days, it is doubtful that any child may reasonably be expected to succeed in life if he is denied the opportunity of an education. Such an opportunity, where the state has undertaken to provide it, is a right, which must be made available to all on equal terms (*Brown v. Board of Education*, 347 U. S. 483 1954).

Thus, the court declared that public education is the primary guarantor of a child's future participation in democratic society, as both citizen and professional. If education is critical to "good citizenship," justice cannot tolerate exclusionary or discriminatory practices.

Framing the right to education in terms of *opportunity*, the Court required that access be offered on equal terms. The crux of the Court's decision lay in its proposition that segregated schooling is, by definition, unequal. Continuing from his previously quoted opinion, Chief Justice Warren wrote:

We come then to the question presented: Does segregation of children in public schools solely on the basis of race, even though the physical facilities and other "tangible" factors may be equal, deprive the children of the minority group of equal educational opportunities? We believe that it does. ... We conclude that in the field of public education, "separate but equal" has no place. Separate educational facilities are inherently unequal (*Brown v. Board of Education*, 347 U. S. 483 1954).

Declaring segregated schools to be "inherently unequal," *Brown* struck a decisive blow against legally sanctioned white supremacy. In doing so, it supported the ideal of integration of schools in democratic society, linking equality of educational access and opportunity for all students with that integrationist ideal.[1]

In the half century since the *Brown* decision, much has been written about why the decision failed to make equal and integrated schooling a reality in the land (see Balkin, 2001; Bell, 2004; Fine et al., 2005; Ladson-Billings, 2004; Wells et al., 2004). It is not my intention to review this vast literature here; rather, I want to draw attention to several key assumptions of the decision that reverberated in the discourse about integration at City

Friends and Parks—assumptions that framed the schools' responses to inequalities.

Critical race scholars have argued that, while *Brown* addressed de jure racial discrimination and affirmed a child's right to attend schools that were not intentionally segregated by race, it did not require that remedies address the structural conditions of racial oppression or be measured in terms of educational outcomes for African-American children (Bell, 1987, 1995, 2004; Freeman, 1995; Ladson-Billings, 2004; Ladson-Billings and Tate, 1995). Derrick Bell (1995, 2004) proposes that, in ignoring questions of educational effectiveness and focusing on desegregation, civil rights lawyers' approaches to litigation, as well as court-fashioned remedies for educational inequality, have failed to confront the real and ongoing inequity of pre-*Brown* schools: the systematic oppression of African-Americans and the construction of white domination throughout the process of education (see also Fine, 1997; Fine et al., 2005; Ladson-Billings, 2004). This lack of attention to systematic oppression of African-American and other subordinated groups, and white accrual of privilege and power resonates inside schools where, as a close examination of City Friends and Parks will show, educators often focus on increasing access to the school or classroom, rather than on the practices within those spaces that act in exclusionary ways.

A second assumption of the Court's—one that echoed loudly at City Friends—envisioned education as an assimilating institution, one that would "awaken the child to cultural values" and "help him to adjust normally to his environment." This mention of "cultural values" referenced a normative national culture, one to which all citizens could, at least in the ideal, belong. Lifting the discriminatory barriers to education was a critical component for undoing the historical legacy of racial oppression and realizing the unfulfilled promises of democratic participation. The language of *Brown* indicated an invitation to participate in the dominant culture, but did not suggest that that culture would itself be or need to be reshaped by such expanded participation. As City Friends grappled with integration as a justice claim, it initially clung to this assimilationist vision.

A third key assumption rests in the way the Court framed the wrongs of segregation in terms of the negative effects on children of color. Chief Justice Warren wrote, "[T]o separate them from others of similar age and qualifications solely because of their race generates a feeling of inferiority as to their status in the community that may affect the hearts and minds in a way unlikely ever to be undone" (*Brown*, p. 195). Racial integration was considered crucial for promoting black students' self-esteem and sense of being fundamentally equal to all others. In focusing on the damage done to African-American students, the power and privilege that white students accrued under segregation remained invisible. City Friends and Parks both offer rich sites from which to examine the consequences of this tendency in our quest for educational equity to focus on the students who are disadvantaged by schooling, thereby ignoring the institutional practices that co-create power and privilege on the one hand and inequality on the other.

Despite the limitations of the Supreme Court's 1954 decision, *Brown* embodied an important public discourse about educational justice. Subsequent to *Brown*, the idea that segregation is inherently unequal reverberated throughout the educational world. Advocates for other groups of students who were traditionally marginalized or excluded from schools and institutions of higher education echoed the language of *Brown* and the Civil Rights Movement to argue for educational justice on similar terms. Arguing that sex-segregation violated the equal protection clause, gender equity proponents fought to have girls and women admitted to powerful, publicly supported all-male institutions (see *Virginia v. United States*, 518 U.S. 515 1996). In addressing the needs of students labeled with disabilities, federal laws (Education for All Handicapped Children Act, 1975; Individuals with Disabilities Education Act [IDEA], 1990) were premised on the standard that children labeled with disabilities should be educated in integrated classrooms to the greatest possible extent (Gartner and Lipsky, 1987). This call for educating children labeled with disabilities in integrated classrooms with their nondisabled peers has been advocated even more strongly in recent years by proponents of full-inclusion policies, like the educators at Parks who were committed to these ideals (Biklen, 1992; Kluth, Straut, and Biklen, 2003; Lipsky and Gartner, 1996, 1997, 1999). Thus, the integrationist ideal of liberal civil rights discourse has permeated multiple movements for educational equity.

City Friends and Parks offer two different examples of how educators struggled with this justice claim in practice. These two ethnographic portraits also illustrate, from a practice standpoint, the cogent critiques of integrationist approaches to educational justice (Bell, 1987, 2004; Ladson-Billings, 2004). They portray how justice claims based around the demand for integration often fail to uncover the invisible, systemic ways that educational practices reflect dominant patterns of power and privilege. To see the limitations is not, however, to give up on the vision of just and diverse school communities; rather, it is to affirm the critical importance of inextricably intertwining the ideals of integration *and* justice. Ladson-Billings has suggested that we might "use *Brown* as a hypothesis for a new future"—a call for understanding that "real education is impossible in isolation from diverse and critical perspectives (2004, p. 11).

## City Friends: Accessing Elite Education, Building a Diverse Community

In February of my first year of research at City Friends, Cheryl Andrews, an African-American teacher, asked me to begin observing her ninth grade algebra class. She was concerned about an edgy atmosphere—an atmosphere that she believed was related to the dynamics of race and class among students. Ninth grade students came to this algebra class through two routes. Approximately half had been at City Friends for middle school and had, unlike the remainder of their peers, taken a pre-algebra course. All these students were white. The rest of the students were incoming ninth graders, a majority of whom had not had the opportunity to take algebra because it had not been offered in their previous schools. With one exception, these students were African-American and Latina. The majority had received scholarships through the school's Community Scholars program. From my first visit, I was struck by the rightness of Cheryl's observation about the discomfort and awkward tone of this class, one that often slipped over into race- and class-infused tensions and conflicts. In that first class, as one African-American boy, who was dressed in a tan jacket and pants approached the board, a white girl whispered as he passed by, "Safari boy"; the girls around her, white and African-American alike, laughed and continued to discuss this under their breath. Over the course of the spring, I witnessed white students challenge Cheryl in ways that smacked of racial overtones, and a few groundlessly accused her outright of playing favorites with African-American students. Students of color expressed their shock at the ways that white students spoke with their teacher, perceiving the casual, demanding interactions as a mark of disrespect for elders. A particularly telling incident occurred one day when the students were involved in a community service project: making sandwiches for a local shelter for homeless men. The desks had been pushed together, with jars of peanut butter and jelly and bags of sliced bread strewn across them. The students were upbeat, joking with each other as they prepared and wrapped the food. Maya, a wiry, energetic African-American girl, lightheartedly chided Andrew, a small, self-confident white boy, for making an imperfect sandwich: one corner was cut off. Suddenly the tone changed. Andrew retorted, "These are for people who eat rats out of garbage cans." Maya flared, "That doesn't mean they should have to eat any old thing."

The tone in Cheryl's classroom reflected tensions and conflicts about race and class that were pervasive across the school. As City Friends sought to become a more racially and socioeconomically integrated community, teachers and students struggled with competing values, perspectives, and assumptions that often implicitly, and sometimes explicitly, structured their interactions. This was difficult work, more so, as I argue, because of the initial approach City Friends took to integration: one that promoted the values and interests of dominant social groups and asked students of color and students from low-income families, who represented only a small minority in the community, simply to adapt to that culture.

## Historical Context

The Civil Rights Movement was directly responsible for propelling questions about racial integration and increased educational access for students of color to the front of City Friends's agenda. Even in a context that was exclusionary by design, civil rights discourse permeated City Friends's institutional consciousness, as it did in other elite schools and institutions of higher education, demanding that educators confront the inequalities inherent in maintaining a racially and socioeconomically isolated community. The school's first move was to renew its commitment to the city and to the neighborhood in which it resided. In the late 1950s, the city, like other U.S. cities, saw growing numbers of white residents move to the suburbs. City Friends's neighborhood had begun to change due to this exodus. Fearing a larger demographic shift, the Quaker Meeting was faced with a critical choice. The Meeting had been offered a large piece of land, in a nearby suburb, upon which to relocate the school. Tom Whitman, the current Head of School, described the decision the Meeting made:

> The decision to stay was the core. You understand they were offered land. We turned it down. Huge tract of land. But the Meeting said, "No." This is 1961.[2] The neighborhood is changing. The Civil Rights Movement is heating up. You have to put [the decision] in the context of the day. The Meeting at that point was standing up for civil rights, standing for integration. This is when Old Town [a nearby neighborhood] is forming that whole [intentionally racially integrated] neighborhood up there that still exists. Dutch Hill [the school's neighborhood] had changed almost by then. Racially at least. I don't know about economically. The Meeting said, "No, we believe in the city. We believe that we can make a difference in this community. We believe we can be of help here. This is our historic home. We're not leaving."

Acting on an ethical commitment to racial integration and service, the Meeting bound City Friends to its historic neighborhood with the hope that the school's presence and relationships with the community would offer a vital resource to the region.

The context of the Civil Rights Movement confronted the community with the contradictory nature of working for racial integration elsewhere, while maintaining an almost exclusively white, upper-middle-class school community. City Friends's first response to the call for integration was to create a small color-conscious scholarship program. The Community Scholars Program, which offered full scholarships to students in fifth grade and above, was intended to increase the number of students of color who attended City Friends (at that time, hovering around 5%) and support wider socioeconomic diversity in the community.

In a brochure to commemorate the program's 30th anniversary, a white City Friends alumnus, parent, and major benefactor of the Community Scholars Program recalled its inception in the following way. Speaking of the 1963 church bombing in Birmingham, he said:

> We, of the enlightened, in Old Town and Dutch Hill were horrified and enraged by this outrageous act by those "terrible rednecks" down South, and we began to discuss what we could do, what kind of aid package we could create to send to Alabama. Then there occurred one of those magic moments which rarely happen but do happen. [We realized] that the problem was not Birmingham or Little Rock, the faraway "them" in the Deep South. Our problem was not [the Southern one] but rather the [Northern one]: our very own neighborhoods, our own hearts and minds.

These words suggest how the Civil Rights Movement, while explicitly focused on fighting legal segregation, generated, at least for some people, broader moral questioning about patterns of racial segregation and inequality that existed across the nation. He continued:

> If one wanted to do something to try to improve relations between and among races, a good place to focus our attention might very well be [here] and in the very school in which we were deeply involved, where our children were growing up and being educated. This specific event, this heartless, cruel bombing reinforced the school's earlier decision to remain in [the neighborhood] rather than moving to a beautiful suburban campus which had been offered us. And it prompted the school to begin the Community Scholars Program instead of sending a "Care package" to Birmingham.

The creation of this program reflected a local response to a certain set of justice claims that were sweeping across the nation. Emerging from the Civil Rights Movement, these claims were rooted in the language of racial integration and racial harmony, and of "improving relations between and among races." For those who initiated it, the program, born a decade after the *Brown* decision, was an acknowledgment that racial inequality and segregation were problems not only elsewhere within the American legacy of slavery and Jim Crow, but rather blatantly within their own community.

City Friends, like other elite institutions, initially responded to the ethical demands leveraged by the Civil Rights Movement with a circumscribed scope and definition of racial/socioeconomic integration. The Community Scholars Program offered scholarships to approximately four new students each year. At its 30th anniversary, the program counted 127 scholars among past recipients, and the number of Community Scholars at any given time hovered around 30 students; however, by that time the school did not depend on the Community Scholars Program alone to increase the racial diversity of the student body. During that same period, City Friends had sought to build a more racially diverse community by recruiting middle- and upper-middle-class students of color. Between the 1960s and the mid-1990s, it increased its overall enrollment of students of color from the earlier 5% to just below 20% of the total population. By the 2002–2003 school year when I conducted my follow-up research, the population of students of color had increased to 26%, and by 2005 it had grown to 30%.

Similar to other private institutions across the country, City Friends adopted color-conscious admissions policies (like the Community Scholars Program and the enrollment goals for students of color) as a necessary step toward building a more racially and economically diverse school community. Initially, the school did not anticipate the ways that it would be challenged to change in response to the shifting demographics of the school community. It assumed that increasing access was a sufficient response to the goal of integration. By the mid-1990s, practitioners at City Friends were engaged in contentious debate over racial diversity and integration in the context of an elite educational institution. In response to the multicultural assessment plan (MAP) process described in Chapter 2, the school was forced to revisit and expand its notions of diversity. Slowly, members of the community came to realize that the school's commitment to a racially diverse community remained elusive, with serious consequences for students and faculty alike.

### Envisioning a Community of Excellence: Assimilating Diversity

The contentiousness of the 1990s evolved because the school's early efforts to become a more racially integrated community hailed diversity without challenging its normative practices. The school had worked on increasing access to City Friends and all it had to offer, but it had not interrogated or transformed the school's educational practices. Focusing on individual achievement and merit, and maintaining a particular view of excellence, the school had created an environment, as I will show, that aimed to invite students of color to participate seamlessly in the most elite institutions of higher education and in the process, left these students feeling that they were perpetual outsiders.

What was the dominant discourse about diversity? What was the ideal community imagined by City Friends? What role did diversity play in this ideal community? This ideal community was reflected in the school's philosophy statement and its overall admissions policies, as well as in those color-conscious programs that aimed explicitly to increase racial and economic diversity. The school's statement of philosophy embodied two clear directives: an adherence to fundamental Quaker values and a pursuit of excellence.

> We are a Friends School ... founded on the belief that there is that of God in everyone. Together, love and respect for each individual provide the premise for all that we do. We regard education not as training for a particular way of life, but as part of a lifelong process, and as we guide and encourage our students in their personal growth, we try to cultivate and support in them principles that Friends have long considered to have lasting value. Among these are truthfulness, simplicity and self-discipline, the resolution of differences without violence, and respect for diverse heritages and experiences.

As discussed in Chapter 2, the foundational Quaker belief that "there is that of God in everyone" implies a vision of community in which the individual is of paramount concern. It is love and respect for each person and "the diverse heritages and experiences" individuals bring that, at least in the ideal, drives all else. This belief in the inherent value of each and every individual reflects an overarching ethical commitment to the fundamental equality of all persons.

This commitment drove a vision of equity that primarily focused on the individual rather than on groups. Thus, the school's Quaker philosophy played a contradictory role in supporting the quest for greater educational equity. On the one hand, the Quaker commitment to nurturing the uniqueness of each person in the community lent great strength to the school's mission to respect and value all children and, by extension, the diverse cultures, values, and experiences they brought to the community. At the same time, this focus on the individual sometimes made it difficult to recognize patterns around race and class that left some students and teachers feeling that their concerns were not addressed, whereas students from dominant racial and socioeconomic groups continued to accrue academic and social benefits from the existing system (Fine, 1997).

If Quaker theology provided one anchor for the school's philosophy, the pursuit of "excellence" provided another. The statement of philosophy ended on this note:

We encourage all members of this community to develop their capacities to the fullest extent possible. In academics, in athletics, in the arts and in human relations, we value this excellence, recognize it, encourage it, and stress our obligation to share it. Knowing as well that learning works by example, we look for excellence in each other and in ourselves. This search keeps us striving.

This language of the search for excellence permeated the school's environment. The school grounded its definition of excellence in a college preparatory mission that was, by its own admission, narrow. As Tom Whitman, the head of school, put it, "Our mission is not any school. There are schools where college prep means a range of colleges. But you look at our unique mission. Our mission's profile is very, very narrow. We're in the most competitive world." Practitioners at City Friends explicitly prepared students for academic success defined in terms of the most elite colleges and universities. In a speech to the faculty, Tom Whitman described the responsibility practitioners had for helping students succeed in that world. Referencing the school's motto, "Behold, I have set before thee an open door," he stated:

> That niche that I talked about is a pretty narrow door to send a lot of kids through. We talk to our kids and we say, "Uh-uh, you do it our way," and we put them through this tiny door. That open door we set before them, it's not a ballroom door. It's a small closet door, whatever the image. But how do we validate kids so they feel they can go for it?"

Learning to "do it our way"—to pursue excellence within circumscribed boundaries—provided students with the navigational skills to sail through the gateways of the most prestigious institutions of higher education. The challenge Tom posed to the faculty was how they could "validate" all students so that they would feel capable of striving to fit through that narrow passageway. Faculty members must direct their efforts toward ensuring the success of each individual student.

The commitment to racial and socioeconomic diversity at City Friends was often framed in direct relation to the mission of providing students access to the cultural capital (Bourdieu, 1984) necessary to walk through the narrow gates of the elite institutions of higher education. City Friends, like similar institutions, interpreted the ethical claims that emerged from the Civil Rights Movement as an obligation to provide educational opportunities for individual students from groups that traditionally had been excluded (by race, ethnicity, or socioeconomic status) from the school. The exclusionary practices of prestigious educational institutions violated a basic premise of civil rights discourse about education: that all students should have access to equal opportunities. Within this framework of access and opportunity, City Friends asked itself how it could prepare students who traditionally had been excluded from or marginalized in elite educational settings to function successfully in that world. In one important sense then, City Friends was implementing color-conscious admissions and recruitment policies to provide a "color-blind" education—one that would offer all its students, regardless of race/ethnicity or class, a similar opportunity to gain entrance into prestigious colleges and universities. Thus, educational equity was conceptualized in terms of equal treatment: The school provided individual students with the same opportunities to be successful in the most elite tier of the educational system.

The school's dominant usage of the term "diversity" contained within it a certain idea about integration. Language about valuing a "diverse" community was highly evident throughout official documents, policies, and individuals' talk. The long-range plan, for example, stated:

> We admit students who: are capable of thriving in a rigorous program; are racially, economically, socially and religiously diverse; are children; are males and females; come from a variety of family structures; have different, sometimes competing, values; have ambition; have a willingness (along with their parents) to belong to this community and to share the School's commitment to the city.

The long-range plan referenced a vision for a student community that was diverse along a variety of axes. Although these differences admittedly involved "sometimes competing values," one strand running through the language was the tendency to treat these differences as being of equal weight. Being male or female, African-American or white, rich or poor, or Christian or Jewish were qualities that students brought with them to the school; however, official school policies often did not recognize these qualities as necessarily interrelated or related to students' potential for academic success. Moreover, all these differences were to be joined together under the common goal of belonging to and sharing in the mission of the City Friends community.

The diverse qualities students brought to City Friends were understood to contribute to the vitality and complexity of the school community; however, it was a core similarity shared by all students that provided the basis for educational practice. All students, regardless of their diverse qualities, must show the intellectual capacity to perform in "a rigorous program." Tom Whitman described an Admissions Committee meeting in which teachers had responded to a question about the qualities they were seeking in a candidate:

Several people said, "I want a kid that is strong enough in some place that they can take on the work of the school and do all of it well. They don't have to be great at everything, but they've got to be able to have enormous strength in some place that they have the reinforcement to take on the challenge."

In the midst of all their differences, the common bond among all students must be the capacity and willingness to engage with the particular intellectual tradition of the school.

Ideally, then, the school viewed itself as creating greater educational access to offer all students the same opportunities, specifically to become future leaders of society. City Friends intended to prepare all its students to be leaders, regardless of their race or class. A report from the School Committee cited, for example, the following purposes for the Community Scholars Program:

> The purpose of this program is to offer able, selected, neighborhood African-American, Asian-American, and Latino-American boys and girls an education that develops their potential, *to help provide mainstream society with minority leaders*, and to educate, in depth, both white students and students of color in the problems of working and learning together. (emphasis added)

The Community Scholars Program sought "able, selected" students of color: children who shared an academic profile with all the City Friends students. This search reflected the school's meritocratic vision of education: that education should provide opportunities for talented students to succeed. Moreover, the preceding passage expressed important assumptions about the goals City Friends had for this particular group of low-income students of color, as well as its vision of a democratic society. The Community Scholars Program had the dual goals of building a cadre of people of color who would become leaders of "mainstream society" and educating students across racial lines to work together productively. These goals reflected one vision of democratic society put forth by the Civil Rights Movement—one that imagined that someday we would live and work productively across racial/ethnic lines.

City Friends's invitation to leadership, however, was oriented squarely toward "mainstream society." As the statement of purpose for the Community Scholars Program suggests, the school did not aim to prepare these students for leadership in their own communities. Admission to the school was explicitly an invitation to membership in the dominant, white society. Tom Whitman argued, "You're choosing us because we're offering something that acculturates you to the dominant culture." This idea that students and their parents are "choosing" City Friends is an interesting one given that, in actuality, the school made choices about students and families based on a set of relatively narrow criteria for admission.

Once admitted, academic pursuits were the means through which students joined this leadership club. For example, Ethan Hayle, a white art teacher, described the acculturation process for students who do not come from upper-class backgrounds:

> I would say the culture of the school overwhelms them really. I mean, whatever values someone might bring in that were class-based would be overwhelmed by the values that the school upholds. In some large way, the school really values student involvement with the institution, with the school. That the most important thing to do as a student is to be on board with the school's project [to ensure admittance to an elite college or university], and then under that, I would still say that academic performance comes first.

Ethan, like many other practitioners at City Friends, viewed the school culture as simply overpowering any differences between students' school and home environments. The "school's project" demanded that students yield to its purposes and assimilate to the existing culture. From Ethan's perspective, however, this did not put students from marginalized groups at a necessary disadvantage:

> One way of immersing yourself in gaining a sense of being part of the community is doing well academically, so certainly one avenue for kids who didn't have the same means economically to find a place would be if they were strong in the classroom.

Although City Friends was admittedly a school dominated by the upper and middle classes, Ethan proposed that pursuing academic success allowed all students to carve out an important place in the community. The classroom was, in his view, at least potentially a level playing field—a space unmarked by race, class, or gender differences.

The college preparatory mission of the school permeated every classroom in which I observed. From art to science, English and social studies to math, teachers taught students fundamental principles of the disciplines at hand. Seventh graders learned about symmetry and complementary colors in their art class. In science class, they set up experiments to investigate electric currents and built suspension bridges for a national science competition. In history courses, they used college-level texts and primary materials. In English, they studied the vocabulary of literary criticism and wrote extensively, learning various genres of essay and fiction writing.

Classrooms were often sites of not only intense activity
ment, but also of the pressure of grades and test prepa
Many practitioners at City Friends expressed the be
of intellectual pursuits could be a neutral invitation f
academic excellence, even though with few exception?
school curriculum was heavily focused on the tradit..
Matthew Volker, a white administrator reflected on his own experiences as
a former student at City Friends:

> When I was sitting in class, I never would have picked up that all we
> studied were European males. It just never would have occurred to
> me, possibly because I'm a white European male. But I wonder too, if
> I, as an English teacher, could say, "Here is excellent literature. There's
> a whole broad swath of literature that represents every culture, every
> race. I am merely teaching this and using it as an example. We could
> use any one of these." Rather than, "Okay. I'm going to pick one from
> every single one so that everybody feels comfortable; everybody feels
> validated."

For Matthew, the nuances of race, gender, and class were incidental to
the pursuit of "excellence." Group identities could be cast off as students
joined in serious intellectual endeavors of any subject. Not everyone needs
to feel "validated" or "comfortable" to engage in the necessary academic
work. Implicit in Matthew's words rests an idea of excellence that was woven
throughout the dominant institutional discourse at City Friends. Excellence was interpreted as referencing objective qualities that exist outside
the cultural and historical contexts within which works are produced.

City Friends cultivated not only a certain type of student, but more
important, a particular type of person (Bourdieu, 1984). Tom Whitman
spoke of the acculturation process:

> There will be a bias toward that more-traditional canon because it
> educates kids to a certain culture. And it's also the way you speak.
> It's the way you interview. It's not—it's deeper than "Can you learn it
> through other means?" It's also a sense of being comfortable in that
> culture. Which is a lot of what our students get taught how to do.
> How to present themselves. How to be articulate about their ideas in
> language that is familiar to an admissions officer at Harvard.

One of City Friends's educational goals was to invite students to participate seamlessly in white upper-class culture. Tom Whitman argued this
is what the majority of students and their parents, including families of
color, were seeking:

our mission is culturally biased, to be sure, culturally biased toward a white upper-class culture. So that even as we try to make ourselves more friendly to a variety of people, more available to a variety of people, the core curriculum has got to have an element of that culture. Even the students who complain—this year's senior African-American students are going to Cornell, Wesleyan, Penn. They're not going to Lincoln. They're choosing not to do that. They are staying in the system because they believe, rightly, and I would argue, rightly, that in the American way of life, that's going to open up more doors to them in the long-term future.

Assuming a meritocratic society, City Friends worked to prepare all its students for such a life (see Fordham, 1991).

For some practitioners at City Friends, this unabashed commitment to prepare students of color to succeed in the most elite colleges and universities reflected a particular assumption about remedying injustice. Given that one great failure of U.S. democracy has been the persistent exclusion of people of color as well as working-class and poor people from the most elite schools, opening up access to those educational institutions moved society closer to the ideal of meritocracy. Thus, at City Friends, the justice claim for integration supported a vision of increasing access to "excellent education" as a morally necessary and viable goal. This vision, however, did not call into question the definition and parameters of excellence.

Clearly, the goals of the Civil Rights Movement were infinitely broader and more democratically based than those reflected in private school education, which is exclusionary by nature. Yet, the justice claims around racial and socioeconomic integration at City Friends, while admittedly quite limited in scope, drew upon ideas generated in discourses of the Civil Rights Movement and in Chief Justice Warren's argument in *Brown*: that equal access forms the basis for practicing justice, and that all students, regardless of race, should have the same educational opportunities to participate together in dominant schools and society. Political philosopher Amy Gutmann (1996) has argued that in a democratic society, color-conscious admissions policies are vital and justifiable practices because they ensure that schools and universities serve essential social purposes of developing diverse leadership for a diverse society. In her 2003 ruling opinion for the Supreme Court, Justice Sandra Day O'Connor echoed this argument in her support for the University of Michigan law school's race-conscious admissions policies (*Grutter v. Bollinger*, 2003). Color-conscious policies support the growth of integrated educational spaces that are essential for building broad participation in a democratic society. City Friends perceived its mission within this framework.

## Contesting the Meaning of Integration

At the same time, this orientation toward integration into dominant white cultural practices was deeply contested at City Friends. Cynthia Wright, an African-American teacher, stated the central definitional problem poignantly:

> I often cringe whenever I hear Tom Whitman say this is a diverse school. I mean I guess you can say theoretically and philosophically that we do have diversity, but then it strikes me I must have a really different definition of diversity because, to me, diversity isn't 20 people in a room and 2 of them are different because of their gender or their culture or their ethnicity or their accent. They're just a minority, but that's not diversity at all.

With these words, Cynthia pointed to the fact that, despite genuine concern and considerable talk about "diversity," City Friends was still a predominantly white institution. For Cynthia, *diversity* in this context simply signaled the presence of a few representatives from other racial and ethnic groups, without significantly shifting the status quo. Cynthia's analysis was shared by many of her colleagues and signaled their concern that simply adding a few individuals or pieces of curriculum reflecting traditionally excluded groups did little to radically reconfigure the institution's relationship to the dominant white culture or to address issues of racial power and privilege (Carby, 1992; McCarthy, 1993b; McLaren, 1994; Mohanty, 1989-90). All the practitioners of color I interviewed, and some of their white colleagues, expressed frustration with the school's definition of integration.

Practitioners who were critical of the school's approach questioned the strength of its commitment to creating a student and faculty population that was truly diverse. Ruth Bliss, an English teacher and member of the school's Gender Audit Committee said:

> We talk a real good game. We do a real good job in saying that we're interested in being multicultural. But when it boils down to actually being a diverse community, we seem to consistently make decisions, whether they be hiring decisions about the faculty or enrollment decisions of the student body that belie that mission, that somehow conflict with what we have said we want to do.

Ruth pointed to the disjunction between the rhetoric and reality of building a more diverse community. Recognizing that the school's concerted effort to increase racial/ethnic diversity was never premised on a vision of a truly integrated community in which whites might not continue to be the majority, Cheryl Andrews went even further: "I'd be curious to see just at what point it becomes, you've reached a plateau of diversity."

Critical race theorists point to the limitations of civil rights discourse that fails to address the systematic oppression and exclusion of African-Americans in educational (and other) institutions (Bell, 1987, 2004; Crenshaw, Gotanda, and Thomas, 1995; Ladson-Billings and Tate, 1995). In a similar vein, critics of City Friends's approach to integration and its language around diversity questioned the school's capacity to create a racially, ethnically, and socioeconomically equitable community in the context of what was, by definition, exclusionary education strongly tied to a system of white power and privilege. They suggested that, although the school had adopted the language of diversity and multiculturalism, it had not seriously challenged itself to confront systemic aspects of oppression.

These critics argued that the dominant cultural norms and assumptions of the school perpetuated the exclusion and marginalization of people of color in the community. The school's definition of "academic excellence" contributed to this exclusion and marginalization. The failure to critically explore the definitions of excellence was manifest in the ways that children were evaluated for admission. In the MAP self-study described in detail in Chapter 2, the admissions subcommittee wrote a set of queries for the school community, which clearly illustrated this point:

> Should City Friends be more academically diverse? Is intellectual or academic elitism consistent with multiculturalism? Should we lower our admissions standards to attract a more diverse racial and cultural student population? Do we need to consider tracking in all disciplines?

The admissions subcommittee assumed that seeking "a more diverse racial and cultural student population" would entail "lower[ing] admissions standards," and, as a result, raised up for consideration the question of instituting tracking (a system of differentiating levels of classes). Because of the assumption that there is only one standard for academic excellence, the Admissions Committee raised questions about the intellectual capabilities of students from underrepresented racial/ethnic groups.

These queries illustrate a central problem that many schools and universities confront as they seek to become more diverse communities. Educational institutions often assume that the criteria defining excellence represent neutral objective measures against which all applicants can be evaluated. When the underlying norms, values, and standards that guide those definitions of excellence remain hidden from view, certain applicants appear different and deficient (Minow, 1990; Young, 1990). Failing to examine the relationship between the definition of academic excellence and particular racial/cultural practices, the system of white racial power and privilege that makes multiculturalism seem incompatible with academic excellence cannot be challenged. Some practitioners at City Friends argued that a racially and economically integrated community that would be truly equitable could not be achieved as long as the school was playing with a deck stacked heavily in favor of upper-middle-class white interests. For them, it was the very definition of excellence, and the ways this definition systematically excluded particular groups of people, that needed to be examined.

Some teachers noted that the school's unstated assumptions about academic excellence also worked at cross-purposes to its goals of hiring more faculty of color. Several teachers suggested that hiring practices provided another example of how the school's paramount values often outweighed any commitment to diversity and integration. Ruth Bliss argued:

> Every position that opens has—will always have the parameters of excellence, and the way the institution views excellence in a candidate will always be Harvard, Yale, Ph.D. [Those] will always be the criteria of the dominant culture. This is just my take on it. It's probably highly subversive, but my take on it is as long as we use those criteria to establish excellence, we are limiting our pool significantly. But if we are able to look at excellence in a broader definition, not eliminate excellence, not sacrifice excellence, just allow that there is a wide range of excellent institutions there. Let's take the A+ teacher from wherever. I think every single time I've seen someone hired, it's been, "Okay, the next time we're definitely going to hire a person of color." They just hired a history candidate who is not of color. You know every one. But that history person has to be a Classics major. How many African-American Classics majors are there? Okay, so there's going to be a rationale behind every non-hire; but ultimately, some of these hires have to be people of color.

Ruth proposed that rigid definitions of excellence limited the school's choices in hiring faculty of color. From her perspective, the school valued in its teachers the same credentials it was preparing its students to acquire. She pointed to the ways that these credentials, rather than representing objective or neutral criteria for excellence, reflected particular markers of white race privilege. Cheryl Andrews concurred, arguing that "the point is, you've got to be careful about how narrow your resources are as far as who you're looking to [hire], what institutions you're looking to." Ruth, Cheryl, and other colleagues felt the effects of unacknowledged, powerful criteria for academic excellence that made it difficult for the school to support its stated goals of creating a significantly more racially diverse faculty. They indicated a fundamental struggle at City Friends about the definition of a "diverse" community in the face of a strong commitment to a particular definition of "academic excellence" that maintained white power and privilege.

Practitioners who were critical of the school's approach to diversity saw a need to address race and class oppression at a systemic rather than individual level. As Cheryl Andrews put it, "This insistence by Quakers that we treat each person as an individual. Well, if I tell you that there are several individuals who have a similar issue, let's not negate that in treating them as individuals. If they say something is an issue, you respect that." The strong strain of individualism threaded through Quaker theology—and emphasized at City Friends—at times worked against a systematic analysis of power and difference. Focusing on the individual left a sparse vocabulary for examining the experiences that people might share by virtue of their group membership.

Students and practitioners of color often felt profoundly conflicted about what it meant to belong to the community. Most of the students of color I interviewed said they had come to City Friends to gain knowledge about, and access to, the elite, white world. Speaking of their reasons for being at City Friends, Charlene and Tanya suggested:

Tanya:      It's all a learning experience for us, you know. Once you're out in the real world, you're not always going to land that job where they'll all be black people. Once you get out in the business world, you're not going to be surrounded by minorities. This is definitely a learning experience.

Charlene:   Yeah. I think City Friends is not a bad place. It's a learning place. If I would have went to an all black school, I probably wouldn't know how to interact, or how to act with white students.

Tanya and Charlene felt that learning required acquiring specific knowledge about how to work with white peers. For many students of color, City Friends provided the opportunity to gain necessary skills to join the dominant society.

If for some students this education offered survival techniques for working in a multiracial world, others hoped that academic success at City Friends would open new options for their future. Julia, one of the few Latino/a students in the high school, spoke of why she persisted at City Friends despite her frequent encounters with racism and feelings of isolation from friends at school and at home:

It's because I know I'm getting a great education, and I don't—I mean like it's pretty hard, but I think I'm coming away with a lot more than what I'm suffering here, whatever. I don't really think I'm suffering, but it's—because I want to be successful. I know, because I don't live in a very good neighborhood. I don't want to stay there my entire life. I want to be successful. I really want to do something. I don't want to sit there and be like a welfare person. Because I know a lot of people who just blow it off. I know so many people who have gotten pregnant, already been married.

Julia's words expressed the alienation she suffered in living between worlds. The struggle she felt seeped through her language in the hesitations and changes of direction: "and I don't—I mean like it's pretty hard, but … whatever." She was, however, reluctant to name her experience as "suffering." Caught in a world at home that she saw as narrowing her choices to becoming "a welfare person," Julia had chosen to stay with the path City Friends could offer her. This was a path that sought to guarantee individual success in the dominant society. It was an education that often reinforced, rather than challenged, Julia's notion that it is a person's choices that make the difference between being a success and being a "welfare person" or pregnant teen. In making the decision to remain at City Friends, Julia found herself increasingly separated from her community at home, reporting, for example, that her friends teased her for talking "white" (Fordham, 1996).

The dominant framework through which City Friends defined its ethical commitment to creating a more racially and socioeconomically diverse community was one that equated equity with access to an educational environment that would teach all students the explicit and implicit rules for success in the dominant society. Therefore, students of color often found themselves painfully caught between conflicting perspectives on the world.

Donald Powell, an English teacher, often worried about the detriment to the students of color he mentored: "It's always difficult to make that choice ethically in terms of what we ask our kids to sacrifice as they adapt to become [City Friends]ers." Donald was troubled by the moral weight of the transformation process that students of color, in particular, had to undergo to be successful at City Friends. He argued that many of these students were caught between unsatisfactory options. He noted that students of color often spoke longingly of leaving City Friends:

It's almost a given that there's going to be a number of kids who are talking about leaving. Their parents may not know anything about it. There's been no actual plans to make it happen. But just to have that, "I want to get out of this place." To have that option to even imagine. To vent and then go to the next class and do the best you can on the quiz is real indicative of some of the straddling.

For many students of color, staying at City Friends often involved imagining being elsewhere, holding onto some part of the self that did not belong to City Friends. Donald continued:

> Because, you know, "I don't really want to be at that other place because no one gives a damn or I'll get lost in the population, or I'm not learning anything there." And yet, to be some place you can feel in some ways familiar with the environment, the setting. It's really interesting this mutation that's created between that public and private school, between these two very different worlds and cultures. *And it makes you some of both and not all of either. You know the idea of being a person without a country is very real.* And you create this middle ground that sometimes is characterized by bitterness and resentment for both environments. Plus you don't adopt either one, and neither one adopts you fully. … *There really needs to be something of you in that home place that is yours, that you feel ownership for. That you don't leave and feel like it was just a room.* (emphasis added)

By trying to mold themselves to City Friends's definition of a model student, many who did not come from the dominant culture were stranded between worlds. They had been shaped enough by City Friends that they no longer fully fit in their home worlds, yet they could never be completely of the school's world (Du Bois, 1903/1989). Donald argued that students of color should not simply be asked to inhabit this other space—this white school—without a sense of belonging and ownership. For students of color, learning to navigate the dominant society, with its nearly invisible system of racial power and privilege, could be dangerous and costly (see, for example, Brayboy, 2004; Cary, 1991; Delpit, 1995; Ladson-Billings, 1994; Nieto, 1996). Donald and likeminded colleagues battled one of the major limitations of conceptualizing integration, in terms of the right for students of color to participate in dominant educational settings without an insistence on the transformation of those institutions.

Donald Powell was not the only teacher to worry about the cost of belonging to City Friends. Many practitioners struggled with how to help students of color to survive and take advantage of what City Friends offered, while simultaneously working for the school's transformation. Mike Knight, the director of curriculum, described a dilemma he faced:

> [It's] the difference between coping with the present and transformation for the future. And it's a tension because, for instance, let's say that the school is racist, as it is, of course. But do you teach a kid to survive that racism by acculturating and teaching skills, and

supporting them through things like that? Of course, you want to help kids survive an institution like this. And that means assuming that the institution is fixed and the individual has to change. And, in some ways, that may even impede the transformational work because it's validating a vision. At the same time, the here and now, the practicality of kids coming in here and doing well and surviving demands that you do some of that. So I think that's a real tension. How do you deal with the present without ensuring the practice of dealing with the present as the way the institution deals with multiculturalism?

This tension suggested the limitation of framing justice in terms of integration and diversity. Without a concomitant change in institutional culture, educators find that they must teach students survival skills and, in the act of doing so, may reinforce the very structures that require transformation. Moreover, as long as diversity is understood to be a property only of the people marked as different, they bear the burden of change.

Of course, as I demonstrate in Chapter 5, becoming a more diverse community would, in turn, force the school to begin to confront its culture as a white institution, precisely because teachers and students of color and some of their white allies would ask new questions. The school's hiring practices, structures of support for students of color, and curriculum content would be carefully interrogated. Over time, the school's history of working toward a more racially diverse community reflected a subtle change in its perspective on integration. In the early years, the purposes of creating a more racially and socioeconomically diverse community were framed primarily in terms of benefits to students of color and those from low-income families who would gain access to all that elite education had to offer. By the mid-1990s, the school community was beginning to ask about transforming the institutional culture to reflect more fully the values and perspectives of its students and faculty of color. The school was moving toward an explicit focus on difference as the grounds for exploring justice. This shift toward justice based on recognition of difference is explored in Chapter 5. In what follows here, I turn my attention to Parks and explore integration as a justice claim in relation to students labeled with disabilities.

## Parks: Full Inclusion, Integrating Disability

On a frigid day in late January, Martha Silverman, a language arts teacher at Parks Middle School, introduced her sixth and seventh grade students to a Socratic seminar. The class had been studying poetry, and on the previous day,

Martha had turned to the work of Paul Lawrence Dunbar. Martha was deeply committed to teaching students about racial oppression; her curriculum was focused on historical and contemporary manifestations of racial injustice and the struggle for freedom across multiple international contexts.

Martha's classroom conveyed a feeling of partnership between students and teacher. The room was comfortable and inviting. The large back wall was covered with artwork, posters of popular teen idols, and writings that students had chosen to display for their peers. Class opened every day with "Connections"; facilitated by a student, this was a time for anyone who wished to share a thought or concern uninterrupted by peers or teachers. Chairs and desks were arranged in a large circle around a colorful carpet on which students often lounged as they read novels, listened to their peers during Connections, or met in small groups to work on assignments. Books lined the shelves and were also stuffed in a cabinet. Student work was on display on every available surface. A veteran teacher, Martha had a direct and commanding presence laced with a huge amount of love and humor. Martha was well loved by her students, who felt she both respected and challenged them.

Martha began the Socratic seminar on Dunbar by reminding the students of what they had discussed about the poet during the prior lesson, pointing particularly to the dilemma Dunbar faced as an African-American poet whose white editor wanted to please a white audience. She explained to the students that she was going to read a poem by Dunbar, "We Wear the Mask," and ask them to discuss their interpretations of the poem. She emphasized that everyone would have a chance to participate, and that the goals of the seminar were not to argue or contradict each other but to support interpretation with direct reference to the text they each had in front of them. After reading the poem to the class twice, Martha posed the question: Do you think Dunbar is encouraging people to wear the mask or not?

What followed was a thoughtful, animated, respectful, and intense conversation among the students. As budding adolescents, many of them felt directly connected to the poem's idea of hiding one's true self from the world's gaze. It took a little longer for students to come to understand that Dunbar was referring to the mask that black Americans wear in the face of racial oppression. Guiding students to stay focused on the text, Martha taught the class how to do a close textual analysis, even as she supported this group of African-American, white, and Asian-American youth to discuss common and disparate aspects of their adolescent lives. With two exceptions, all the students participated in the Socratic seminar, and in the final moments of the class, those two students were challenged about their silence by their peers. Thus, all students were called upon in some way to be active, engaged participants in this lesson.

During the approximately 45 minutes of the Socratic seminar, every student in the class was made visible as each contributed his or her perspective to the discussion. What was made invisible were students' differences along the lines of (dis)ability. Several students in this class were labeled as learning disabled, and one boy was identified as autistic. In addition, a majority of students were not reading on grade level as measured by standardized tests, even as several others tested at college reading levels. All these differences became irrelevant—at least temporarily—because the Socratic process invited each person's participation.

This scene and others like it were commonplace in Martha Silverman's language arts classroom. Martha embraced a variety of pedagogical practices that offered all her students a path to engage meaningfully with literature and its large ideas. Martha struggled, too. For example, she worried about her capacity to teach some of her students to read, and she was deeply troubled by the degree to which standardized testing would determine her students' futures. In response to these concerns, she always sought new practices that expanded possibilities for creating an inclusive classroom. Pedagogical practices like the Socratic seminar reflected moments in which a vision of an inclusive education—integrated across different approaches to learning—was imaginable.[3]

## Integration and Disability Rights

At Parks, the struggle to create a community integrated by disability posed some of the most troubling questions for practitioners. As discussed in Chapter 2, in response to a budget cut, Parks had recently adopted the practice of full inclusion, which integrated students labeled with disabilities into all classrooms. Before this full-inclusion policy, Parks had offered several self-contained special education classrooms and a resource room for children identified with disabilities. The large budget cut had forced the school to rethink its program, however, and, drawing on the principles of the Coalition of Essential Schools, it had moved to a full-inclusion model.

This change in Parks's program reflected shifting national trends in educational policy for children identified with disabilities. It was only in 1975 with the Education of All Handicapped Children Act (Pub. L. 94-142) that the federal government finally guaranteed children identified with disabilities the right to free and appropriate education. This law, which was changed in 1990 to the Individuals with Disabilities Education Act (IDEA) (Pub. L. 101-476) and reauthorized in 1997 and 2004, required that children identified with disabilities be educated in the "least restricted environment." It specified that to the greatest extent possible, children identified with disabilities must be educated in classrooms with nondisabled peers. Federal law further specifies that, where accommodation in general education classrooms cannot be attained, children labeled with disabilities must be offered a continuum of placement options and supplementary services to meet their needs. Thus, federal legislation, in addressing the education of children identified with disabilities, posited an ideal of integrated classroom communities.

Rather than a realization of this ideal, the "least restricted environment" clause, along with the mandate for a continuum of care, led to a proliferation of special tracks, classrooms, and schools for children identified with disabilities in the public (and private) spheres. By the late 1980s, some researchers and advocates for children identified with disabilities began to argue that special education tracks and classes offered inferior, inequitable educational opportunities (Gartner and Lipsky, 1987).

Throughout the 1990s, schools and districts across the nation began adopting full-inclusion practices in response to the growing evidence that students labeled with disabilities had been denied their rights to education in the least restrictive environment. Advocates support full inclusion on both educational and ethical grounds. They argue that children placed in special classrooms and tracks fail to make significant academic gains (Gartner and Lipsky, 1987). Moreover, echoing the spirit of *Brown*, they propose that segregated classrooms violate a democratic ideal of integrated communities; that separate is indeed inherently unequal (Lipsky and Gartner, 1996; Skrtic, 1991); and that the special education population includes a disproportionate number of students of color (Donovan and Cross, 2002; Losen and Orfield, 2002). Thus, the ethical arguments in favor of full inclusion represent a specific claim for educational equity: that all children should have equal educational opportunity and access.

This is an argument that supports the ideal of integration.[4] The education of children with special needs, like the needs of children of color under legal segregation, had proven that separate was not equal. Advocates of an inclusive approach propose that, in the interests of equity, children with special needs should be served in the same classrooms as their peers (Biklen, 1992; Kluth, Straut and Biklen, 2003; Lipsky and Gartner, 1996; 1997; 1999).

Importantly, advocates warn against an interpretation of full inclusion that focuses primarily on placement as the marker of equity (Rizvi and Lingard, 1996). Integration of children labeled with disabilities into "regular" classrooms without a concomitant change in pedagogical and curricular practices does not lead to inclusive education. Rather, it leaves students identified with disabilities vulnerable to having their academic and social needs ignored or unmet. Integrating children labeled with disabilities into all classrooms challenges educators to confront rather than ignore difference. In theory, inclusive education simultaneously acknowledges the essential equality of all persons and recognizes and values our differences as learners. Thus, fundamental to the argument for inclusive classrooms for students identified with disabilities is a more complex understanding of integration as a justice claim than the ideal offered in the early years of civil rights advocacy to end racial segregation. The ideal of integration held by disability-rights advocates requires not only access to mainstream schools and classrooms, but also significant changes to those environments—changes that recognize and value our differences as learners.

In practice, however, this vision of integration remains difficult to implement, particularly when, as was the case at Parks, full-inclusion policies are implemented in the face of budget cuts rather than with an increase in resources. Parks offers a site in which to examine closely the tensions that emerge as practitioners struggle with viewing students as "the same, but different." That is, through practice, it is possible to see the difficulty of acknowledging our fundamental equality as persons without either denying our differences or viewing certain differences as individual deficits. The following section examines how educators' support for integrating students labeled with disabilities into mainstream classrooms was eroded by two forces. First, the school had few resources to support fundamental changes in how teachers organized their classroom practices. Second, a pervasive medical discourse of disability located the "problem" of difference in the bodies and minds of particular individuals (Gartner and Lipsky, 1987).

*Imagining Integrated Classrooms; Rejecting "Branding" and "Segregation"*

Parks's full-inclusion policy embodied one ideal for equitable educational practices: that all children be served in the same classroom. Its adoption of this policy was consistent with the philosophical principles of the Coalition of Essential Schools embraced by the school. The principle that a school's goals should apply to all its students, along with the principle acknowledging that students differ, supported Parks's decision to address a major budget cut by integrating children with and without special needs in all classrooms.

Many practitioners willingly embraced the move to a full-inclusion model. Martha Silverman articulated a strong critique of special education as a program:

> I've been in the school system since 1963, and there was always special ed. And, from what I've read and from what I've studied, there

is no evidence that children in special ed. ever improve. I think kids rise to the occasion. And I think when you tell them they're limited, then they behave limited. And I think they're taught in a limited way. So I think the idea of inclusion is good for that. Because I mean there was nothing that proved they were benefiting from being segregated, and by being segregated, there was also the stigma that they were segregated. And so I think only negatives came out of that.

Martha invoked the language of segregation to argue against special education classrooms and tracks. For her, as for other advocates of full-inclusion models, special education classes had served to *segregate and thereby stigmatize* children identified with disabilities. From her perspective, segregated classrooms communicate to children that they are "limited"—inferior to children without disabilities. In linking segregation to stigmatization, Martha echoed Chief Justice Warren's argument in *Brown*. Segregation, in and of itself, engenders feelings of inferiority. She argued that, segregated and stigmatized, these students have also been "taught in a limited way." She believed that the curriculum in segregated special education classes tended to be less rigorous and more focused on a narrow, skills-based approach to learning. Thus, in her view, special education classes perpetuate, rather than remedy, educational inequality. Martha, like several of her colleagues, viewed integration of students labeled with and without disabilities in all classrooms as an equity practice.

Speaking of his support for full inclusion, David Waters, stated:

I like [full inclusion] for the most part. I don't like kids being branded. And I think for some of them it's been a godsend. Because here, they are in a regular classroom with other kids, and they're working and they're having some success. Nobody makes fun of them. And we don't say anything special. This [curriculum] is what we all are doing.

Like Martha, David used strong language to argue the case for full inclusion. Referring to special education as "brand[ing]," David, an African-American history teacher who had a strong commitment to teaching his students about injustice, invoked comparisons to slavery, concentration camps, and animal farming. Integration into regular classrooms, by contrast, offered "some success" and an absence of teasing and scapegoating.

David and Martha both referenced an important implicit aim of integrated classrooms and communities: promoting children's self-respect. They articulated a belief that segregated classrooms, organized around children's differences, compromise children's self-respect by implying that they are somehow deficient—an argument that reverberates with Chief Justice Warren's ruling opinion in *Brown*. Children in special education classes get the clear message that they are "limited" and easily become the butt of other children's teasing. Respecting others and respecting oneself are integrally related educational aims and important aspects of equity.

Some teachers questioned the validity of categorizing children as "special education." Lisa Bird, a social studies teacher, was acutely aware of the relationship between race, class, and special education. As a long-term substitute, Lisa had come to an analysis of special education through her experiences across a wide variety of city schools. She argued:

> See now, my problem with special ed.—it just seems to me that somewhere along these kids' lives, a boat has been missed. And it's not necessarily that they are quote unquote special ed., regardless of if they've been tested. I've been subbing for four years, but in those four years, I've seen diverse schools. And I have seen so many children who are so illiterate, it is amazing. And, I know they are not all special ed. I just feel it. I know too many people who have been labeled throughout their lives "special ed." whose standards in the classroom have been lowered their whole lives. And their whole lives they've been stigmatized as being special ed. I don't think it's that we're getting a group of kids who are special ed. I think we're getting a group of kids who've been cheated, and now each year, the teachers are trying to catch up.

Lisa interrogated the special education classification of many children she had taught. She felt sure that the majority had been mislabeled. Rather than casting "illiteracy" as an outcome of a child's "disability," she pointed to discriminatory practices that "cheated" children out of a fair and decent education. Inequitable educational experiences, not children's disabilities, were culpable for children's miseducation. Starting with a focus on children's similarities, Lisa argued that a majority of the differences that students manifest in school develop as result of educational inequalities. One articulation of inclusion, then, emphasized the shared qualities of children as learners.

A fair, decent, and equal education for *all* children was what proponents of full inclusion advocated. Melanie Post, the principal, talked about how she had tried to build a school culture that would philosophically support the decision to teach all children in the same classrooms:

> We've also had conversations after [the decision]. And, I'm trying to undo the notion that's been in place for 25 years that special ed. teachers are different, and that special ed. youngsters, particularly mildly handicapped youngsters' learning needs and the pedagogy to address those needs is substantially other than what good teaching

or good teachers look like. That is a huge mistake that special ed. made when [Pub. L.] 94-142 went into effect.

Melanie explicitly argued for a definition of "good teaching" as that which addressed the needs of all young people. From her perspective, the law regulating the education of children labeled with disabilities had mistakenly proliferated separate special programs rather than supporting a vision of good and equitable education for all. A strong advocate for public education that aimed at full and meaningful participation for each child, Melanie had worked hard to build a school culture that would embrace full inclusion on moral and pedagogical grounds. Moreover, she proposed that viewing special education students, particularly in her view "mildly handicapped" students, as fundamentally different from their peers is problematic. For Melanie, Lisa, and other Parks practitioners who supported full inclusion, integrated classrooms, by focusing on children's similarities, uphold a fundamental democratic ideal that all children are equal and are to be treated that way.

## Equality: Practicing Sameness or Differentiation

There is a critical tension here—a recurring theme that cuts across the three justice claims explored in this book. In educational *practice*, it is difficult to hold a commitment to the equality of all persons while simultaneously acknowledging our differences. Focusing instead on students' fundamental equality—equality that is implicitly reflected in the refusal to segregate students by virtue of disability, race, gender, and so forth—often equates equity with same treatment and leads to a refusal to examine taken-for-granted educational practices. This was certainly the case at City Friends when the Quaker commitment to the fundamental equality of all persons led the school to question its exclusionary admissions practices without interrogating its broader educational culture.

At Parks, acknowledging the basic equality of all learners often led to thinking about full inclusion as treating all students the same by offering them the same curricular and pedagogical opportunities. David Waters indicated this approach when he stated that teachers "don't say anything special" about the students, and that they ask all students to participate in the same activities—"this is what we all are doing." With few exceptions, my observations of educators' practices confirmed this tendency to engage all students in the same classroom activities. Chapter 4 addresses fully the assumption implicit in David's words and in many of the practices I observed in classrooms: that one way in which equity is served is by treating everyone the same. What is important here is David's indication that integrating children with and without disabilities must be accomplished without acknowledging differences either directly (in speech) or implicitly through curriculum and pedagogy. He suggested that students identified with disabilities should have the opportunity to participate in the same environment as their peers and be taught with the same curriculum and pedagogy.

Melanie, on the other hand, envisioned inclusive education as one that simultaneously acknowledged children's similarities and their differences. As she worked with teachers and children, she advocated an approach to teaching that was designed to acknowledge the wide human variability in approaches to learning. Melanie believed that good teaching could and should address the diverse needs that students brought to classrooms. Rather than focusing on integration of children labeled with disabilities as primarily a placement decision, she sought to develop a vision of classroom practices characterized by flexible, diverse strategies for pedagogy and assessment. Along with some of the teachers at the school, she advocated an approach to full inclusion that demanded significant changes in the approach to curriculum and pedagogy—changes that would create multiple entry points for all learners.

Some teachers remained skeptical of educational research in support of inclusive classrooms. For example, at one faculty meeting in which Melanie introduced professional articles about differentiated learning, the four teachers with whom I sat were dismissive of the idea that teaching a widely diverse group of learners was an achievable goal. However, in some classrooms, teachers were experimenting with new practices, for example, cooperative grouping, partner reading, or books on tape, as strategies to support students identified with disabilities to participate fruitfully in curricular activities. Many teachers also worked with students individually, seeking to help them tackle the assignments.

The inherent tension here between two visions of equitable education—one that emphasized "same" treatment and one that focused on the diversity of learners—reflects another set of contending justice claims that are more fully the subject of Chapter 4.

Despite Melanie's efforts to build a professional climate in which teachers embraced differentiated educational practices (Tomlinson, 1999) that would support the full-inclusion policy, three years into the program, every teacher I interviewed[5] thought the academic needs of the special-education-labeled students were, for the most part, not being met. Many felt the program had benefited students who formerly had been placed in special education classes by improving their self-esteem and removing the stigma attached to being labeled; however, none believed it addressed the academic needs of the students. Despite her strong advocacy of the principle of full inclusion, Martha Silverman, for example, argued that the academic needs of their students were not being met by the program as it was implemented at Parks:

> I do feel, however, that we've cheated the kids by not providing remedial help to those who need it. I mean there are kids here who are in desperate need, and we can't pretend that they are just going to get it by osmosis or by sitting next to somebody who is MG [mentally gifted]. We are *not, we are not* doing well by these kids.

In interviews, teachers again and again expressed their feelings that they were unable to meet the "range" of needs of their students. Many spoke of "teaching to the middle" by not providing challenges for "gifted" students or "remedial" support for those in need. Whereas many general education teachers were left feeling ineffectual, at least one of the former special education teachers was sad that she had been forced to abandon children who needed her and whom she felt she had previously served well:

> As a special ed. person, it really hurts my feelings of sensibility as far as seeing kids that we could be doing more for. But because we don't have the structure, because we don't have the manpower, we're not reaching those kids the way we should be. I'm afraid we're going to see a lot of these kids leaving us in eighth grade that are still not literate ... and in a way, I take that personally because that was really my role at one point in the school to work with special ed. kids.

Rather than creating the opportunity for teachers to build alternative classroom practices and new pedagogical strategies that might have strengthened their abilities to meet a wide variety of students' needs, the move to full inclusion under forced circumstances and impoverished conditions left teachers deeply troubled about their students' academic learning.

However, I risk overstating teachers' negative responses to the new structure. Despite a general feeling that the program was struggling, coupled with a widespread distrust of research supporting full inclusion, many teachers simultaneously expressed the idea that a philosophy that envisions an integrated, diverse learning community was one they supported. They identified the problems with the program as clearly due to economics:

> We're missing a vital piece in most inclusion models and that is the resource. Most of the models out there or other people that are succeeding with inclusion, they have the personnel that are freed up to work with kids either in the classroom along with the classroom teacher or in small group instruction.
>
> The main reason [for not supporting the program] is because the children have no resources. We don't have a resource teacher. We

don't have aides that could work with them. … I just don't think it's what inclusion is supposed to be.

Many teachers recognized that true inclusion models required new resources to successfully meet the learning needs of all students. Parks's experience with its full-inclusion program reflected, in large part, the profound inequalities of an inadequately funded urban educational system. Within this broader system of inequality, integrating students with and without disabilities in mainstream classrooms becomes a placement decision—an assimilationist stance similar to that adopted by City Friends toward the admission of students of color—rather than a real opportunity for equity.

### Disability and the Discourse of Medical Diagnosis

Without underestimating the impact of these structural conditions of inequality, I suggest that it is not only a lack of resources, but also a way of thinking about the difference of disability, that limited the effectiveness of the full-inclusion policy. At Parks, the justice claim embedded in full inclusion and based on an ideal of integration offered an argument for building equity by focusing on similarities between children. However, it was pitted strongly against a medical discourse of disability (Gartner and Lipsky, 1987) that focuses on difference and has a tenacious grip on educational thinking and practices. I refer here to an understanding of disability that positions differences as a problem located in the bodies of particular children, rather than in the relationship between an individual and the contexts that make differences stand out (Baker, 2002; Carrier, 1986; Gartner and Lipsky, 1987; Luna, 1997; McDermott and Varenne, 1995; Mehan, 2000; Mehan, Hertweck, and Meihls, 1986; Minow, 1990; Rizvi and Lingard, 1996; Slee, 1999; Varenne and McDermott, 1998). This discourse is embedded in legal approaches to disability and education, under which children can only receive special educational services with a recognized disability diagnosis. This pervasive approach to disability and education seems self-evident. Children in need of special services must be identified to have their needs addressed.

The medical discourse profoundly influenced many of Parks's practitioners' ideas about full inclusion. Strong institutional forces sustained this medical approach to learning diversity. Special education brought greatly needed additional resources to the school. In one meeting that I observed, the school district's special education supervisor commended Melanie Post for knowing how to "play the numbers game." Melanie knew that to maintain the current level of staffing, a certain percentage of students had to be tested and subsequently identified as needing special services. For Parks, as for many schools, special education monies offer crucial fiscal and personnel resources. There is, however, an important assumption underlying special education funds: that what is due is due to the individual, rather than, for example, to the school or district. Woven throughout the fabric of the special education system is a powerful force that centers attention on the individual student and on differences located within the person.

Many practitioners at Parks felt that, in large part, their struggle to educate children well was a reflection of the underdiagnosis of disabilities. These educators believed that many students who could be classified as "special education" had not been properly tested and identified. Commenting on his own ignorance about which students had been designated "special education," Tim Fraser, a white teacher, stated:

> I bet I don't know all of [the special education students]. I suspect if we followed the school district's public guidelines on who qualifies as special ed., meaning kids at low ability and kids at high ability as well, we would probably find that there are far greater numbers of students who qualify than we label. My cynical view is that more are not [identified] because of the economic implications. It costs more to provide for special ed. than it does for quote normal students. The kids who were labeled special ed in the school were only the most glaring examples that simply could not be ignored.

Tim believed that the school district's desire to save money led to a situation in which many students were not identified and labeled properly. Tim mistakenly understood special education to identify children with low or high ability. He had lost a critical piece of the definition of learning disabilities: a discrepancy between what a child is assumed to be capable of (ability) and how she or he is performing (achievement). However, his definition, in accordance with a medical view of disability, framed special education in terms of clearly identifiable categories of children who are different from the majority of their peers.

Other teachers expressed similar beliefs. David Waters, a strong supporter of full inclusion, spoke about disability in this framework:

> A lot of them should be in special ed. who aren't labeled. At some point, I forget who is on the [special ed.] list and who's not. I'm looking at behaviors and the production, and I'm saying isn't he on the special ed. list? Well, he should be. But he hasn't been tested or his parents don't want him to be. Sometimes it's a guessing game.

Special education labels represented identifiable categorical "differences" among students. David felt he could intuit the qualities that set some students apart; these differences could be confirmed by the outside measurement of tests. Throughout the data, practitioners expressed similar beliefs that differences in students' learning (manifested, for example, through their "behaviors" or "production") represented differences in individual bodies and brains.

For many practitioners at Parks, part of the difficulty of implementing a successful full-inclusion program rested in their sense that children labeled with disabilities represented a fundamentally different category of learner from children without disabilities. Thinking about disability as a medical diagnosis, many practitioners feared the children in special education needed a different kind of expertise from what they could provide. Tim Fraser, for example, lamented, "I don't personally feel qualified to work with kids that are labeled special ed … I don't know how to deal with that. I feel, in some cases, the kids are just not being helped as much as they should be." From Tim's vantage point, children identified with disabilities required a specific kind of teaching expertise that he simply did not have. Many teachers expressed similar feelings of vulnerability, stranded without the necessary tools to help children succeed. One consequence of the lack of resources to build a full-inclusion program that served students well was that teachers felt overwhelmed and unsuccessful, a condition that did not support them to rethink their fundamental assumptions about disability.

Failing to challenge many teachers' beliefs about disabilities, the full-inclusion program also did not yield major changes in their curricular and pedagogical practices. For example, Ann Page, one of the social studies teachers, discussed her understanding about how the full-inclusion policy was implemented and the impact on her teaching as follows:

> [Full inclusion] was done one year at the beginning of the year. It was like, "Okay, we've gotten rid of special ed. classes." We used to have a resource room and two special ed. teachers. Okay, it's inclusion. And they just put the students in our rooms. There was no transitional period. There was no, "Okay, these students have been in special ed. or these have IEPs [individualized educational plans]" and to go through each one of those students and to know *what their problems or special needs were. We were not given that information.* And so to me, there was a disadvantage to the teacher and to the child. (emphasis added)

Ann described the way the decision to move to an inclusive model was imposed without professional conversation and development strategies to help teachers meet students' specific learning needs. Ann focused on her need for "information" about students' "problems and special needs." While I agree that teachers need to focus attention on the variability of individual learners, one detrimental outcome of a medical approach to disability was reflected here in the tendency to think in terms of the "problems" particular children have. Ann continued:

And so the child was frustrated and definitely I was frustrated ... and I was told [by the principal], "Well, really your lessons should be to the point. You should be able to tailor your lessons to meet the needs of all the students no matter what level they are." That's a bunch of crap. *You tell me what's wrong with the student. You tell me what their needs are, and I'll try to do my best to address it.* (emphasis added)

Ann argued that a lack of attention to specific pedagogical techniques for children labeled with disabilities left students and teachers feeling equally frustrated. She countered Melanie's admonition that teachers should create approaches to curriculum that are flexible, so that all students would be able to learn with an insistence on paying attention to "what's wrong with the student." From Ann's perspective, knowing "what's wrong with the student" would indicate particular educational strategies for each individual that she could then attempt to implement. The medical discourse of disability focuses on diagnosing and treating individual differences. It rests expertise for knowledge about individual students with outside experts, rather than with classroom teachers. Moreover, reverberating throughout this discourse is a perspective that registers differences as deficits—as "problems" with individual children who are different from "normal students."

However, in pointing to this deficit orientation, I do not want to lose sight of the critical fact that this medical discourse of disability also implies an approach to educational equity. A fair and just education is one that focuses on each student's identified differences to provide instruction that addresses his or her particular needs. Ann and Tim (and many of their colleagues) worried that the new full-inclusion policy, in failing to give them tools to address individual differences, had abandoned children identified with disabilities without adequate expertise and academic support for their learning. Viewing disability through a medical/diagnostic lens can also suggest that a different, possibly even separate, education is needed. If children identified with disabilities represent a different class of learners, then they need a different kind of education.

Framing differences as qualities within the individual appears a natural and incontrovertible way of thinking about disability. A person with a disability is different because her or his body or brain works differently from those of the majority of people. Deaf people have ears that do not hear; blind people have eyes that cannot see; people with reading disabilities have brains that function in such a way as to interfere with their learning to read easily.

There is, of course, truth to the statement that deaf people are different from hearing people by virtue of some quality of their physical being. Denying that such differences exist would be patently absurd. However, thinking about disability in terms of differences located in the bodies of individuals fails to describe the relationship between a person and the environment in which he or she lives that makes some differences matter and not others (McDermott and Varenne, 1995; Mehan, 2000; Mehan, Hertweck, and Meihls, 1986; Minow, 1990; Rizvi and Lingard, 1996; Varenne and McDermott, 1998). Shifting perspective to focus on the dominant norms and assumptions of the environments we inhabit casts a different light on how we understand disability.

McDermott and Varenne (1995) cogently argue for a radical re-conceptualization through the lens of "culture as disability." Culture as disability suggests that we must understand disability as a "display board" for the fault lines of our culture. Differences become apparent in specific cultural arrangements that are organized around one kind of person and not another (see also Minow, 1990). One example used by McDermott and Varenne is a historical study by Nora Groce (1985) about 18th- and 19th-century life on Martha's Vineyard. At the time, a significant number of people in the community were born deaf; however, both deaf and hearing persons were completely integrated into the life of the community because everyone signed. The community was organized in such a way that the physical difference of deafness was not a difference that counted. It was extensive tourism from the mainland that made deafness a difference that mattered. McDermott and Varenne demand that we ask how differences come to matter in specific cultural and institutional contexts. They bring the "culture as disability" lens to an understanding of how differences come to matter in schools.

Understanding difference to be a product of the relationship between what a person brings to an environment, and the demands of that environment provides a critical lens for re-viewing disability. It offers an alternative way of thinking about the problem of disability that attends to how classrooms are set up to accommodate some children's ways of learning and not others'. Consider learning to read. Children learn to read in a variety of ways and at different ages. For some, the process is easy; others struggle. The demands of a literate society and the structures of schooling as we know it make some ways of learning to read stand out as disabilities (rather than as variability in how children approach reading). It is the dominant assumptions of a majority of schools and classrooms that make reading matter the way it does (Hehir, 2002; McDermott and Varenne, 1995; Varenne and McDermott, 1998). Most schools expect, for example, that children will read on a certain developmental schedule, that learning will be primarily text-based, and that reading instruction does not need to vary greatly to take into account the needs of all the children in the classroom. Children who do not fit the timetable or instructional models stand out and, more significantly, are often shut out by an over-reliance on text-based learning.

Viewing difference in relational terms offers us a way to cut through the two tendencies for dealing with difference: ignoring it or locating it in particular bodies (that are then interpreted as being deficient). Building truly inclusive classrooms demands a careful examination of normative classroom practices that stigmatize and exclude some children. Shifting our scrutiny from the child to the invisible norms and assumptions of the classrooms suggests ways to build inclusive practices that account for the wide variability in human learning, thereby creating integrated classrooms that offer all students meaningful access to learning.

### Integration and the Public Imagination

True integration moves beyond desegregation—beyond removing legal barriers, and simply placing together students of different races. It means bringing students together under conditions of equality, emphasizing common goals, and deemphasizing personal competition. ... True integration in our schools, then, is transformative rather than assimilative. That is, while desegregation assimilates minorities into the mainstream, true integration transforms the mainstream. (Powell, 2005, p. 297–298)

Might it be a place to argue that real education is impossible in isolation from diverse and critical perspectives? (Ladson-Billings, 2004, p. 11)

Integration, a word that has a quaint ring to it, continues to echo well beyond the walls of Parks and City Friends, through a range of educational debates about justice. Educational activists continue to fight for the rights of students labeled with disabilities to be included in mainstream classrooms (see, for example, *Gaskin v. Pennsylvania Department of Education*, 2004), arguing for reconstructing inclusion as a transformative policy that challenges normative educational practices (Isaacs, 1996; Lipsky and Gartner, 1999; Rizvi and Lingard, 1996; Slee, 1999). The struggle to keep racial integration of public schools alive continues with varied success as courts across the country have ruled differently on the question of whether race can be considered a factor in school assignments (Powell, 2005). In some places where race has been ruled an unacceptable basis for school assignment, public school educators committed to integration have moved to use socioeconomic diversity as a race-neutral means to maintain racial diversity in schools (Flinspach and Banks, 2005). Institutions of higher education across the country have looked to the Supreme Court's rulings in *Grutter v. Bollinger* (2003) and *Gratz v. Bollinger* (2003) as guides for developing policies aimed at increasing racial/ethnic diversity on campuses. Detracking efforts are based on the observation that schools with multiracial/multiethnic student populations are often internally segregated, with disproportionate numbers of students of color from marginalized groups filling low-track and special education classes (Artiles, 2003; Donovan and Cross, 2002; Eitle, 2002; Lucas, 1999; Mickelson, 2005; Oakes, 1985); detracking aims to create integrated classrooms with rich educational opportunities for all, not just some, of the school's students (Fine et al. , 2000; Wells and Serna, 1996; Welner and Oakes, 1996).

The strength of indifference and active opposition to policies and practices based on a commitment to integration suggests the ongoing struggle over what kinds of schools, and, by extension, what kind of society, we desire. The ugly history of white communities across the country actively and violently fighting desegregation orders and fleeing the nation's cities to avoid integrated schooling reflects the profound legacy of racial discrimination and oppression. There is evidence that white families continue to withdraw from integrated schools through residential and school choices (Holme, 2002; Powell, 2005; Wells and Holme, 2005) Detracking policies face fierce opposition from elite parents who silence conversations about the internal segregation of schools by arguing in terms of merit (Wells and Serna, 1996). In higher education, while some institutions such as the University of Michigan have fought long and hard to maintain race-conscious admissions policies that aim to create and maintain racial/ethnic diversity on college and university campuses, this remains embattled territory. In 1995, the Regents of the University of California eliminated color-conscious admissions policies; students from marginalized racial/ethnic groups are underrepresented in the University of California system (Crosby and Blake-Beard, 2004; Jones et al., 2002). These various sites of opposition to policies that aim to create more diverse classrooms, schools, and universities signal the significant threat that integration, as a justice claim, poses to the existing inequitable conditions inside schools and in our society at large.

At one level, the fight for integration—reflected in affirmative action policies at colleges and universities and desegregation, detracking and full-inclusion policies in K–12 schools—is about creating opportunities for students from traditionally marginalized communities to have access to richer, more challenging educational experiences. That is, the goal of these policies is not integration in and of itself, but, rather, opening up the kinds of educational experiences that have historically been reserved for white middle- and upper-class students, as well as students who are not labeled with disabilities. Integration is intended as a pathway to educational opportunity.

At another level, social activists often invoke a larger vision: They embrace the value for all students of living and learning in diverse communities as a central goal for democratic education. We can hear this claim echoed strongly, for example, in the *Grutter v. Bollinger* decision. In that decision, Justice O'Connor writes of diversity as an important value for creating leadership in a democracy. I view the ruling opinion as encompassing a limited and narrow vision of justice because it does not address deeply entrenched patterns of racial inequality; the *Grutter* decision is hardly aiming for the scope of change that *Brown* imagined in theory, if not in practice. However, as a decision that comes in the midst of the retreat on the part of many courts from endorsements of race-conscious educational remedies to inequalities, *Grutter* importantly argues for racial/ethnic diversity as a critical social good in a democracy (Powell, 2005).

Conceptualized most broadly, integration across the lines of race/ethnicity, class and disability offers a vision for truly transformative classrooms and schools—places where the existing power hierarchies can be interrogated and dismantled, and where all students can participate fully in meaningful and significant educational experiences (see, for example, Fine et al., 2000; Lipsky and Gartner, 1999; Orfield and Eaton, 1996; Wells and Serna, 1996; Welner and Oakes, 1996). Classrooms and schools that are integrated by race/ethnicity, disability, and other dimensions of difference are key sites for learning to work across differences, hopefully in ways that can truly transform society.

I urge us to hold on to, rather than abandon, this impulse to view integration as an important aspect of educational justice and take seriously Ladson-Billings's proposal that "real education is impossible in isolation from diverse and critical perspectives" (2004, p. 11). The lessons from City Friends and Parks suggest that integration remains an important value to educators, but the road to what Powell calls "true integration" requires fundamentally transforming existing educational practices to serve the goals of educational equity. Certainly, as the lessons from Parks demonstrate, a key component of this vision is a commitment to create equitably funded and well-resourced schools. Equally important, these examples illuminate a need to examine more carefully our assumptions about and approaches to difference within our school communities. The experiences of these two schools indicate that *diverse and critical perspectives* must work together for integration to serve the goal of equity. Simply being present at the table does not automatically shift the normative culture of educational practice, but without diverse perspectives, there is little hope for widespread transformational change.

CHAPTER **3**

# Equal Standards

In the spring of 1996, the atmosphere at Parks was palpably tense as the third-year students prepared for eighth grade graduation. Students joyfully anticipated moving on to high school, but felt deeply frustrated by new requirements for graduation. These new requirements asked students to demonstrate their learning in ways they had never before encountered. Graduating students were asked to compile a portfolio of proficient work in each of their four subject areas and to conceptualize and engage in a research project of their choosing. For this project, students had to pose a researchable question, become experts on their topics through traditional library research, and conduct a small field study. Their research culminated in an exhibition project that included a five-page written paper and an oral presentation that was judged by teachers and other adults in the community.

The portfolio and projects reflected Parks's new approach to curriculum and pedagogy. On the cutting edge of reform movements sweeping the nation, Parks had adopted one set of standards for curriculum and assessment to which all its students would be held. Throughout the spring, eighth grade students and teachers struggled to understand and engage with the new standards-based approach to reform. Many students had difficulty with the assignments. Some, especially those with less developed reading, writing, and research skills, found the projects and portfolios confusing and difficult. Others felt overwhelmed by the many new skills they needed to learn and implement to complete the projects and portfolios in a timely fashion. Many responded by ignoring assignments and deadlines. Teachers were frustrated by students' apparent lack of engagement with the tasks at hand and were particularly troubled by the quality of the work they did receive from many students. The teachers' deepest concern was how to assess the widely disparate performances of their students.

How does this struggle over new graduation requirements relate to questions about justice and difference? Embedded in Parks's new approach to curriculum and assessment rested a justice claim: Equity is served by holding equal standards for the education of all students. Parks's adoption of equal standards for all students evolved from its work with the Coalition of Essential Schools and reflected a growing national movement for educational reform based on equal standards. This justice claim evolved in response to the observation that educational inequality across the lines of race, ethnicity, class, and disability resulted, in large part, from the impoverished, low-skill curriculum and pedagogy that marginalized groups of students too often receive in the United States (see, for example, Anyon, 1980; Gartner and Lipsky, 1987; Lipman, 1998; Oakes, 1985; Olsen, 1997). In response, Parks, like many other schools across the nation, decided to offer all its students the same rich, innovative curriculum based on a clearly delineated set of equal standards. Moreover, a critical element of this justice claim is that schools must pay attention to student outcomes as a measure of equity. It is not enough to claim that all students have been exposed to equal standards; educators must build a school culture that supports students to meet them. The justice claim for equal standards focuses on student outcomes as an indicator of educational equity. The claim pushes beyond the limitations (discussed in Chapter 3) of access as a measure of equity; rather, it suggests that schools must create the conditions under which students can benefit from the equal standards.

In practice, however, the shift toward an outcomes focus implied by the justice claim for equal standards is complex and contradictory. Parks's experience with implementing equal standards for all students illuminates a central dilemma of practice in relationship to difference. As the new standards and assessments unfolded, educators found themselves faced with troubling questions. When all students were held to equal standards, many did not meet them. Should all students be held to the same standard for assessing outcomes, with the result that some students would not meet the proficiency requirements? Or did fairness require acknowledging learning diversity among students and designing different means of assessment that could account for students' learning styles and their development over time? Teachers wanted to acknowledge student diversity and growth over time. However, they also feared that shifting criteria for assessing students' outcomes would reestablish unequal standards and leave some students, particularly youth from historically marginalized social groups, unprepared to navigate schools and society successfully. Faced with student diversity, a tension evolved in practice, between standardizing expectations and differentiating them—between treating students the same or differently.

This chapter, perhaps even more than those on integration and recognition, illustrates the messiness of working for educational equity in contexts saturated with social inequality. The ideal, reflected in the Coalition-inspired reforms at Parks, that all students should be offered an equal and expansive education, expresses a faith in all students' capabilities to develop the knowledge, skills, and competencies needed to be creative and engaged participants in a democratic society. Focusing on student outcomes as part of this goal is intended to support the development of a professional culture inside schools that attends to learning and learners in ways that make it possible for all students to achieve the standards (Darling-Hammond, 1997; Wheelock, 1998). In practice, as Parks's story will demonstrate, designing educational reforms around equal standards is a thorny process. As educators turned to student outcomes in relation to the standards, tension arose around treating students the same or differently.

This chapter explores this central dilemma of practice that teachers faced: Does treating students the same or differently constitute equity? Rather than simply viewing this dilemma as a result of standards devolving into standardization, I explore how everyday practice-based contradictions arise in relation to three major issues. First, as described in Chapters 2 and 3, Parks faced a serious lack of resources to support the development of learner-centered education (Darling-Hammond, 1997). Second, educators expressed conflicting discourses about learners: Is learning a matter of students' choice and agency, or is it limited by individual "ability"? These discourses—discourses that resonate across the field of education—imply a deep ambivalence about whether we truly believe that all students are capable of meeting the challenges of an equal and enabling education. Finally, I reflect on the limitations of adopting standards intended to help students navigate successfully in schools and society, without interrogating whether, in fact, it is possible for all students to succeed in schools, given the structural inequalities of our social order. That is, I suggest we need to view standards critically and understand the norms, values, and assumptions embedded in them—norms, values, and assumptions that may guarantee that differences continue to track inexorably into educational inequalities. Before exploring Parks's experience with equal standards, I situate the school's work in the broader national movement for equal standards.

## National Discourse about Standards and Equity

All, regardless of race or class or economic status, are entitled to a fair chance and to the tools for developing their individual powers of mind and spirit to the utmost. This promise means that all children by virtue of their own efforts, competently guided, can hope to attain the mature and informed judgment needed to secure gainful employment and to manage their own lives, thereby serving not only their interests but also the progress of society itself.

We do not believe that a public commitment to excellence and educational reform must be made at the expense of a strong public commitment to the equitable treatment of our diverse population. The twin goals of equity and high-quality schooling have profound and practical meaning for our economy and society, and we cannot permit one to yield to the other either in principle or in practice. (National Commission on Excellence in Education, 1983)

The 1983 report from the National Commission on Excellence in Education on the state of education in the United States set forth an agenda for the nation's schools that wove together a concern with equitable and excellent education *for all*. *A Nation at Risk* argued that U.S. schools were failing to educate students to high academic standards that would guarantee they could compete successfully in the changing global economy, which increasingly depended on "knowledge, learning, information and skilled intelligence [that] are the new raw materials of international commerce." Moreover, the report acknowledged the historical inequalities of race and class and the necessity of addressing educational equity for "our diverse population." The report proposed that the nation's schools desperately needed reforms that would simultaneously remedy the existing inequalities of race and class, and the general "mediocrity" of U.S. education. *A Nation at Risk* set the tone for the next two decades of public discourse about education and helped shape policy initiatives aimed at reforming schools across the United States. Parks's venture into a curriculum based on equal standards for all students must be located within this broader national context of educational reform.

*A Nation at Risk* ended with a set of recommendations that included a framework for content standards for high school graduation. The idea that education should be based on clear and coherent standards, whereby all students should be expected to achieve, became central to school reforms in the decades following the report's publication (see Jennings, 2001). By the mid-1990s, when I began my fieldwork at Parks, standards were the rallying point for educational reforms in school districts across the nation. Examples abound. The National Council of Teachers of Mathematics (NCTM) completely overhauled its recommendations for mathematics education based on a set of standards for curriculum, instruction, and assessment (NCTM, 1989, 1991, 1995; Romberg, 1998). In 1994, President Clinton signed into law the Goals 2000: Educate America Act (see Goals 2000, 1994), which put standards at the forefront of the national discourse about school reform. Systemic reform efforts in major U.S. cities were organized around content and performance standards to which all students would be held. The No Child Left Behind Act of 2001 (see No Child Left Behind Act, 2001) directly tied federal funds to schools' capacities to ensure that all students meet equal academic standards as measured by standardized testing. *A Nation at Risk* and the school reforms that evolved in its wake introduced a justice claim into public discourse about education: holding all students to equal standards—ideally those reflective of the highest quality education—is a key component of equity.

Admittedly, standards are conceptualized in a variety of ways and are used to leverage vastly different educational reforms. Advocates of bottom-up reforms would use standards as frameworks within which local professionals can develop high-quality, innovative curricula and pedagogy tailored to individual students and particular communities (see Darling-Hammond, 1997; Meier, 2000; Sizer, 1992; Wheelock, 1998). Parks offers an example of this kind of bottom-up reform. Others see standards from the perspective of top-down initiatives that are intimately bound up with strong accountability systems (see Barth et al., 1999; Fuhrman, 1993; Haycock, 2001; Murnane, 2000; Ravitch, 1995). Some of the efforts to use standards to leverage reform, specifically those that depend on high-stakes testing, have been called to task for perpetuating rather than remedying educational inequalities along the lines of race and class (Lipman, 2002, 2004; McNeil, 2000; McNeil and Valenzuela, 2001; Natriello and Pallas, 2001). Certainly, those who advocate equal standards as a means to ensure equity by promoting strong professional communities and rich, innovative curriculum and pedagogy at the local level (see for examples, Chase, 2000; Darling-Hammond, 1997; Falk, 2002; Nash, 2000; Wheelock, 1998) find little common ground with the top-down legislation of President George W. Bush's No Child Left Behind legislation, which is highly dependent on accountability through high-stakes testing. However, this legislation also advocates equal standards as a path to equitable education, stating its purpose as "ensur[ing] that all children have a fair, equal and significant opportunity to obtain a high-quality education and reach at a minimum, proficiency on challenging, State academic achievement standards and state academic assessments." (No Child Left Behind Act, 2001).

My purpose here is not to enter into a detailed discussion of the debates that have been raging about standards and their effects in terms of building more equitable schools (see Chase, 2000; Meier, 2000; Murnane, 2000; National Research Council, 2002; Noddings, 1999; Ravitch, 1995; Thernstrom, 2000). My concern is specifically with three key assumptions of the justice claim that undergirds the movement for educational standards. In no way do I want to imply that proponents of bottom-up approaches to reform share the same educational vision as reformers advocating top-down policies, especially those who support punitive accountability measures; however, I suggest that, despite highly variable and contentious approaches, discourse about standards shares key assumptions about educational equity.

First, even advocates of wildly disparate views of standards-based reforms believe that schools should hold equal standards for all students. Standards are intended to change the kinds of education students actually receive in the nation's classrooms. The justice claim for equal standards moves beyond the question of access to educational institutions and classrooms to address what happens inside schools and classrooms. Equal standards are ideally supposed to guarantee that, wherever a student may be located, his or her learning experiences will reflect high-quality education.

Second, the justice claim for equal standards attends heavily to educational outcomes. Outcomes serve as the measure of educational equity.[1] Thus, evidence of education equity does not lie simply in whether all students have access to a curriculum based on equal standards. Rather, it rests with whether all students are able to achieve those standards (see especially Coleman, 1968; Howe, 1997 for explication of different approaches to educational opportunity).

There is, then, a common concern among proponents of standards with students' achievement outcomes; however, the significance of these outcomes and assessment of students' educational achievement is defined in dramatically different ways and for very different purposes. Top-down educational reform initiatives usually advocate holding schools responsible for student achievement through standardized testing and strong accountability systems. Many proponents of top-down reforms deem strong accountability systems necessary because, they argue, without such measures there would be no mechanism through which to make ... all schools accountable for teaching all students to the same standards (Barth et al., 1999; see also Elmore, Abelmann, and Fuhrman, 1996; Linn, 2000). These reform models imply that without the requirement of policy initiatives that hold schools accountable for student achievement, there is no way to leverage radical changes in schools that historically have failed to educate children well. Critics of this approach caution against accountability systems that over-rely on test scores and use narrow measures of students' knowledge, especially single-measure standardized tests. They suggest that these accountability systems increase failure and dropout rates, and tend to narrow the curriculum for students in schools with poor test scores (see, for example, Center on Educational Policy, 2006; Heubert, 2001; McNeil, 2000; McNeil and Valenzuela, 2001; National Research Council, 1999; Natriello and Pallas, 2001; Neill, 2003; Shepard, 2000; Thompson, 2001).

Advocates of bottom-up initiatives that use standards as a framework for reform have embraced the need for multiple measures of student achievement, especially focusing on developing more authentic performance-based assessments through which students can demonstrate their grasp of the broad educational standards (Chase, 2000; Darling-Hammond, 1997; Falk, 2002; Sizer, 1992; Wheelock, 1998). Recognizing that people have diverse ways of learning and expressing what they know, authentic assessment proponents suggest that, while all students should be expected to achieve certain standards, the means through which they demonstrate their competencies should be multiple, flexible, and reflective of "authentic" applications of students' knowledge. Moreover, the purposes of assessing student learning are to help teachers tailor curriculum and pedagogy to meet the needs of individual students. Parks's reform efforts drew on this approach to assessing student outcomes.

Standardized testing and authentic assessment represent conflicting notions of student achievement outcomes and deeply divergent ideas about the goals of education in a democratic society. However, *they share a belief that the measure of educational equity lies in the results* (see Howe, 1997). Within this framework, it is insufficient simply to say that children have access to equal opportunities if their outcomes continue to be widely disparate.[2]

Thus, the disparate arguments for using equal standards to leverage educational reform rest upon two important shared tenets: equal standards should be applied to all students, and the measure of equity lies in student outcomes. Ideally, there is a third critical component to standards-based reforms: an infusion of resources to schools that guarantee the conditions within which high academic standards can be fostered (Chase, 2000; Darling-Hammond, 1997; Falk, 2002; Korhhaber and Orfield, 2001; Porter, 1995; Wheelock, 1998). These conditions include sufficient resources (for example, personnel, materials, and services) and excellent professional development opportunities for educators. Many would argue it is the continued failure to provide adequate resources for schools serving poor children and children of color that makes the greatest mockery of commitments to equality of opportunity (Hilliard, 1998; Kozol, 1991, 2005 ).

Thus, the justice claim for equal standards is organized around three important strands: equal standards must be applied to all students' education;

the measure of educational equity is in students' outcomes; and (in some manifestations of this discourse) schools must be given adequate resources to implement these standards.

At Parks, the initial implementation of equal standards grew out of a bottom-up approach to reform inspired by the school's membership in the Coalition of Essential Schools. In the early years, before it was subject to a district-wide reform effort, Parks had maximum flexibility in its approach to standards-based reforms. Parks envisioned equal standards as frameworks for directing high-quality and innovative curricula, and aimed to build pedagogical practices tailored to the diverse needs of its students. Despite this flexibility and commitment to creating an environment that was "learner-centered" (Darling-Hammond, 1997), as the justice claim for equal standards unfolded in everyday practice, it raised complex questions for addressing equity in relation to difference.

## Equal Standards in Everyday Practice

Educators at Parks were determined to make curricular changes that would guarantee that all their students left well prepared for high school. When they talked about educational inequality, educators expressed deep concerns about the large number of students who did not gain the knowledge and skills needed to be successful in high school and the workforce. As discussed in Chapter 2, Parks's educators viewed "learning diversity" as the difference that made the greatest difference in student achievement; the wide variability in how students learned and what they knew and could do was most troubling to the teachers. Educators understood these differences to be related to class and racial inequality in the United States— structural inequalities that affected the quality of education their students had experienced before their arrival in middle school. Parks's practitioners aimed to disrupt the recursive relationship between educational and social inequalities, and make a difference in their students' life trajectories by developing a rigorous, high-quality program for all.

Like many of their colleagues across the nation, Parks's practitioners embraced equal standards as a path for improving educational outcomes. Parks's affiliation with the Coalition of Essential Schools had engendered new thinking about the school's curriculum and pedagogy. Guided by the Coalition principle that "less is more," the faculty had considered carefully the essential knowledge and skills they wanted students to have mastered by the end of their tenure at Parks. Describing the plans for curricular reform to parents, Melanie Post, the principal, wrote that through "these standards [the school seeks] to create a rigorous learning community with high expectations of achievement for all of our students." The language of standards, rigor, and high expectations for *all students* signaled the under-lying justice claim with which this chapter is concerned.

During the year before my arrival, Parks's practitioners had worked collaboratively to write content and curriculum standards for each of four domains: communications, mathematics, science, and social studies and citizenship.[3] The standards on which they agreed emphasized the development of students who would be active writers, problem solvers, investigators, and knowledgeable citizens. For example, the communications content standards called for students to "use effective research and information management skills; write creatively for a variety of purposes and audiences using appropriate and varied conventions; and analyze and make critical judgments about various forms of communication." Science standards included "investigate the relationships of science and technology; and evaluate and generate potential solutions to environmental issues." These few examples, reflective of the larger set of content standards and their accompanying curriculum standards, suggested a commitment on the part of Parks to knowledge grounded in meaningful work and a vision of socially responsible participation in community life. Parks had also moved to an assessment system, based on rubrics, that set out clear criteria for proficiency and gave students a chance to rework assignments until they met the proficiency requirements. The school had chosen an assessment system that, in the ideal, embodied the belief that, with the right guidance, all students would be able to meet the criteria. At Parks, practitioners worked hard to foster education that was rich, challenging, and engaged in social critique and action.

Across the disciplines, teachers were implementing new approaches to curriculum and assessment. In Martha Silverman's English class, students read many novels and learned tools for formal analysis. They wrote essays analyzing the books, but they also expressed what they had learned through visual and dramatic expression. They wrote in a range of genres: research, persuasive essays, fiction, poetry, and so forth. Through all these activities, critique and revision were the norm. Moreover, Martha encouraged the students to be "critical friends" to each other; she taught students how to give and receive feedback on works-in-progress that would help with revisions. In Tim Fraser's science classes, students learned how to observe the natural world, searching for patterns and making hypotheses. Students engaged in scientific inquiry, setting up and conducting a range of experiments. Hannah Stein usually had students work in cooperative groups, taking a problem-solving approach to mathematics. In David Waters's social studies classes, students posed important questions about power and oppression, learned research skills to investigate the issues, and worked to present their conclusions through essays, demonstrations, and dramatic performances. As they implemented new curricula, teachers used team and faculty meetings to ask for formal feedback from their peers on their lessons and assessments. Thus, reflective inquiry guided teachers as they implemented the new standards for students.

The eighth grade graduation requirements described at the beginning of this chapter also exemplified the school's new standards. Eighth grade students spent the spring semester intensively focused on their "I-Search" research projects. Each teacher worked closely with a small group of advisees to help them develop an appropriate research question, find resources about their topic, and design manageable interviews or surveys they could conduct in the field.

During the final months of the school year, I often found teachers and students engaged in serious conversations about these projects, as in this scene described in my field notes:

> Students spent the whole morning working in their Family Groups on their final projects. I found Sharon Brice (an African-American language arts teacher) meeting with Renee (a small, soft-spoken, always fashionable, African-American girl) on her "I-Search" questions and the outline for her final project about abortion. I listened to Sharon guide Renee to fine-tune her questions: "Are you asking about abortion in the city, state, country or world?" for example. Sharon has a nice way with students, taking their questions seriously, probing for clarity. Later Christine (the wiry, dynamic African-American self-described computer whiz), who is doing her project on herpes, worked with Sharon to think through interview questions she will ask a doctor over her spring break. Sharon suggested a series of questions and talked with Christine about taping the interview so that she might be able to listen carefully afterwards. Again there was a nice way in which Sharon—even while suggesting interview questions—really safeguarded the search aspect of this project, never giving Christine answers that Sharon might already know.

As Sharon worked with the girls, she sought to strengthen their understanding of the research process. She helped Renee develop a research-able question, while advising Christine on how to translate her broader research questions into an interview protocol. Through all this, Sharon never usurped the project, remaining respectful of each student's capacity to decide on and answer her own questions. This anecdote offers a glimpse of the type of academic pursuit in which teachers hoped all students would engage through the I-Search projects. Christine, who was considered by teachers to be one of Parks's strongest students, and Renee, who was learning-disabled labeled and considered one of the most vulnerable, were both provided an opportunity to engage in the same project which had been designed to put students' interests at the center of learning the research process.

To graduate, students were each expected to demonstrate their knowledge and skills by fulfilling the same proficiency requirements.[3] Christine, Renee, and their peers were expected to demonstrate what they had learned through a written report and an oral presentation. Thus, the graduation project embodied key components of the justice claim for equal standards, by offering each student the same rich, demanding curriculum and looking to student outcomes as a measure of equity. The idea is that implementing a rich, challenging curriculum for all students is an insufficient guarantee of equity if there is no attention given to whether students meet standards for performance. The focus on student outcomes as a critical component of educational equity, however, pulled practitioners in two directions, creating a dilemma for everyday practice.

## Equal Standards in the Face of Diversity: The Dilemma of Practice

As teachers implemented a curriculum that expected that all students would engage in the same intellectually challenging work, the educational reforms generated new questions about difference and equity. As the reforms unfolded, educators' discussions about equal standards for all students were intimately interwoven with questions about learning diversity and worries about all students' capabilities to meet the new standards. A curriculum based on setting equal standards for all students raised difficult questions, especially in relationship to students' educational outcomes. How should teachers understand or respond to the fact that many students appeared disengaged from the project of schooling or seemed unable to meet the proficiency requirements? Was it fair to expect all students to be assessed by equal standards for proficiency, given that they started with very different knowledge, skills, and experiences? At the same time, how could teachers assess students by different standards without leaving some children unprepared for high school and beyond?

A few educators at Parks advocated cogently for an assessment system that would allow students to demonstrate what they knew through multiple expressive media (painting, performance, and so forth), thereby proposing that assessment should be responsive to students' different strengths. However, a majority argued that all students must be assessed by the same performance standards. The eighth grade graduation requirements reflected the latter approach: All students were expected to produce a written paper and an oral research presentation that met proficiency standards. Importantly, these performance standards were intended to prepare students for the academic work they would be expected to do in high school and beyond.

As the school implemented a curriculum based on its new standards, many teachers voiced concerns and frustrations about the persistent "problem" of learning diversity, as they observed that most of their students found the new approach difficult and did not meet proficiency standards. Questions about learning diversity became particularly compelling for eighth grade teachers as their students struggled to meet graduation requirements. Because students spent most of the spring working on their final projects, conflict between teachers and students increased noticeably. Teachers felt exasperated with students who missed deadlines, evaded work, and turned in projects that did not meet the requirements. They expressed disappointment and anger that as of early May, half of their students were not meeting the standards for graduation. Teachers worried about what they should do. Would they refuse to graduate half the class if the students' projects did not meet the proficiency requirements?

At the same time, many students resented the overarching focus on this single project. They challenged the decision that the key requirement for graduation was a proficient exhibition project. Would none of the rest of their work count if they were unable to complete the exhibition project to their teachers' satisfaction? As one boy put it, "All that work we did, math homework and that stuff, don't none of that count for graduation?"

Teachers often found themselves at odds with the principal over what equal standards should mean in practice, particularly in relation to assessing students' performance. This conflict was palpable at a team meeting in mid-May at which the principal and the teachers of the graduating class discussed their dilemmas about standards and assessment. Sharon Brice, the language arts teacher, came to the meeting with a question from her students, who had been asking whether they would have a chance to redo their papers if they were not proficient by the time the final draft was due. This question opened up a difficult conversation. Tim Fraser, the science teacher, strongly advocated a firm stance in relation to the deadline. He argued that meeting deadlines is an important skill to learn, and that the students had been given sufficient opportunities to make their work proficient. Tim believed that "the students were choosing not to avail themselves of opportunities." The other team members agreed with him, arguing that students needed to learn these standards because of expectations they would face in the "real world." Melanie Post, the principal, advocated a different perspective. She asked the teachers, "What's enough time? What's the lesson if you don't let [the students] work on the papers more?" Her explicit goal was to retain as few students as possible. She felt it was in students' best interests to work and rework their papers until they met the proficiency standards. She emphasized that it was the teachers' responsibility to make sure all students met the standards however long that took. Tim and his teammates worried that students would get the wrong message from this approach. They feared that students would learn that they did not have to take the standards seriously and would not take responsibility for meeting them.

Underlying the disagreement between the teachers and the principal were two different ideas about what constitutes fair educational practice: treating all students the same versus different and individualized treatment. In this team meeting, the eighth grade teachers advocated the first approach. Students must know that they were all required to meet the same performance standards for graduation. From the teachers' perspective, students needed to learn to meet requirements to survive in high school and the workforce. The school must prepare students to take on the types of responsibilities that would be demanded in the world beyond Parks. Failing to hold students to final deadlines by which time their work had to be proficient would teach them that the equal standards did not apply to everyone—a lesson that would do students a disservice in the future. Melanie pushed for a different view. She felt that students must be given every last chance to complete work proficiently. From Melanie's perspective, teachers must be responsible for continuing to provide students with opportunities to succeed. She advocated an approach that looked to each child's circumstances and needs.

As the exhibition date drew nearer, the eighth grade teachers were once again in conflict with Melanie over what they would accept for the final projects. As before, Melanie argued that equity demanded considering individual students' differences. Melanie was an ardent advocate of standards; in fact, she had pushed the faculty to define a set of content and curriculum standards for the school. However, she viewed standards as an endpoint toward which students might take different paths. Melanie understood those paths to vary, given students' different learning styles, needs, and interests, and she imagined that different students might reach the standards at different times. She argued strongly for an assessment system that would evaluate each student in terms of overall growth and development. Moreover, she wished teachers would allow students to demonstrate what they knew through a variety of media, rather than assessing them primarily on the basis of a five-page research paper and an oral presentation.

Many teachers, however, felt that the graduation project and their expectations for students were undermined by Melanie's insistence on making every effort to allow students to pass by shifting standards, expectations, and deadlines to an individual basis. They wondered: Shouldn't all students be able to write a five-page paper? How could they grade as proficient projects that did not meet the standards of the state's writing rubric for a well-reasoned and coherent paper? Teachers worried that assessing students by different standards did not constitute educational equity, but rather reinforced a system of low academic achievement for some students. Many teachers were wary that the continued failure to hold all students to the equal outcome standards reflected racist educational practices that did not expect enough of children of color.

This conflict between advocacy for flexible approaches to learning and assessment and commitment to providing all students with the same expectations and opportunities for academic achievement represents a real equity dilemma for everyday practice. The question facing practitioners was how to deal with the diversity of actual learners, given equal standards and assessment measures. This dilemma was highlighted during the final exhibition projects of the graduating students. The projects held all students to the same performance standards. All students were expected to meet proficiency standards on the five-page written research paper as well as on the oral presentation accompanied by a visual component. Because the standards were juxtaposed with the diversity of skills, interests, and learning styles students brought to the project, however, teachers struggled to make sense of how to assess individual students' performances.

Parks's practitioners struggled with several specific questions. Given the range of skills students had demonstrated when they began their research, could they all be expected to produce a proficient final product? What were the implications of holding different students to different standards? Which expectations were nonnegotiable (for example, deadlines, typing, proficient writing style and grammar, accurate information, interdisciplinary connections)? The following excerpts from my field notes provide a sample of the range of final exhibitions:

Andy is a ham. His presentation on the Vietnam War was definitely disjointed, but he told the story from the perspective of a hippie protesting the war, played the part fully, and enjoyed himself. He had lots of disconnected bits of information about many aspects of the war (some more accurate than others). He needed help with the organization. He had a nice variety of media: a hippie outfit, a colorful poster he had made of a man burning a draft card, music from the 60s, clips from Forrest Gump. Andy began his presentation by introducing himself and then stating, "My father, Sunshine, who was a hippie at the time will be giving the presentation today." He then dressed himself in a longhaired wig, headband, tie-dyed T-shirt and vest, and turned on a Jimmi Hendrix piece. Andy's talk included describing Eisenhower as a "far out cat" who believed in a domino theory; discussing the tropical climate of Vietnam; citing 2 million U.S. deaths; describing napalm as a "chemical substance that sticks to anything in sight and burns"; referencing the burning of draft cards and the Black Panthers's critique of the war; and more. He strung these various statements together, interspersed with music and the movie clips. Andy and I had a chance to chat about his performance. He told me he was very nervous and sweaty doing it. He liked his poster. He likes to draw and told me he'd run out of a lot of markers doing his poster. Finally he told me it was "a shame, all those people dying—and for no reason."

Andy's exhibition project allowed him to play up to several of his real strengths: his acting talent and his love of music, color, and drawing. He seemed interested in the time period and enjoyed taking on a different persona. At the same time, his presentation entailed a string of disjointed and often inaccurate pieces of information.

Mona's exhibition project was quite different:

Mona spoke about the work of architects. She had the most visual aids of any presentation to date. She had blueprints for floor plans, tools architects use, renderings of buildings, and an architect's portfolio. She had made two posters—one showing three levels of architects and their salaries. The other was incredible. She had hand drawn with such precision three [of the city's] buildings, blown them up, and painted them on a poster. Mona is thinking of becoming an architect. She spoke slowly, clearly, and a little hesitantly, but she did not read from her notes. She was very straight-faced during her presentation. It was well organized and provided a lot of information about how one gets to be an architect, what they do. Finally, she summarized the biographies of three famous architects.

Mona's presentation reflected her interest in architecture and drawing, her clear organization skills, and her great attention to detail. Although she did not appear completely at ease with her oral performance, it was a competent, well-articulated, and traditional presentation.

Khallid's project reflected yet another outcome of these final exhibition projects:

Despite the teachers' persistent frustrations that students were not deeply engaged with the process of the research project, in the end, most students took their final presentations very seriously. Khallid, for example, whom I have never seen but fooling around in class, presented quite earnestly, about heroin and marijuana. He read from note cards, a little hesitantly, but well. He might not have been clear on every bit of information, but the presentation, which was quite short, was also focused on the effects of drugs on the body. Hannah Stein [a white, veteran math teacher who was his advisor] told me later that his paper was a "disaster." She said she had finally resolved herself to the fact that it was never going to be truly proficient. So, she "cut a deal with him" that he would write about one of the two drugs. They went through the paper and organized it. She asked him when he'd have it completed. He told her Monday, and she said Tuesday was fine and that he could hand write it since he doesn't have a computer at home.

For Khallid, the oral presentation gave him an opportunity to show a different side of his usual comedic personality. His presentation was short but organized and allowed him to demonstrate more mastery than did the written component of the project.

Andy's, Mona's, and Khallid's very different exhibition projects illustrate well the difficult and painful question that teachers kept asking: What does it mean to hold all students to equal standards? Mona's represented the most traditionally academic type of presentation: a focused talk about becoming an architect, with appropriate visual aids such as tools of the trade, charts, and drawings of famous buildings. She had clearly demonstrated the criteria for proficiency. Andy and Khallid raised critical issues for teachers about standards and assessment. During many of my classroom observations up until that time, both boys were frequently in trouble with their teachers. They often appeared bored or were fooling around with friends and were almost always among the students who had not turned in assignments; however, they approached their presentations differently. Andy, who from my many observations loved acting, pretense, and fantasy, threw himself wholeheartedly into the role of a hippie telling the tale of the Vietnam War. Khallid shifted from his usually jocular persona into that of a sober lecturer. How, teachers wondered, should they assess the boys' performances? Should they be judged against absolute standards or against some standards of growth? Ultimately, Andy was not allowed to graduate on time. He had to work to make his project proficient over the summer. This decision grew out of the team's belief that Andy could, with some effort, meet the proficiency requirements. In Khallid's case, Hannah Stein decided to change the proficiency standards as set out in order to create more reasonable goals for him. These goals were tied to Khallid's development in skills and knowledge. Hannah's decision, as well as similar ones made for other students, grew out of teachers' knowledge of their students' strengths, vulnerabilities, and *growth as learners*. Khallid, for example, had come to Parks reading well below grade level, and although he had made more progress in three years than he had in the previous six years of schooling, he still was not reading on grade level. Given this knowledge of his growth, should Hannah refuse to pass him?

In the end, rather than measuring "success" in identical terms for every student, many teachers considered individual students' demonstrated growth and change; however, they did this with great reservations. They worried that they were reestablishing a system of low standards and expectations for some children—a system that would perpetuate educational inequality. Teachers were fully aware that there might be a damaging message in these shifting standards—one which suggested to students that they need not or could not meet the expected academic standards. Furthermore, teachers feared that grading students' work as proficient based on where they had started—rather than against some set endpoint—risked jeopardizing their academic success in the future as they moved into high school and beyond without necessary academic competencies.

Martha Silverman expressed this conflict well:

> I went to a conference and I brought student writing, and people were looking at it. And my question was, is this stuff that I marked exemplary really exemplary? And in the cases that I gave them, only one of them was truly exemplary. And I realized that I was grading it exemplary based on what I know about the kid. One of them was by an eighth grader who is autistic. And for him, I thought this was incredible, and so I graded it exemplary. And there was another young lady who never wrote, who submitted the paper five times—wrote about her grandfather's death. And it brought me to tears. And so I graded that, by the fifth time that was exemplary writing for her. And what this panel of people said is, "You just have to hold to the rubric. You still have to hold to the rubric, and you can't let that other stuff get in the way." And it raised a question for me. If we're really supposed to personalize education and we're really supposed to get to know kids well, is it fair to say that we can be their coach and their adjudicator?

Martha's struggle was engendered by contradictory, albeit interwoven, beliefs about student achievement outcomes. One idea is that "exemplary" references fixed, measurable objective criteria. Students' academic achievements are assessed against those criteria, and all students are treated the same. Learning is measured in terms of a fixed endpoint, and the teacher's ultimate role is to judge students' successes or failures against the set criteria. In the field of education, standardized testing best exemplifies this way of thinking about student achievement outcomes.

How, then, does a teacher consider difference? The autistic child? The white working-class girl who had never written an essay in her academic career until she entered Martha's classroom and then plunged herself into five revisions of an essay about her grandfather's death? When she shifted her focus to the individual student, Martha viewed learning in terms of each person's strengths, vulnerabilities, and development—a stance embedded in the principles of the Coalition of Essential Schools to which Parks belonged. As a teacher, Martha's role, then, became one of facilitating growth over time.

Aware of the constant tension between looking to external standards for academic achievement and attending to the educational growth of each individual student, Martha and her colleagues were caught in a dilemma of practice. Should all students be assessed against the same performance standards, or should education attend to each individual's strengths, vulnerabilities, learning styles, and growth? As Martha probed this dilemma, she raised a set of key questions: What is the purpose of education? What is fair? What constitutes just treatment of students? What is the role of a teacher?

As educators at Parks worked to create just educational practices through equal standards, then, they faced an irresolvable struggle. Holding all students to equal standards and performance expectations perpetuated unequal outcomes; some students did not meet the goals. Judging students individually, however, threatened to send them out into the world unprepared to meet the challenges ahead. Further, it risked reinscribing low expectations for some students, thus treating them as less capable than others. The dilemma of practice in which teachers often found themselves caught reflects what feminist legal scholar Martha Minow has called the "dilemma of difference." She writes:

> [W]hen does treating people differently emphasize their differences and stigmatize or hinder them on that basis? And when does treating people the same become insensitive to their differences and likely to stigmatize or hinder them? ... The problems of inequality can be exacerbated both by treating members of minority groups the same as members of the majority and by treating the two groups differently. The dilemma of difference may be posed as a choice between integration and separation, as a choice between similar treatment and special treatment, or as a choice between neutrality and accommodation. (1990, p. 20–21)

Minow argues that this dilemma results from the broader, inequitable social arrangements that make differences matter in the way they do (see also Scott, 1988; Varenne and McDermott, 1998; Young, 1990). The recurrent struggle that teachers faced over whether treating students the same or differently constitutes justice is, I suggest, tied to other deeply rooted ideas and inequalities that must be exposed if we are to move beyond this dilemma of practice.

## Sources of the Dilemma of Practice

The dilemma engendered by the justice claim for equal standards was bound up inextricably with three key issues. First, the school's strapped resources profoundly affected teachers' capacities to help all students meet the new standards, just as it had made successful implementation of full inclusion nearly impossible. As I have explored this issue at length in Chapter 2, I will only touch briefly upon the impact that scarcity had on implementation of standards-based reforms. Teachers' struggles about how to assess students' academic outcomes were connected to their dismay at not having enough personnel or resources to have a sufficient impact on students' development as learners. The majority of students at Parks had reached middle school without being successfully taught to read or to use fundamental mathematical concepts. Teachers were deeply concerned about this. However, they felt keenly that without extra personnel and more professional development about teaching reading and mathematics, they could not adequately address literacy and numeracy needs and guarantee that all students would make enough progress to meet eighth grade proficiency standards by graduation. Without a commitment to equalizing resources across schools and school districts, the justice claim for equal standards cannot, in practice, constitute a real opportunity for providing students with an equitable education (see Howe, 1997). Expecting that equal standards will lead to equal outcomes without addressing the inequalities of resources across schools can hardly meet any democratic ideal for equity (Kozol, 1991, 2005).

The broad inequalities of class and race/ethnicity in our society severely limit the impact local schools can have in remedying educational and social inequalities. However, the dilemma that emerged as educators at Parks implemented its new standards was also deeply bound up with a second issue: the discursive construction of learners. The dominant underlying discourse about the relationship between the individual child and learning—at Parks, as at many schools—reflected key assumptions that sustain the dilemma of difference. This discourse suggested two competing and yet interwoven explanations for academic achievement: that achievement was related to students' unfettered agency to choose success or that it reflected fixed limitations on individuals' capacities to learn.

The third issue that I discuss is that standards-based reforms cast the claim for justice primarily in terms of providing students with a fair chance to *compete within existing schools and society.* The school's efforts, as well as the dominant approaches to reform across the nation, aim to prepare students for success in what many Parks educators repeatedly referred to as the "real world." This "real world" is, however, one that is continually reconstituted around the failure of some children. Understanding the roots of the dilemma of practice that educators continually faced demands interrogating the values and assumptions invisibly woven into our educational standards.

### Conceptualizing Learners

Discourse about the relationship between learners and academic achievement reflects a complex and contradictory set of assumptions about choice and capability as sources of inequitable educational outcomes. This complexity resonates in the words of Peter Elliot, the counselor, describing the difference that posed the greatest "problem" for the school:

> That diversity of how people—how empowered they feel, their ability to resource in the world around them, to connect with the resources— I think is the greatest diversity that poses us a problem. That's across racial, economic lines. Parks works best for kids who can resource, who can take what's available here and use it. You know, there's Andrew. As I understand it, his mother was an addict. He's living with a grandmother now. He's been through tough stuff. But she's a resource now in his life. Real solid. And he comes in. He's got some social maladaptations. But he's getting it. I can see just how he's able to take it in and grow with it. There are other kids that have nourishment barriers up that won't take. They are so broken and damaged in some way that they are resisting everything that is here for them. And we don't have the resources I don't think, either in the school, or in ability to work with the family to make an impact on them. So we miss some of them. I think it's those who come here with the ability to resource. You know, somebody used the analogy one time that you go to the supermarket and the manager says, "Here. Take the basket and you can fill it up with everything and it's free. Put whatever you want in the basket and when you get to the check out, there's no charge for it." And a lot of these kids come out with an empty basket. They just can't organize themselves to fill up their basket here.

In the analogy of the supermarket, Peter Elliot compared public school to a free market where all children have equal access to goods. Public school is the place where students are given the opportunity to acquire equal life chances. For one short time, goods are free, and everyone is allowed to "fill up their basket" with as much as they can. The problem that leads to a diversity of academic outcomes is some people's inability to collect the goods. It is, according to Peter, people's differential "ability to resource in the world around them, to connect with the resources" that leads to unequal academic outcomes. Interestingly, Peter used the word "resource" as a verb. Resourcing is something one does for oneself. It is action and indicates choice. Resources are not provided, but rather willfully chosen. Moreover, Peter does not suggest that it is the responsibility of schools to teach students to "resource."

Peter argued that the reason some individuals cannot "resource" is that "they are so broken and damaged in some way that they are resisting everything that is here for them." Peter acknowledged that students do not all come to the free supermarket of schooling on an equal footing, and he placed responsibility for their inability to "resource" with individuals' "nourishment barriers" and with the causes of their "damage." Peter spoke earlier in this interview of the "level of trauma and disassociation" that existed in communities he perceived as torn apart by materialism, television, drugs, and violence. For Peter, the "problem" of resourcing, and thus unequal academic outcomes, is located in individuals, their families, and their communities.

A critical piece of this framework is that Peter, like many others at Parks, constructs the school as a *possible* site for equalizing life chances among students. The goods are free; the baskets are available. Students simply cannot, or do not, make appropriate shopping choices. Peter's words highlight two interwoven assumptions about academic success: that it depends crucially on individual choice and that some individuals are unable to choose because of some kind of internal limitation (such as prior life traumas). Unequal academic outcomes, then, are a consequence of differences individual students bring to school with them (by virtue of their individual, family, or community experiences). The differential academic outcomes are not viewed as an outcome of the processes of schooling.

At the same time, Peter complicated this picture by hinting at the school's role in producing academic outcomes. Perhaps, he suggested, the school shelves are empty, or at least not fully stocked. "We don't have the resources I don't think, either in the school, or in ability to work with the family to make an impact on them. So we miss some of them." As Peter shifted to use "resource" as a noun, he implicated, importantly, the ways that students' academic outcomes are constructed in the interaction between what students bring to school and what the school does or does not provide. Public schools, in fact, may not be the free supermarkets where all children can receive equal access to societal goods. Given a poorly stocked system, schools function to provide goods and care to those students who arrive with more resources in the first place.

Keeping in mind, then, that a profound lack of resources undermined educators' capacities to address the needs of diverse students, I want to focus here on fundamental beliefs about learners (implied in Peter's supermarket analogy) that undergird the dilemma of practice that emerged as teachers implemented equal standards for all students. The question of whether students should be treated the same or differently in the face of equal standards is related in complicated ways to conflicting notions about learning and human capacity. The belief that fairness is achieved by holding all students to the same standards is premised to a large degree on the idea that, given the right conditions (rich curriculum, good pedagogy, high expectations), students can choose to succeed in school if they so wish. This idea of relating academic outcomes to choice lives side by side with another prominent educational discourse: that a set of (innate) abilities constrains students' capacities to achieve. If abilities are different, then equity may not be served by expecting everyone to meet equal standards.

### Constructing "Success" as Responsible Choosing

*Choice* and *responsibility* were words that often framed the teachers' understanding of students' academic achievements. The belief that academic success or failure was related to choices that children or their parents had made was represented throughout educators' thinking about students' learning outcomes. The eighth grade teachers' narrative reports reflected this way of understanding their students' academic engagement. Teachers wrote about students' "successes" and "failures" in terms of choices the young adolescents had made—choices about effort and commitment.

Teachers wrote of successful students in the following ways:

> Of Rashida: "Rashida has made remarkable progress. She has become a serious and diligent student."

> Of Christine: "The seriousness toward school that Christine has demonstrated thus far has been exemplary. You and your child are to be commended. Christine has consistently demonstrated ability to accept personal responsibility for her actions."

> Karen was described as "a hard worker. An asset to her group."

> Rachel's "pattern of good behavior and helpfulness continues. She takes pride and responsibility for her work."

"Diligence," "seriousness," "pride," "responsibility," and "hard work" characterized these successful students' attitudes toward academic endeavors. Success was constructed as a series of qualities that the individual brought to her work. She, and by extension her family, were seen as responsible for the positive outcomes. Looking at academic outcomes through the lens of choice, schools are responsible for laying out the tasks to be undertaken, and students who choose to work hard can accomplish the expected goals.

The following examples are representative of teachers' comments about students who were not meeting academic expectations:

Of Adam: "Unless Adam is as *committed to his own success* as you [his parents] and I are, it will not be achieved" (emphasis added).

Of Carl: "Carl appears to lack *motivation to produce quality* work" (emphasis added).

Of Peter: "He has the ability to produce quality work in all subject areas. However he *chooses to socialize*, not only before and after class, but also during class. As a result he does not focus on whatever is being taught and his work is below average" (emphasis added).

Of Jerry, "If Jerry expects to be successful in completing final work, he must be more *diligent* about all tasks. His performance is inconsistent. Jerry needs to refocus his efforts and bear in mind that graduation *is entirely dependent upon him*" (emphasis added).

Of Renee, "Renee is doing very little of anything in school and is *more interested in her appearance* than she is in her academic improvement. Renee is not working up to her potential. She must *buckle down* and focus if she expects to do well" (emphasis added).

The words I have emphasized in these passages portray a common explanation that permeated teachers' narrative accounts about academic disengagement. At the center of this discourse lies the assumption that students choose to engage in the project of schooling in ways that produce academic "success" or "failure." Unfortunately, despite decades of research on education demonstrating that academic outcomes must be understood as the situated product of the institutional structures of schooling (see, for a few examples, Anyon, 1980; Oakes, 1985; Rist, 1970; Varenne and McDermott, 1998), the notion that individual choices are responsible for achievement outcomes maintains a strong grip on educational thinking.

Students are, of course, active agents in their engagement with schooling. As many authors have shown, students accept, resist, or transform the academic agendas of schools (see, for a few examples, Connell et al., 1982; Dehyle, 1995; Erickson, 1987; Fine, 1991; Fordham, 1996; Lee, 1996; Valenzuela, 1999). As teachers observed many of their students consistently "goofing off" in class, rarely completing homework assignments, and simply not working on their final exhibition projects, they had good reason to wonder about the "choices" students were making about engaging with the project of schooling. However, the terms around which "choice" gets constructed in educational discourse interest me. Effort, commitment, and diligence are viewed as key aspects of choosing academic success. The idea of a strong and necessary work ethic is evoked by the language of "buckling down" and "producing." The energy for these activities is presumed to be the individual student. The individual student is viewed as dependent on him/herself, and success is his or her "own." Within this framework, choices to "socialize" or prioritize one's "appearance" become explanations for particular academic outcomes. Such choices are seen to *precede* rather than reflect academic disengagement. Thus, from one perspective, students are in some sense presumed to be free agents choosing success and failure, unencumbered by either the lives they live outside school, the specific relationships they form within the school walls, or the way school and society are structured.

The notion of choice is bound up with "taking responsibility" for one's success or failure. Students were commended for their willingness and reprimanded for their refusal to take responsibility for their academic outcomes. For example, Nadia's narrative report read:

> She has demonstrated real effort. Even though the results may not have been completely satisfying, continued effort will pay off. Nadia has demonstrated ability to accept personal responsibility for her actions, a mark of a maturing young woman, to be commended.

Responsibility for success was credited to particular behaviors of the individual. Effort, especially repeated effort, will inevitably "pay off." A key assumption is that school, and by extension society, are meritocratic places where hard work will be rewarded. Contrast this with a narrative report about Khallid:

> Khallid consistently demonstrates inability to accept personal responsibility for his actions. When I question him about his behavior, the inevitable answer is someone else is to blame. Maturity demands accepting responsibility for one's own actions.

Thus the "mature" student is independent and responsible for her or his actions in the world. Undergirding these narratives about students' academic performance rested a set of important assumptions that preserve a belief in meritocracy. Effort will be rewarded. Individual students are responsible for making choices that lead to academic success and failure.

This idea that students' academic outcomes reflect the choices that individuals make contributed to the tensions that arose at Parks around standards-based reforms. For example, the disagreement between the eighth grade teachers and the principal that I described earlier in this chapter reflected conflicting views about choice and its relationship to academic outcomes. The teachers argued that by setting clear standards, they had created the conditions that allowed students to choose to succeed; students who did not meet the standards had refused to act responsibly. Melanie Post disagreed and argued for a more negotiated view of academic achievement: Ultimately, it was the adults in the community whose ongoing efforts would support all students to become proficient. Rather than resting with the individual alone, Melanie suggested that academic success and failure are co-constructed through relationships between students, teachers, curriculum, and pedagogy.

Equal standards, to some degree, are intended to create equitable and enabling conditions that help students to choose participation and academic success. Ideally, as proposed by Melanie, equal standards set expectations not only for what students will be able to do, but also for the kinds of learning environments teachers develop to ensure all students can successfully reach those standards. However, the idea that *individuals* choose success is embedded deeply in the ideology of U.S. schooling. Without interrogating the contexts in which choice and agency are made possible, this ideology often blames individuals for academic underachievement. In their disagreement with the principal, many teachers drew upon this implicit assumption to argue that, once a clear set of standards was established, it was students' responsibility to meet them. In some part, teachers' arguments for holding students to the same expectations were premised on the idea that they could choose to be academically successful if they so desired.

### Difference as Fixed Qualities of the Individual

There is, at the same time, deep ambivalence in educational discourse about whether, in fact, all learners have the same capacity for choosing success. Running alongside the discourse of choice, a second, contradictory belief has a tenacious hold on educational discourse about learners: Academic achievement is related to "ability," which is viewed as a fixed, intrinsic quality of the individual. Ability indexes some innate capacities and limitations that shape how and what students are capable of learning. Framing ability within the individual person echoes the medical discourse of disability explored in Chapter 3. The notion that individuals have fixed capacities for achievement is reflected, for example, in the educational tendency to group students within and between classrooms according to "ability" differences. My field notes offer a starting point for examining this assumption:

Hannah caught up with me early in the morning and invited me to her class for the second day of some problem-solving activities. She described this activity as part of her own move to try and let go of some control. Her blackboard was lined with folders that contained Xeroxed copies of logic problems. Each folder had a bold label: "easy," "medium," "hard," "lovely girls," "for friends of numbers," "will the real items help," "party time," and "a real puzzler." Hannah began class by pointing out to her students that she had displayed some new problems that they might work on. "Notice," she addressed the class, " I haven't labeled the [new problems for today] easy, medium, hard." She then described the various problems. "In 'lovely girls,' you're asked to figure out who is the cheerleader and the class president. So it shouldn't be that hard. 'For friends of numbers,' that means you know them real well. This is another one, 'a *real* puzzler.' It's from a game from a time when lords paid serfs in grains of wheat."

Hannah Stein, a very experienced math teacher, was working hard to change her practice. Having spent much of her career teaching students who had been grouped by what she called "ability," Hannah had been rethinking her practice to work with more heterogeneous classes. The preceding example expressed conflict about making this change. For Hannah, having students choose from a set of problems represented a move toward less control on her part. All students would not be working on the same problems at the same time, as was usually the case in her class. However, Hannah was both resisting and caught within the framework of "ability levels." After initially labeling problems "easy," "medium," and "hard," Hannah tried the next day to use more neutral nomenclature. In the end, she could not resist "telling" the students which problems were easier or more difficult. As will be described in depth next, what lay embedded in the hints she gave is a view of students in terms of three corresponding groups: easy, medium, and hard problems become activities designed to meet low, middle, and high students' "abilities." Although a climate of Coalition-led school reform had made, as one teacher put it, "ability grouping a dirty word" at Parks, teachers found themselves deeply challenged by these new ways of working. As they struggled to understand the diversity of learning styles and academic engagement that students manifested, practitioners often remained captive to a discourse that slotted children's capacities for learning into three distinct categories: "highs," "middles," and "lows."

Highs, middles, and lows are believed to be distributed across three unequal sets of learners: a small group referred to as "bright" individuals, a larger group considered to be "low end," and the majority somewhere in between. For example, in response to a question from a parent about how she formed groups for cooperative learning, Hannah Stein stated, "I don't measure. It's more observation. Then picking my highs out, then middles, then lows." These categories seemed so real that observation allowed Hannah to discover her "highs," "middles," and "lows." Many other teachers conveyed their idea that three discrete groups of students existed within a "range." Jane Paterson, a white science teacher, stated:

> I find that the range I have to teach sometimes feels overwhelming. There are occasions where I think I'm getting everybody. But it's not that way most of the time. The group that's hardest for me is the group that has low skills, and sometimes I feel like I'm beating my head against the walls. And today was one of those days, so I'm feeling it pretty strongly. And, the other group is the group that are very bright, who, you know things do come very easily to, are very interested, value a challenge. And um, once in a while, I think I give something that gives them a good run for their money, but most of the time that's not how I feel.

Thus, the "range" consists of those with "low skills," those who are "very bright," and an unnamed group in the middle.

This idea that students can be identified in terms of a range is intimately related to the construction of human intellect as measurable in terms of a normal curve. In another example, David Waters referred to this ubiquitous belief in the normal curve as an accurate representation of learning diversity. David lamented the fact that "we do not do a very good job for our very bright kids. I'm always trying to find ways to challenge them, but then if we point just to them, that great mass in the middle gets lost." David implied here the notion that these groups fall in the shape of a normal curve, with his description of "the great mass in the middle." He was expressing a belief in the existence of a strong centralizing tendency. The "average person" or "common man" is an invoked category here. Although the image of a distribution of learning diversity along a normal curve lies silently below the surface, in educational practice this range has been sliced into three unequal groups ("highs," "middles," and "lows").

The question for teachers was how to teach these slices. As represented by Jane's previous quote, most teachers expressed a belief that they could not successfully meet the needs of the entire range of students. Many felt, as Jane did, that they did not know how to "reach" the most academically struggling students. Martha Silverman said:

> Where I struggle and where I don't feel good and where I feel I have failed really is in the kids that are on the very, very low end where I just know I haven't given them enough to make a difference in their lives in terms of their skills.

Martha's feelings of frustration and failure were shared by many of her colleagues. David Waters expressed a similar feeling of helplessness: "There are some [students], there's absolutely nothing we can do. If the child can't read at all, I don't, I *can't* help you. I *can't* help you." At the same time that most teachers felt they were not meeting the needs of struggling students, they also worried that they did not "challenge" students at the "bright" end of the range enough either.

There was a close relationship between language that framed students in categories of "low" or "low skill" and teachers' sense of efficacy in the classroom. Attention to teachers' language choices demonstrated their feelings of ineffectiveness in relation to particular groups of children. Teachers spoke of feeling they had "failed" or were "unqualified"; they were "overwhelmed" and "struggling." Teachers were deeply concerned about students' basic reading and math proficiencies. Tests administered district-wide indicated that Parks's students' performance was improving steadily; however, the slight improvements over time that these and other assessment measures documented were scarcely enough to allay practitioners' worries.[4] As practitioners felt overwhelmed by both the increasing needs they perceived their students to have and the ever-decreasing resources to which Parks had access, many teachers utilized discourse that located difference within individual students. "High," "middle," and "low" came to define qualities located in the bodies of individual students, rather than being seen as categories created within the context of schooling (see, for similar discussions, Erickson, 1996b; McDermott and Varenne, 1995; Mehan, Hertweck, and Meihls, 1986; Varenne and McDermott, 1998).

Thinking about human capacity in terms of differences located within the individual learner suggests a concept of educational equity as treating students differently in accordance with their specific abilities. When teachers struggled over how to assess their students against a set of equal standards, they were engaging the central question of whether same or different treatment constituted equitable educational practices. Undergirding this struggle is a fundamental tension in educational discourse about whether learners are fundamentally the same or different. Resting within this debate is another more critical question: Do learners have free agency or are they limited by their innate "abilities?" These are, I suggest, the wrong questions, for they continue to locate educational outcomes with the individual students.

## Equal Standards in the Context of the "Real World"

The questions about whether learners are free or constrained and whether equity is served by similar or different treatment in the face of equal standards are circumscribed by the broader context of vast social inequality within which schools operate. Standards are usually framed as a strategy for helping all children compete successfully in the "real world" (high school and the workforce beyond). Under the best circumstances, schools adopt the kinds of standards that promote the development of rich, complex knowledge and skills that support students to effectively negotiate schools and society. Through its emphasis on communication and inquiry across disciplines, Parks sought standards that would teach its students to participate successfully in dominant social practices. Preparing all students to negotiate schools and society successfully is a critical component of building equitable, educational practices (see, for example, Darling-Hammond, 1997; Delpit, 1986; Mehan et al., 1996).[5] However, the justice claim for equal standards leads to the dilemma of difference when it fails to interrogate the existing values and structures of schools and society (Minow, 1990).

The justice claim for equal standards, at times, devolves into an argument for standardization, and when it does, it doubles as an unabashed excuse for the seemingly inevitable hierarchy of educational outcomes. Tim Fraser, who was exasperated with the persistent academic underachievement of many students, argued:

> I think our academic standards around here can be tightened up quite a bit. Even though we say we have high expectations of the kids, in practice the expectations turn out to be lower. I think what we can do is just put our expectations in place in the beginning of each year and then just stick with it, and *let the chips roll where they may*. Some kids will probably not be able to meet them. But I think unless you put the standards out there, nobody will meet them (emphasis added).

Tim did not struggle in the same way as some of his colleagues with the question of how to judge student work. For Tim, setting equal standards and expectations for all offered at least some of the students the opportunity to be academically successful. However, in contexts like Parks where many students arrived with few academic tools and the school had few resources to support their learning needs, equal academic standards—conceptualized as preestablished and assessed in uniform ways—persistently translated into the kind of triage system suggested here: Equal standards should be established so that at least some students would be able to achieve them. It is key to pay attention to the assumption, embedded in Tim's words, that failure was a natural part of this system: "Some kids will probably not be able to meet them [the standards]." Furthermore, academic outcomes appear to be somewhat arbitrary—a matter of the "chips roll[ing] where they may"—rather than a fairly predictable consequence of the dominant social order.

In the context of reforms led by rhetoric like "no child left behind," Tim's words might strike a discordant note—a seemingly callous indifference to the inevitable failure of some children. I want to caution against such an interpretation for two reasons. First, in practice Tim was a caring and innovative teacher who worked hard to engage all students in the process of scientific thought and practice. Moreover, and more important for the argument I am pursuing here, is that Tim's words referenced the heart of the debate about the definition of educational equity. When educators and politicians frame educational equity in terms of a justice claim for equal standards—that all students will be offered a curriculum based on the same high standards—what assumptions do they hold about what constitutes evidence of fair outcomes? Is fairness evidenced by all students having the same *opportunities* for achievement? Or must they demonstrate equal achievement outcomes? What kind of schools and society are assumed by the justice claim for equal standards?

For many teachers, including Tim, reforms based on equal standards represented an honest attempt to provide students with tools necessary for success in the "real world"—a phrase repeatedly invoked by Parks's practitioners. Lisa Bird, a staunch critic of schools and their role in producing academic failure for low-income students of color (see Chapter 3), described her practice as follows:

> I do present options for failure and succeeding because I just think it's realistic. And you know, being a minority you learn that you're going to have failure, and I don't like to protect students from that. I like them to see—I think learning failure is just as good as learning success. Because if life is presented to you, if you're sort of in a sheltered environment, where options are just open, and failure isn't presented to you, then you sort of live in like a never, never land. And then, when you go out into the real world, it starts hitting you. I've used different tactics with them as far as dealing with them on their level and grading them according to their ability. But then I ask myself, "Is that realistic? Am I presenting success to them, whereas in actuality it's really not success?"

Lisa's words referenced the intertwined nature of the contradictory ideas about learning and human capacity discussed previously. On the one hand, notions of choice are fundamental to explaining academic achievement. Lisa wanted to teach her students that success and failure are "options." At the same time, she expressed the assumption that some internally located "ability" sets the limit on achievement. The phrases "dealing with them on their level" and "grading them according to their ability" introduced the idea that every student might not in fact be able to opt for success. With the concepts of "level" and "ability," difference is located once again, as the property of individuals.

Caught between options and ability, Lisa articulated the central dilemma of everyday practice with which she and many of her colleagues struggled constantly. Lisa pointed out that to treat each student individually—differently—in terms of his or her "ability" risked presenting some students with "success" where the "real world" would see failure. However, holding them to the "real-world" standards—treating them similarly—demanded that some students would fail. This plan would reestablish inequitable academic outcomes among students. For activist teachers at Parks, the dilemma of practice arose out of a deep sense of duty. They believed in the importance of acknowledging students' differences and nurturing each child's growth and development. At the same time, they wanted to prepare all students to meet educational standards that would support students to negotiate successfully in the "real world." In everyday practice, there is a palpable tension between attending to particular students and their different learning trajectories and having all students equally prepared to navigate successfully in schools and society.

I suggest that getting out of the dilemma of difference requires that we interrogate more closely the "real world" for which students are being prepared (Minow, 1990). Framing justice claims around equal standards for all students does not necessarily unmask the patterns of structural inequality that produce differences and make a hierarchy of educational outcomes appear inevitable. Young (1990) argues that the dominant theoretical framework for justice restricts itself to questions about the equitable distribution of social goods (be they material resources and wealth, social positions like jobs, or nontangible goods like self-respect and power). The rationale for standards-based reforms can be understood to fit within this distributive frame. Educational inequality is, in essence, understood to be about the unfair distribution of educational goods. Inequality results from the fact that students have been offered different educational standards that lead them to be more or less equipped to function successfully in school and society. What makes the unequal distribution of educational goods particularly glaring is the fact that it usually tracks along the lines of race, class, gender, and disability. In this frame, equal standards can remedy this inequality because they offer *all* students the same educational goods. Standards set guidelines for the knowledge and skills that all students are expected to acquire and for the assessments through which students are to demonstrate what they have learned.

This focus on getting all students to meet equal standards, however, often avoids the question of whether, in fact, success for all is a possible outcome—or even a goal—of the dominant structures of schools and society. To some large extent, success *and* failure—a hierarchy of academic outcomes—are assumed an inevitable part of schooling (Varenne and

McDermott, 1998). Success and failure are part of, to use Lisa's words, "the real world."

When I began my fieldwork, the Goals 2000: Educate America Act of 1994 legislation (Goals 2000, 1994) framed the national context within which local reforms were being formulated. Goals 2000 articulated the objectives of standards-based remedies for educational inequality as follows:

> The academic performance of all students at the elementary and secondary level will increase significantly in every quartile, and the distribution of minority students in each quartile will more closely reflect the student population as a whole.

The goal of reform, then, was to guarantee that everyone was learning more, but there was no assumption that the hierarchy of educational outcomes would disappear completely. In fact, fairness is conceptualized here in terms of making sure the distribution of children from traditionally marginalized groups is more equitable across the hierarchical system.

One useful way of unpacking the assumptions behind the justice claim for equal standards is to do a thought experiment. What if we had the resources to offer all students equal standards and enabling conditions in their schools to meet those standards? What if we actually could create an educational system in which academic achievement outcomes were not so disproportionately distributed along the lines of race, class, gender, and disability? What if we could reach the aims set out by Goals 2000? Would that represent equity? Are differential outcomes acceptable as long as they do not follow entrenched patterns of social inequality? Would we have overcome the "problem of difference"—the tendency for certain differences to track inexorably into hierarchical outcomes?

Let me extend the thought experiment even further. The No Child Left Behind Act of 2002 (NCLB) mandates that all children will demonstrate, "at a minimum, *proficiency* on challenging State academic achievement standards and state academic assessments" (NCLB, 2002, emphasis added). NCLB claims to be unsatisfied, as was Goals 2000, with mere progress in each quartile, but requires that students be proficient in those areas of the curriculum that are assessed. More questions arise. How is proficiency to be defined? Is it defined in terms of a norm, and if so, by definition, won't some students fail to meet that norm? Are all students expected to be proficient at the same time? Or do we expect that children develop differently and therefore may demonstrate proficiency according to variable schedules? How will we account for the different ways children learn? Moreover, how will we attend to young people's different passions, interests, and inclinations? Will we listen to children and adolescents, as well as families and communities, and their goals for education as we develop the standards to which students will be held? Or will equal standards elide into standardization? *Can equal standards attend to differences?*

Herein lies the limitation of framing justice claims in terms of equal standards for all students without interrogating the values, assumptions, and norms those standards entail. In asking how we might more equitably provide students with the tools necessary for academic success, we act as if, in the "real world" in which we live, "success" were possible without its corollary "failure" (Varenne and McDermott, 1998). Young (1990) argues that one fundamental problem with the distributive approach to justice is that it fails to interrogate the social structure within which the distribution of goods takes place:

> Many discussions of social justice not only ignore the institutional contexts within which distributions occur, but often presuppose specific institutional structures whose justice they fail to bring under evaluation. (p. 22)

The justice claim for equal standards aims to offer all students the kind of education that only few have traditionally had. It does not attend explicitly to the ways that schools and society are structured to produce and reproduce educational inequality.

In a world that distributes educational success in such glaringly unequal proportions, the question of equitable distribution of educational goods is certainly relevant to justice claims. For Parks's practitioners, providing all students with a rich, challenging curriculum was a moral stance they were compelled to take. In a world in which survival often depends on having certain knowledge and skills, to do any less than try to prepare children to meet those demands would be irresponsible and damaging. In a world that distributes privileges along clearly demarcated lines of "difference," ethical action demands working to change these patterns. In a society with fewer and fewer guarantees of jobs that pay decently and more and more people abandoned without a social safety net, providing all students, especially those from subordinated or marginalized groups, with the valuable academic tools and credentials (embodied in standards) that might allow them to survive the cruelty of this world constitutes moral action. The words of one teacher, Mary Davis, and her sense of urgency about this mission echo in my mind: "[Young people's] chances have been sliced down to where now the battlefield—the playing field is indeed equal. There is nothing out there for anybody, unless we prepare them."

The question, however, is whether it is in fact possible to prepare everyone to negotiate successfully schools and society. What does it mean to prepare all children to be successful, given a deeply stratified society? Mary Davis's initial choice to describe this as a "battlefield" offers an apt metaphor for understanding the problem. Is it conceivable that all could survive the battlefield? Varenne and McDermott write:

> How are we all to escape both success and failure? ... Most research-ers let themselves be caught by parents and politicians who want to know why particular children, and particular kinds of children at that, fail more often than others. The answers that make sense to those who ask the questions range from theories of inherent intel-ligence to theories of political injustice. The theories are different in emphasis, but they mostly work with the given categories and thus reconstruct a world in which success and failure remain a fact of life and in which whatever else may happen ... children will be identified as having succeeded or failed. ... We hope to show that school suc-cess and failure are not simple consequences of the way the human world must be. It is a cultural mock-up. (1998, p. xiii)

As long as we focus on whether individual children or particular groups of children succeed or fail in schools, we fail to interrogate the values and contexts that make hierarchy seem a natural, rather than constructed, aspect of our schools and society.

Viewing standards as educational goods to be possessed (achieved) obscures the ways they reflect specific values and ways of knowing that are the outcome of particular social relationships (see Minow, 1990; Young, 1990). In failing to view standards as markers of socially constructed val-ues and relationships, the justice claim for equal standards threatens to perpetuate, rather than remedy, the "problem of difference." Focusing on standards that are necessary for success in the "real world" obscures the fact that our social order values a very narrow range of human capac-ity, making failure an inevitable corollary to success. We end up focusing on whether students have or do not have these "goods" or "skills," and whether they meet or do not meet the standards. Consequently, we often do not recognize that standards embody social processes that value hierar-chically certain ways of knowing but not others, certain bodies of knowl-edge and not others. This hierarchical valuing of different ways of knowing sets up relationships between students; it marks some students as successes and others as different or failures. In schools, this means that regardless of race, class, etc. (although usually coincident with it), children are judged on whether they have or do not have, and whether they learn or "fail" to learn, a limited set of "tools" or "skills." Increasingly in schools across the nation, in the face of budget cuts and high-stakes accountability systems, this set of standards has been pared down to include only the fewest ways of knowing and expressing, focusing primarily on skills and disciplines considered economically necessary (literacy, mathematics, and science).

I want to be clear here that I am not arguing against an equal and equally enabling education, as well as the power of certain academic tools (literacy and numeracy, for example) for all children. I am, however, suggesting that we must always understand standards as embodying values and assumptions that must be made explicit to create educational environments that nurture all students. When the only question is whether a student has achieved or has not achieved a standard, then the only answer is success or failure. I propose that it is only by interrogating the values and assumptions embedded in our standards and our assessments of learning that we can create educational environments that truly reflect multiple values and ways of knowing.

## Equal Education in Policy and Practice

As a justice claim, equal standards offer a powerful corrective to a legacy of educational inequality. Standards have been embraced broadly, by educators, policy makers, business interests, legislators, and citizens, as a tool for combating the uninspiring, reductive education to which too many students (particularly in low-income schools, low-track classes, and special education) have been subjected. One ideal, embodied in the justice claim for equal standards, is that all students should have an education that develops their capacities to become creative, effective, and, hopefully, critical citizens in a democratic society. Our hope for realizing full democratic participation depends on such a vision of education.

In everyday practice, as Parks's experience portrays, the justice claim for equal standards proves complicated in the face of difference. Parks was, in some important aspects, an ideal site for making equal standards work for all students. As a Coalition school, Parks had in place many key elements to support the development of what Darling-Hammond (1997) has called "learning-centered" and "learner-centered" schools, for example, academic standards focused on concepts and critical skills and a strong professional culture built around team-teaching. The principles of the Coalition of Essential Schools offered the school a language for simultaneously holding a commitment to offering all students an empowering education and attending carefully to their differences.

Melanie Post and some of the teachers drew upon these principles to advocate for an education that would take each individual's strengths and learning trajectories into account when planning activities and assessing performance. However, putting these principles into practice proved contentious as students' "differences" became visible in the face of the standards to which they were being held. Some teachers worried that assessing students through different means, or focusing on their overall development rather than their endpoints, would reinforce a system of inequitable expectations for learning and would leave students unprepared to navigate the demands of high school and the workforce. The contentious debates between these educators reflect gritty struggles of practicing for equity in the everyday. In practice, the justice claim for equal standards surfaced tensions and contradictions—tensions and contradictions that are, as I have argued previously, inherent to practicing for equity in contexts of inequality (see also Abu El-Haj, 2003b).

In the current national climate in which the call for equal standards has been conflated with educational outcomes as measured by standardized tests, Parks's story should serve as a cautionary tale. In the early stages of its reform efforts, Parks had considerable flexibility to determine its curriculum and assessment measures. Work with the Coalition of Essential Schools inspired many educators at Parks to think expansively about the purposes of education and the scope of its curriculum. Teachers worked collaboratively to explore ways to address students' different learning styles and to document their development as learners. Of course, teachers' capacities to work with students in ways that could support their growth and development were seriously constrained by the limited resources of an urban school district. Nevertheless, teachers were continually planning, implementing, and revising curricular and pedagogical practices aimed at ensuring that all students could learn and benefit from an equally challenging education.

Within a few years, however, the school's capacity to decide on its standards was eroded by a reform effort at the district level. The district's systemic reform plan initially promised local autonomy and proclaimed that "time was the variable" in helping all children achieve equal standards. This promise, however, soon faded. By 2002, even before the No Child Left Behind Act, Parks, like schools across the nation, had lost much of its autonomy and was subject to top-down curricular mandates and increasingly onerous assessments based on standardized tests and high-stakes requirements for graduation.

Proponents of top-down policies that mandate equal standards and strong accountability systems might say that these measures are needed precisely because of the experiences in schools like Parks: Locally devised standards and assessments did not guarantee that all students met proficiency standards in a timely manner, with the result that the cycle of inequality was perpetuated. I suggest, instead, that Parks's story makes visible knotty issues that unfold in real school contexts when teachers work to create equal standards for all students *and* attend to the differences in skills, knowledge, and learning styles that students manifest. This grounded perspective argues against moving further toward high-stakes, standardized accountability systems—systems that some research suggests are narrowing the curriculum, focusing teachers' attention on test preparation and further encouraging a triage system (Booher-Jennings, 2005; Center on Educational Policy, 2006; Lipman, 2002, 2004; McNeil, 2000).

In pointing to these inherent contradictions that emerge in the face of the justice claim for equal standards, I am not arguing that we should abandon the ideal that all people have a right to an equal education, by which I mean an expansive and empowering one. I am suggesting that educators need time and resources to figure out how to teach challenging, meaningful curriculum in ways that support the diversity of learners in their classrooms. More important, educators, preferably in concert with students and parents, need to engage in sustained inquiry to interrogate their implicit beliefs about learning and learners, as well as the norms, values, and assumptions inherent in all educational standards. This idea that all curriculum and pedagogy reflect particular norms, values, and assumptions that must be examined rests at the heart of the third justice claim with which this book is concerned: recognition.

CHAPTER **4**

# Recognition

In the spring of 2003, City Friends mounted its first theatrical production with an all African-American female cast. Responding to a need she saw to showcase the talents of young women who were often overlooked or marginalized in the school's public performances, Kyla Walters, a young African-American English teacher, decided to produce Ntozake Shange's *For colored girls who have considered suicide when the rainbow is enuf.* The show was an enormous success. In the days following the production, I heard many administrators and faculty praise the stunning and inspiring performance the young women had given. The faculty of color with whom I spoke, however, also viewed the performance as reflecting both the strength of the community of African-American students, teachers, and families and the ongoing struggles to address racial inequity in the institution.

The performance evolved as a response to a pattern of drama and musical productions that drew from the traditional canon and consistently overlooked black girls' musical and acting talents. Kyla, with the support of other faculty of color, volunteered her time to create the space for these young women to be visible and celebrated by the whole community. Reflecting on the process, one African-American administrator, Esther Daniels, described the issues the performance aimed to make apparent to the entire community as follows:

> We have just produced this wonderful play, *For colored girls*, and it's wonderful. I agree we should take all the credit. But it's also pitiful that we had to wait for these young faculty members to come here to do this. And the fact that one of the seniors that was in this play was told

she could not sing and there she was beautiful, on stage, singing her heart out and has tried repeatedly to be in plays at City Friends and was just invisible to our drama department, that's criminal. And my heart was so filled for that young woman to be able to graduate from City Friends having her face time. And we give so much face time to so many of these white kids and there's so little face time for kids of color that I could cry. I could sit here and work myself into tears right now. And the fact is that if we in this room don't push the drama department to see what a tremendous gift was given to them, we could go back to the status quo very easily. The kids, black kids, kids of color, could be trying out next year, not being seen. The play could be, you know, you have to affect a British accent in order to be credible.

Described by one black male teacher as a kind of necessary "guerrilla warfare," this play enabled students and faculty of color to perform an unmasking ceremony, making visible an alternate landscape of aesthetics, knowledge, norms, and values that drew upon a rich heritage often hidden from view in a school environment that tended to embrace the knowledge, values, and practices of dominant social groups. Kyla Walters, Esther Daniels, and the many other educators concerned about racial equity worked diligently to push the school beyond the assimilationist framework that had dominated its approach to racial/ethnic diversity.

If, as we saw in Chapter 4, one strand of contemporary public discourse about educational justice argues for equal standards for all students, another equally compelling theme is that a fair and just education recognizes group differences and is responsive to those differences. When Kyla and her colleagues produced *For colored girls* they were signaling, through this "guerrilla action," that the school must visibly acknowledge diverse communities *and* that, for students, "having face time"—being visible in a culturally relevant context—is crucial to educational equity (Ladson-Billings, 1994). This idea that not only individual but also group identities must be made visible in educational settings reflects what Taylor (1992) has described as a demand for recognition. It is to this demand for recognition—of race and gender—that I turn my attention in this chapter.

*Recognition* is a fundamental premise of the practices of multicultural education. Multicultural education encompasses a diverse range of perspectives and strategies for reform, and it is not my intention to review these various approaches (see for overviews, Banks, 1997; 2004b; Gay, 2004; McCarthy, 1990; Nieto, 1996; Sleeter and Grant, 1993). Some educational theorists have cogently argued that multicultural education is often implemented in ways that attempt to manage diversity and, consequently, maintain the status quo (Carby, 1992; McCarthy, 1993b; McLaren, 1994;

Mohanty, 1989–90). Theorists also suggest that multicultural education can be defined in sufficiently encompassing and critical ways to truly subvert educational inequalities (McLaren, 1994; Nieto, 1996, 1999; Sleeter, 1996). This chapter examines debates about multicultural education by looking directly at the implicit assumptions about difference that drove the demands for an education that recognized and was responsive to race and gender at City Friends. Justice claims that are framed around recognition of and responsiveness to group differences hold great potential for shaking up the status quo. Looking carefully inside City Friends, however, I argue that, as a force for change, recognition may be limited by its assumptions about difference. When the educational discourses about race and gender posit a bounded and dichotomous rather than a relational view of difference, dominant groups are not challenged to be part of the process of change.

## Recognition and Multicultural Education

The demand that schools recognize and respond to group differences is not new in U.S. education (see Reich, 2002; Spring, 2004; Tyack, 1974). The current discourse of multiculturalism can be located more specifically, however, within broader critiques of liberalism that address questions about democracy and difference. Contemporary political theorists have explored the ways liberal democratic states across the globe are facing challenges from a new politics of "recognition,"[1] "identity," or "difference" (for example, Benhabib, 2002; Gutmann, 2003; Kymlicka, 1995; Taylor, 1992; Reich, 2002; Young, 1990). Many recent social movements have been organized around group identity and the need for liberal democracies to address group concerns. The literature that discusses the grounds and merits of such challenges to liberal, democratic states is vast and reflects diverse ideological perspectives. It is beyond the scope of this book to review that body of work or to engage the central arguments of current political philosophy. I do, however, want to connect several key themes in the educational discourse of multiculturalism to these broader critiques of liberal democracies.

One core assumption of the multicultural critique of education is that, for equity to be achieved, all students need to see themselves—their cultural stories, history, and values—reflected in the curriculum. This assumption is premised on a notion that one's identity includes not only individual characteristics but also a collective component. Thus, when collective identities are absent from, or distorted by, the school curriculum, students are denied full and healthy participation in their education (see, for example, Bingham, 2001; Friend, 1993; Gilligan, 1993; Gordon, 1993;

Ladson-Billings, 1994; Nieto, 1996). If, as advocates of the need for group "recognition" in public institutions argue, cultural identity is critical to a person's identity, sense of well-being, and capacity to participate fully in society, then the failure to acknowledge cultural identities constitutes an injustice (Taylor, 1992; see also Bingham 2001). Explicating the rationale behind the politics of recognition, Taylor writes:

> The thesis is that our identity is partly shaped by recognition or its absence, often by the *mis*recognition of others, and so a person or group of people can suffer real damage, real distortion, if the people or society around them mirror back to them a confining or demeaning or contemptible picture of themselves. Nonrecognition or misrecognition can inflict harm, can be a form of oppression, imprisoning someone in a false, distorted, and reduced mode of being. (p. 25)

Precisely this sense of the harm caused by the "nonrecognition or misrecognition" of African-American girls at City Friends guided Kyla Walters's decision to stage a production of *For colored girls*. Persistent marginalization or exclusion of African-American students denied these young people opportunities to participate as full, equally valued members of their school community; however, it is critical to understand that at issue here is the recognition of group identity. In a Quaker context, in which, as described in Chapter 2, attention to each individual is a paramount value, Kyla Walters decided to stage a play that specifically acknowledged the collective identities of African-American females.

The demand for recognition of collective identities sets wide parameters for the goals of a just educational community. Focusing narrowly on traditional measures of academic achievement is not a sufficient mark of educational equity. Recognition holds that schools must be responsible for developing young people's cultural knowledge as a key factor contributing to their capacities to participate fruitfully in their education and society at large. Framing justice around recognition means that a school's curriculum and pedagogy must reflect the knowledge, values, assumptions, and participatory modes of the various groups that constitute its community. Proponents of multicultural curriculum and pedagogy are arguing, in a sense, that to learn and succeed academically, education must hold up a mirror in which students can see their collective identities affirmed in rich detail, undistorted by oppressive images of their communities (or by the lack of any images at all). The rationale for recognition as an important educational goal, however, reaches well beyond the affirmation of each and every student. Recognition also aims to create opportunities for social action and increasing democratic participation (for example, Banks, 1997; Ladson-Billings, 1994; Nieto, 1996, 1999; Sleeter, 1996). That is, the knowledge developed as curriculum and pedagogy come to reflect multiple perspectives makes it possible for people to contest collectively the dominant narratives and institutional structures that have maintained the status quo.

Furthermore, multicultural education challenges the idea that any education is or can be neutral. Rather, it points to the particularity of all knowledge and pedagogy. At the heart of the heated debates about curriculum that have raged across K–12 schools, college campuses, and the public arena in the past several decades rests a fundamental conflict over this challenge to neutrality. Multicultural education reveals curriculum that has traditionally been cast in terms of human universals to be grounded in the knowledge and experiences of dominant groups (most often, white male experience). Curriculum is never, therefore, neutral (Banks, 1997; Castenell and Pinar, 1993; McLaren, 1994; Pinar, 1993). In representing the knowledge and experiences of particular groups without naming that particularity, it serves to maintain the existing power structure. This central premise of multicultural education is connected to broader critiques of liberalism charging that the apparent neutrality of liberal democratic states serves to protect the rights of dominant groups (Reich, 2002; Taylor, 1992). Advocates of multicultural education argue that there is no neutral educational position, and, therefore, a just education is one that is culturally responsive, grounded in the multiple and particular experiences of all its students (Banks, 2004a; Ladson-Billings, 1994; Nieto, 1996, 1999; Perry and Fraser, 1993). These multiple perspectives aim to dislodge the dominant narratives, values, and assumptions of educational institutions.

Finally, the demand for recognition invites educational institutions to pay attention to patterns of inequality along the lines of race, ethnicity, gender, class, sexuality, and disability. This demand that we attend to groups contests one of the most deeply held commitments of liberal democracies—the commitment to the individual. In schools, this commitment to the individual—and in particular to individual achievement—masks deeply entrenched systems of inequality. Shifting the focus from individuals to groups raises new questions and possibilities for defining educational equity in ways that address the structural inequalities of schools and society (Fine, 1997; Ladson-Billings, 1994; McCarthy, 1990; McLaren, 1994; Nieto, 1996, 1999; Sleeter, 1996).

This chapter explores how demands for recognition of and responsiveness to difference played out at City Friends in relation to gender and race. The first part examines how advocates for racial equity drew on this claim for recognition to push for curricular reform and the creation of safe spaces for marginalized groups of students. Next, the chapter focuses on the story of a group of high school girls who sought to effect an equitable mathematics education through pedagogical changes that they claimed would recognize their gendered ways of knowing and learning. These two examples are not parallel ones: curricular change was led by faculty interests, while the high school girls made pedagogical demands that were never realized. Through these different stories I ask two critical questions: How can we *recognize* group differences without reifying them? What fruitfully emerges when difference is, instead, understood to imply a relationship between dominant and oppressed groups? I propose a relational model of difference offers us a richer path for enacting multicultural education that includes everyone in the process of change.

## Race/Ethnicity and Recognition

"There needs to be something that says there's a place for you here."
—**Eugene Jones, African-American history teacher, City Friends**

Advocates for racial/ethnic equity at City Friends have focused significant effort on the relationship between school climate and curriculum and inequality. By the 1990s, many practitioners and students were deeply dissatisfied with the assimilationist stance (described in Chapter 3) that seemed to dominate the school's approach to creating a racially and ethnically diverse community. They insisted that City Friends acknowledge that in its current configuration the school was defined by white power and privilege. They argued that the school must fundamentally shift its educational vision to recognize and respect difference and reflect, in the curriculum and beyond, the various historical and cultural experiences of all its members.

### Struggling to Belong: Creating Safe Spaces

As a teacher new to City Friends, Kyla Walters chose to add to her official duties and share responsibility with several female colleagues for convening an affinity group for African-American female students. For many African-American girls, the affinity group offered a collective space for discussion and activism. These girls often felt invisible in the wider school community. For the most part, they were doing very well academically, yet they rarely found themselves publicly acknowledged in awards ceremonies or public performances. Kyla Walters's decision to direct the play *For colored girls* reflected a conscious attempt to jolt the school awake to the unwritten exclusionary practices embedded in its public performances. This was a daring move; staging a play that featured an all African-American female cast risked charges of separatism and divisiveness. Although there were some rumblings of discontent, overall, the community received the play with great enthusiasm.

While the need for such a drama production suggested the ongoing struggles for racial equity, it also reflected changes in the school climate that had occurred between the mid-1990s and 2003. The idea that students of color (as well as gay, lesbian, bisexual, and transgendered youth and students from minority religious communities) needed safe spaces where their collective identities could be recognized and valued had gained increasing acceptance in a school community that had historically felt threatened by these affinity groups. Advocates for racial/ethnic equity had, over time, created an audible discourse around recognition that was challenging the school to move beyond an integrationist approach to difference.

The increasing acceptance of recognition as a legitimate ground for creating just practices reflected a growing acknowledgment in the school community that many students of color continued to feel like outsiders, finding little representation of their collective identities. These students often narrated their lives at City Friends in terms of conscious struggles to carve out spaces where they could survive comfortably enough to get what they wanted from the school. As discussed in Chapter 3, students of color consistently stated that they chose City Friends because they believed it would offer them necessary knowledge for success in diverse work settings in the future. Many of them described the difficult transition to City Friends. Tanya, speaking about fellow members of the school's multicultural students' union, described the transition:

> I think what we all have in common is change. We're all coming from different schools. ... I think public school to private school in itself is a huge change. Let alone the race issue—coming from all black, or actually all black and Hispanic to a predominantly white school. And how I feel here—I don't feel like I don't fit in. I don't feel like I can't sit over there with a group of people. I'm not scared to come to school. I'm not upset to come to school. You just have to make the best of the situation. And yeah, you're here. You might not always want to be here. School is what you make out of it. You don't let others make school horrible for you. You're paying your money or whatever. And you're learning things that you should learn.

Tanya's narrative underscored the complex and subtle work of fitting in as a black student at City Friends. The transition she had made across several social contexts—public to private, black and Hispanic to white—seemed to leave her precariously positioned. Her repeated use of double negatives (for example, "I don't feel like I don't fit in") suggested a tentative connection to the community, one she appeared to have made by force of will. Tanya was determined that others would not destroy her experience at City Friends or prevent her from reaping the benefits she sought.

Her friend Charlene concurred: "They can't make your four years here—excuse my language—hell." Speaking of her own difficult transition to City Friends, Charlene continued:

> I can say right now I feel fine, comfortable. In ninth grade, it was hectic. I didn't want to come to school. I came late probably 300 days … At first I couldn't adjust 'cause I was coming from this black school to this all-white institution where these people were snobs and all of them had money. I came to the realization at the end of the year that if I wasn't capable of working with these people or being here, I wouldn't be here. So, I'm here for a reason. Truthfully, I didn't know much about them, and they seemed to know nothing about me. So, I figure we can learn together. Now, I think I'm comfortable because I make City Friends what I want it to be. I don't concentrate on how somebody feels about me, or sometimes if people face up to me, I kind of deal with it sharp, and they know, "Don't mess with Charlene."

Charlene's words echoed Tanya's determination to make the school work for her purposes. During her first year, Charlene avoided school and felt alienated. She perceived the chasm of race and class to be absolute, defining the school as an "all-white" one in which "all [the people] had money." Against this definition, Charlene was definitely an outsider, different in every way. However, she made a conscious choice to stay and to learn—to create a space for herself in this otherwise strange sea. She did this, though, through sharp delineation of boundaries and constant vigilance toward others when she perceived racist interactions—what she described as "straightening them out."

As I spoke with students of color at City Friends, I heard many talk in similar ways of negotiating territory carefully, in particular, figuring out when to confront or ignore salient experiences of racism. Taneesha, another African-American junior, described finding a comfortable zone in which she could interact with white students:

> And I think just because of the neighborhood I was raised in, because of my family, it wasn't purposeful, that's just how it happened, I was never exposed to other white children, other white people. And when I came here I had to adjust—it wasn't so much a problem for me to adjust, 'cause it was just me. I just came here and went to class. That was in sixth grade and now I'm in eleventh, and I've figured out to what level I'm able to interact with them comfortably; they're able to interact with me comfortably. Sometimes it does take, like Charlene said, stating your opinions sharply and getting it across right away. You have to assert yourself. It's not mean. It's not purposeful. It's just that after awhile that's just how it tends to come out.

Like Charlene, Taneesha self-consciously navigated across racial boundaries; she had learned to "adjust" and find a comfortable level of interaction with "them." This process, however, left much unsaid and unacknowledged until Taneesha occasionally and pointedly burst out of the boundaries and spoke honestly.

Julia, one of the few Latina/o students in the school, struggled to find a place to call her own. Speaking about a conversation with her white best friend, Julia said, "Sometimes I tell [her] you know I really miss my people. I really miss going up to them and saying I had this for dinner last night and them knowing what it is. And there's another part of me that I'm really glad there's different people here because it's so neat when I bring in Spanish food and they go, 'let me try it.' But it's really hard. I really want some of my own people, and at the same time I like to be with other people." Although Julia managed and even appreciated the role she played as a kind of ambassador for "my people," the cost of continual translation—a life between worlds—was high. Julia talked to me of the many times she preserved her few close friendships with white students through silence, by not calling attention to race or racist incidents.

If negotiating the world of City Friends was difficult for girls of color like Julia, it was often more treacherous for boys like her cousin. Julia's cousin decided to leave City Friends after one year because he repeatedly encountered school personnel who did not believe he was a member of the school community and who responded to him fearfully, while at the same time he was struggling with the academic transition from public to private school. His story was unfortunately reflective of the experiences of other boys of color who left City Friends during their middle and high school years; and it represents the school's ongoing struggle to successfully retain African-American and Latino boys through these years (see Duncan, 2002).

Through their choice of words—"my people," "other people," "we," and "they"—the students of color with whom I spoke mapped out separate racial/ethnic territories that often demarcated the social landscape at City Friends. These students described their positioning as outsiders striving to maintain a foothold in this strange land. Michael an African-American junior, argued, "They [white students] dominate the college room, and we can't really go in there. They dominate the front halls so we can't really go there. We have a discussion some time, and we might bring up race and gender and then they swear we're talking about them and trying to gang up like something is going on here. They blow everything out of proportion." Many students of color experienced a sense of being outsiders in terms of both physical and intellectual space.

Students of color also described not fitting in with the dominant social scene in the school. Of course, many adolescents share this feeling of living outside mainstream peer culture; however, many students of color at City Friends described feeling alienated by the vast differences in modes of expression. As one girl put it, "They're too different from me. I don't feel comfortable. I can mingle, say 'hi,' whatever, I can be friendly, but I just can't hang out with them." Students of color distinguished between the ways they preferred to interact socially, pointing, for example, to differences in the kinds of parties that they and their white peers liked to attend or the types of music they enjoyed. Although they recognized that music was an arena of adolescent culture that often crossed racial/ethnic boundaries, the African-American students with whom I spoke said that they did not like to attend school dances because the music usually did not represent the genres they liked. Commenting on a discussion about feeling excluded from the prom, Charlene observed, "Music at the prom, that sounds real petty and insignificant. But it's not. We have to have something."

Echoing their teacher Eugene Jones's words that "there needs to be something that says there's a place for you here," Charlene and her peers recognized the importance of representation and recognition for inclusion in a community. Multicultural education has been taken to task, rightly I would argue, for focusing too often on visible aspects of culture, thus glossing differences within groups and failing to address deeper issues of power, privilege, and domination (Banks, 1997; Erickson, 2001; McCarthy, 1993b; Nieto, 1996). Sharing holidays, foods, and music does little to reconfigure oppressive curriculum, pedagogy, and practice; however, students of color at City Friends and many of their teachers also acknowledged the importance of these more tangible aspects of cultural expression for drawing the boundaries of inclusion into, or exclusion from, the school community. Public recognition of the multiple cultures that constitute a community is a critical aspect of building more equitable educational environments (Nieto, 1996).[2]

In the face of their feelings of exclusion from the dominant community at City Friends, many students of color were drawn to a space they could call their own. The school's Multicultural Student Union (MSU) offered its members both a support group and a space from which to proactively educate the school community about ethnicity, race, and racism. Older members of the group felt a responsibility to support entering students of color and teach them how to survive the transition to City Friends. They argued, for example, that they needed to help younger students figure out how to manage the academic work City Friends demanded. Furthermore, they saw a strong MSU as a vehicle for increasing the number of students of color willing to come to City Friends. Michael put it this way: "If all of us stay here and more come, then we won't be such a minority. If all of them stay here and they see the black kids are united here and they stick together, then other black kids will start wanting to come in. Then we won't have to complain about everything." Stressing the relationship between unity among black students and increasing attendance and retention rates, Michael, like many of his peers, argued for the importance of racial affinity groups, especially in an educational environment that was largely white.

The MSU was not exclusively for African-American students or even for students of color; at times, a few white allies were active members. However, given that the majority of students of color at the school were African-American, the dominant perception in the larger community was that the MSU was a group for African-American students. Students like Julia with few peers with whom she identified ethnically and racially often felt caught between the worlds of white and black students. "It's like they have little cliques here. They have a black clique. It's like if you go into the lunchroom, you'll see all these black cliques and then you'll see the white kids. It's like I just can't find a place."

It is important to pay attention to the ways that educational practices, such as creating safe spaces within which group identities can be recognized—spaces in which students like Michael use the language of being "united" and "sticking together"—can create new boundaries within which other students like Julia "can't find a place." Julia's story raises important questions for educational institutions about organizing for social change around group identities. How should school communities organize to support some students (and teachers) to use the connection with their group identities as a source from which to advocate for educational equity, given that this strategy can leave others caught in the in-between? In many school communities, some members, like Julia, find themselves doubly marginalized as members of an oppressed group and a demographic minority. Moreover, our identities are more complex than can be recognized in groups based on a single dimension of difference. Organizing resistance to domination around group recognition risks hardening permeable boundaries that might serve well as sites for solidarity and resistance.

Despite the limitations of this strategy, a growing number of affinity groups offered important challenges to City Friends's historical tendency to place primacy on individuals. In the six-year period between my initial fieldwork and the follow-up study, several important student, faculty, and parent groups had emerged to offer sites for support and social action around race, ethnicity, sexuality, and religious affiliation. Describing the purposes and effects of these groups, Tom Whitman, the head of school, argued:

Affinity groups have enriched the community. And Quaker notions of the way it's supposed to work say affinity groups shouldn't occur because there is that of God in every individual. If everyone is equal in the sight of God, we should all be equal when we're sitting and talking about something. And I think what we've basically said is that's true, but if you don't feel you have equal right and equal place at the table, then you're more reticent. As soon as things get tough, you tend to back away. And the affinity groups have given kids such a power, just because they have a place.

Affinity groups, then, challenged the community to consider how the Quaker focus on individuals obscured issues common to excluded or marginalized groups. Affinity groups created a forum where people could make visible common issues and injustices that the school needed to address.

The production of *For colored girls who have considered suicide when the rainbow is enuf* was one fruitful outcome of these affinity groups. These alternative collective spaces offered support and a forum for social action for students and teachers; however, affinity groups were still viewed by some with suspicion. Kyla Walters described the language through which affinity groups were often challenged:

That word exclusionary gets attached to certain efforts. The [group for African-American girls], [group for African-American boys], the *For colored girls* performance. How the language of diversity always seems to include that exclusionary piece. So, you're already in this box. If you want to empower yourself by getting together and finding some kind of solidarity, somehow it's exclusionary. That's the best evidence of things not having changed much at all because that shows me that there hasn't been movement in the thought process, in their racial identity development.

In referencing racial identity development (Tatum, 1997), Kyla suggested that as long as whites do not also see themselves as part of a racial group, then they view resistance strategies built around group identity as exclusionary, while the dominant school culture maintains its façade of neutrality and inclusion.

Furthermore, faculty of color noted that whites who do not explore their racial identity cannot see their way to participate in dismantling power and privilege. Discussing the school's approach to diversity in the context of the play, Kareem Nasser, a social science teacher, commented:

It still seems to me that the main model is based on the assimilationist model. And they think they're doing something when they remember to invite people into that model. And then when you say, "You know what? We have a project over here we'd like to work on. "Why are you separating yourself?" Because that's what I had a student say to me. A white student interviewing me for the [school newspaper]. She was saying, "Don't you feel this play, *For colored girls*, don't you think it might be exclusionary?" I said, "What do you mean? I don't understand." She said, "What about white people?" "Well, you got City Friends for one thing. This is your forum. Also, how many of you have come to see what you can do to help out?" "Well, we just thought we couldn't."

Kareem pointedly argued that City Friends was already organized around exclusionary practices and invited this student (and, by implication, many others) to join in the effort to shift the school away from an assimilationist to a truly inclusionary culture. While the growth of affinity groups marked a change in the school climate that had, in the past, been slow to acknowledge group oppression, many faculty of color were quick to point out that City Friends had not put institutional support behind these groups; Kyla Walters, for example, advised the African-American girls' group and produced the play on top of her contractual teaching and extracurricular load. Overall, City Friends had not abandoned its primary commitments to white power and privilege. However, recognition—represented in the practices of affinity groups and the production of *For colored girls*—reflected a challenge to the assimilationist approach to integration as an organizing strategy for educational equity. Inclusion that was substantive and meaningful might be brought about by focusing on, rather than ignoring, differences.

## Race/Ethnicity and Curriculum

Practitioners and students concerned that City Friends needed to recognize and represent racial/ethnic groups to be truly inclusive viewed the curriculum as a key site for change. In schools and universities across the nation, activists have for several decades challenged the curriculum to reconfigure the canon and create a knowledge base more reflective of the full range of human experience. Historically, City Friends, as described in Chapter 2, had built its reputation on a curriculum steeped in the traditional Western canon that critics suggested represented partial and particularized knowledge, perspectives, and values. For students of color, this curriculum created a chasm between the worlds from which they arrived and the one in which they lived at school. African-American high school students, for example, discussed their frustration with a curriculum focused almost entirely on the experiences of white Europeans and white Americans. Michael argued, "The problem I have with the curriculum we have is that we're learning about the culture, the European culture, the Caucasian culture and everything. … And then when do we learn about our culture?" Students in their junior year complained that they had read only one novel by an African-American the entire year (Ralph Ellison's *Invisible Man*). In the high school, only one required history course titled "Comparative Cultures" discussed civilizations other than Western ones. They were upset that the only class on African-American history was an elective, offered only every other year—a course the students with whom I spoke had all missed.[3]

These students were angry that African-American history was rarely discussed outside Black History Month and was almost always portrayed in terms of victimization. As Katie, an African-American junior, put it, "I know slavery has been taught since elementary school. But you know that one month of Black History is not enough." In response to Katie's observations, Maya pointed out, "There's more to us than slavery though. Everybody talks about—we should learn about slavery." Charlene interrupted, "I think in all my years of school from kindergarten I learned about one African queen, and I learned about her through a summer program." These students were arguing for deeper, nuanced, pervasive teaching about Africans and African-Americans reaching beyond minor additions about slavery and Dr. Martin Luther King Jr., to challenge the dominant narratives the school taught.

Moreover, the distanced, analytic stance that dominated much of City Friends's approach to academic literacy denied its role in constructing narratives of power. Katie offered as an example their study of *Invisible Man*. Complaining about the formal literary analysis of the novel in which students were asked to engage, Katie interpreted her teacher as too scared to discuss the real heart of the novel: racism. She said, "The teacher was trying to extend the basis of the plot, Ellison's ideas, instead of going to what he felt about racism and stuff. I think she tried to keep away from that." From Katie's perspective, treating *Invisible Man* with the same formal analytic approach used for all novels was her teacher's way of avoiding difficult, emotional discussions of racist oppression. This strategy left Katie and several of her peers deeply disappointed. They spoke palpably of the pain they felt as the novel made visible the physical and psychic reality of racism. Katie said, "One part of the book was about how he was in a boxing ring with all these people … and to me all that resonated was slavery with whips and chains. And I couldn't read it. I mean I read it because I knew I had to get the reading done. And it hurt to read it."

Katie's words are a powerful reminder of the very different positions we occupy in relation to text. Katie described how, when the class was reading *Invisible Man* she listened, "to white students feel free to say 'nigger,' " while a discussion of racism was simultaneously absent. When an African-American boy objected to a white peer's persistent use of this word, Charlene reported to me that the white student answered, "Why? It's in the book. It's in the book." This response, and the general failure of the teacher to address the deeper questions about race and racism underlying this confrontation, left the incident floating unresolved.

Michael speculated about why schools often avoided in-depth examinations of African-American experiences and serious discussions about racism:

> I think I know why some schools don't get enough about slavery and stuff. I think they might be a little frightened because sometimes blacks get a little riled up about stuff that was going on back then. Because if you look at the movies, sometimes when we see stuff that had happened to us, we get hyped. But I think they fear a little bit about us getting hyped up about that and trying to start something. But basically, most of the kids who want to learn about stuff like that are the educated ones that are really smarter not to start anything because we are going to learn.

Michael ascribed the persistent avoidance of in-depth explorations of race issues in schools to white people's fear that blacks will react violently. Pointing out that the images of violence are socially constructed and unrealistic, Michael argued that black people want to learn more about their history. Michael's insight about white fears, however, indicated the symbolic if not actually explosive potential such works could have in relation to dominant narratives (see, for example, Banks, 1997; Fine et al., 2000).

Undergirding these students' critique of the City Friends curriculum was a demand for reconsideration of how the school configured center and periphery. This was not a simple request that could be accomplished by adding more people of color to the literature lists and history texts. The English curriculum already included at each grade level works by writers of color, white women, and international literary figures. In addition, each spring the school offered a vast elective program which invited scholars from the staff and from outside the school community to teach a range of courses inclusive of multicultural interests.[4] From the point of the view of Jennifer Gerhardt, the white department chair, over the course of the middle and upper school years the English curriculum had built a broad and multifaceted knowledge of African-American literature, "from Ellison's Marxist critique, to Hurston's cultural celebration, to Morrison's treatment of universal, mythical ideas."

The approach to curriculum and pedagogy was certainly an evolving process. For example, in the year following my discussion with students about *Invisible Man* I asked their English teacher, Jennifer Gerhardt, for her perspective. She told me that, when she had initially introduced books by authors of color and white women, she found herself focusing on formal literary analysis to legitimize the literary worth of these traditionally marginalized works; however, she had learned from student evaluations that this attempt was unnecessary and did not serve students' interests. Over time, she had tried to focus more of the discussions on the issues of oppression raised in various novels. Jennifer had shifted from focusing textual analysis around the universality of human experience to recognizing the specificity (alongside the universality) of human experiences that shapes all artistic expression.

From the point of view of some students and teachers, despite the introduction of more multicultural works into the high school curriculum, City Friends had not seriously disrupted the preeminent position of the traditional Western canon and its dominant narratives about the world. Ruth Bliss, an English teacher, discussed this failure to dislodge the status quo:

> Entering this institution, part of what I've experienced is that we talk a real good game. We do a real good job in saying that we're interested in being multicultural, but when it boils down to actually being a diverse community, we seem to consistently make decisions that belie that mission. … When you also have a teacher who is teaching [a text by a person of color] who doesn't buy into the idea that this is the same kind of literary weight as another book, the kids get it. If the teacher doesn't feel it, then the kids get it. They devalue the text in a way that they see the teacher doing it. … The thing to try to do most for me is to not necessarily adopt the perspective of the author, but at least place the author in some kind of structural context, look at the issues that come out of power, of how power is negotiated. And yet when you're listening to a lecture of "the great authors" and one female is listed by a colleague, and no African-Americans, you know, it says at the top of the page "Great Authors!"

Ruth noted the contradictions between talk about being multicultural and consistent subtle messages that defined "excellence" in terms that left the privileged position of white men intact and invisible. She argued for the importance of understanding authors and their works in a "structural context," acknowledging the particular historical, cultural, and political locations from which all art arises, not just that of artists from oppressed social groups.

There were interesting contrasts between students' and teachers' critiques of the curriculum. For the most part, students of color framed their desire for a more representative curriculum in terms of learning about one's "own" cultural history and literature, a stance consistent with adolescent racial identity development (Tatum, 1997). Michael, for example, said, "But before they expect us to learn about their culture, I think first black people as a whole have to learn more about themselves before they can begin to learn about other cultures." The language heard earlier in this chapter when students spoke about finding a place in school—of "us" and "them," of sharply demarcated boundaries—resurfaced as students spoke about curriculum. Many students of color argued for a curriculum in which they could see their culture mirrored through multifaceted, nuanced perspectives, and some, like Michael, suggested that the curriculum must start by building knowledge of students' own cultural groups before extending to teach about others.

In the eyes of teachers who sought to radically reconfigure the curriculum, every curriculum represents a particular viewpoint. They sought to develop curricula that would reflect the experiences of many social groups in order that all students would learn to cross the borders of race/ethnicity (and other dimensions of oppression). They aimed to decenter a curriculum that largely glossed white male experiences as the universal standard, to explore the ways we all participate in the social practices of race/ethnicity.

The first year of my research the newly formed middle school division with its interdisciplinary team approach offered the seventh grade English and history teachers an unprecedented opportunity to create an interdisciplinary multicultural curriculum focusing in-depth and across time on African-Americans, American Indians, Asian-Americans and white women in the United States. As Donald Powell, Eugene Jones, and Cynthia Wright took their students on a yearlong journey into these marginalized territories, they invited them to investigate oppression and prejudice. Many seventh graders found themselves engaged for the first time in a concentrated study of these groups through the lenses of literature and history. The team's multicultural curriculum illustrates the power this approach holds for developing in-depth knowledge about groups that are often ignored or addressed superficially; however, it also surfaced the problematic nature of addressing the histories and literatures of those marginalized by the social order without simultaneously examining their relationship with dominant groups.

The seventh grade teachers pushed the study of oppression in U.S. history from margin to center. For example, in early February students watched the video *Shadow of Hate* in their history class. My field notes chronicled this experience:

The students crowded into class. There were just enough chairs and students sat close together around tables pushed next to each other to form a horseshoe. All chairs were positioned forward to view a television screen. One girl handed out a worksheet with questions they were to answer as they watched this video *Shadow of Hate*. The video outlined incidents chronicling oppression, prejudice and discrimination against many different groups across U.S. history: Native American Indians, Quakers, Baptists, Irish Catholics, Chinese Americans, Japanese Americans, African-Americans, and Jews. ... As Eugene [the teacher] moved to start the video, a white girl asked him, "Isn't today Black History Month?" He replied "every day is Black History Month for me."

This student's question suggested how she had most likely encountered issues of race and racism in her education to date. These topics were usually reserved for Black History Month. Eugene's retort explicitly referenced the shift he and his colleagues were making throughout the seventh grade curriculum. Although this particular video viewing occurred during February, it was one of many lessons throughout the year focused around the history of people of color in the United States. As the lesson continued, students expressed both innocence and shock about events that have fundamentally shaped life in the United States:

Several students asked Eugene questions as the film progressed. Two students at different points asked him "what's lynching?" Eugene responded, "Just watch" until finally there was a picture of black men lynched, with an audible, horrified gasp from several girls. Eugene asked, "Now do you have an idea what lynching is?" Another African-American boy was shocked by the picture of the suicide by hanging of a Japanese-American interned in the camps. Urgently he asked Eugene, "Did they hang themselves? Eugene, did they hang themselves?" Eugene replied, "Keep your eyes on it. Yes."

The brutality of the film appeared to be too much for some seventh graders who had not confronted such vivid portrayals of lynching and suicide before. This lesson aimed, perhaps too abruptly for some early adolescents, to debunk scripts of U.S. history that recounted a simple tale of liberation for its inhabitants. Students were confronted with the tragic realities of racism and discrimination, many for the first time.

The seventh grade English and history curriculum sought to do more than inform students about the experiences of people of color in this country. It also explicitly demanded that students analyze differences in values between dominant and marginalized cultures. Cynthia Wright asked students to consider how American Indian peoples' spirituality grew out of their experiences with the shape of the land in a precolonial period, and she helped them analyze how their own experiences with spirituality compared. After reading *Anpao*, a fictional account of one Native American boy's odyssey, students were exposed to the writings of contemporary Indigenous young people and examined similarities to and differences from their own experiences (Highwater, 1977).

At the same time that they were reading *Anpao* in English class, students were also studying Native American Indian cultures in their history course. Each student was part of a group researching the history and lifestyles of one particular Indigenous nation. Through these reports, students considered the great variations among different nations, rather than viewing Native American Indians as a monolithic group. These projects importantly led students to consider the history of the United States from the perspective of conquered and colonized nations. In their final presentations, some of the students noted the ways particular values, for example, the Arawaks's relationship to the land, "directly clashed with European, [values]." They viewed Columbus from the vantage point of the vanquished and with the dramatic accent of young adolescents: "Columbus wasn't really friendly to them, but they greeted him. He murdered many, hit babies' heads on rocks and brought diseases. Few remain today, except as a bitter reminder of the injustices of those we call our heroes."

The seventh grade curriculum's goal to shift students' perspectives on U.S. history was not easy to accomplish. The focused study of the literature and history of oppressed groups in the United States did not always challenge students to consider the invisible norms and assumptions of the dominant society. The tenacity of these norms and assumptions was evident throughout the majority of the seventh graders' presentations on Native American Indians. For example, references to women were comedic in their naïve assumptions that traditional male tasks were the measure of "work." Alice, a white girl, proposed, "Algonquins were patriarchal. Their women didn't do much. They just cooked and worked in the fields." By defining "doing" as men's work, women's labor was rendered insignificant. Of the Huron, Walter wrote, "Women controlled the tribes. The matriarch decided on the food supply. The men chose to put women to work because why should they have extra people sitting around the house doing nothing? If they could go through labor and raise children, they were tough enough to work." Unlike Algonquin women, Huron women "do a lot." Walter suspected that this was all a clever idea of Huron men, who did not want to have women "sitting around the house doing nothing." In both Alice's and Walter's reports the definition of work was similar and based on their assumptions about the division of the public and private spheres of life. Admittedly, it is demanding a lot of a seventh grade curriculum that it succeed in having students deconstruct their notions about the gendered division of labor; however, these examples serve as a reminder that a focus on "difference" in terms only of subordinate groups can leave tenaciously in place the unstated presumptions of the status quo.

This was even more evident in these Native American Indian reports in relationship to experiences with colonization. Whereas students explored in great detail the history and cultural practices of indigenous people, few made reference to encounters with conquest and colonization and those that did almost always erased European and Euro-American agency in these processes. For example, reporting on the Shawnee, Lisa, a white seventh grader, read, "They were pushed from their great hunting lands to some of the greatest farming lands in the south," and later continued, "they were famous warriors who rallied Native American Indians in the East to go against white men." In reconstructing history as Lisa did, whites were given no direct responsibility for "pushing" the Shawnee off their lands, while the Shawnee appear implicitly to be the aggressors, "famous warriors" who "go against white men." Paul argued of the Algonquin, "They were skilled and crafty and not mean to other tribes, unless they had to be. With the Civil War, their lands were invaded upon, and they fought." Here again the invaders are invisible agents, and as a result the Algonquin shift into position of the active warring faction.

Throughout the many reports about Native American Indians, the seventh graders had researched, in textured hues, the many cultural practices of Indigenous peoples, but the majority consistently either failed to reference encounters with European and white people, or alluded to them in ways that masked white people's responsibility and agency. The distinction I am referring to here may indeed seem trivial, especially in light of an extremely well-thought-out curriculum that had purposely exposed students to the complex and multifaceted histories and experiences of many groups traditionally marginalized in school curricula. I believe, however, that the nuances of these reports show just how difficult it can be to dislodge the dominant narrative of U.S. history and fundamentally reconstruct our knowledge about the nation (for example, Banks, 1997; McCarthy, 1993a; Pinar, 1993). Moreover, I suggest that multicultural education can and must illuminate the relationships between colonized and colonizer; oppressed and oppressor, if it is to make visible the processes through which domination and subordination occur, and truly shift margin to center.

Importantly, there were moments when the curriculum was successful in pushing students to question guiding norms and assumptions. Through explorations of African-American culture and history, Chinese-American experiences with immigration and racism, and women's struggles for equality, Eugene, Cynthia, and Donald directed students to consider events both distant and close from new angles. During a discussion of *The Star*

*Fisher (Yep, 1991)* , a story about a Chinese-American family's experiences in a small town, Donald pressed students to redefine foreignness:

**Donald** asked: "What makes something foreign? Is a person foreign, or does foreign arise from the context?"

**Harry** responded: "Everything is foreign to someone. If we went to China, we'd be foreign."

**Donald**: "Do you have to go that far?"

**Alysia** (a recent transplant from the West Coast) replied: "A New Yorker in L.A. is foreign."

**Donald**: "Where does foreignness come from? Is it a matter of the majority?"

**Nasir**: "You can feel foreign with a group of friends. In everyday life we sometimes feel foreign."

**Carly**: "No one is really foreign. I don't think foreign exists."

**Donald:** "Consider this statement. If everything is foreign, then everything is normal."

Harry and Alysia had been trying to get a word in.

**Harry** finally burst in, "But Donald, there *is* racism."

**Alysia**: "Sometimes foreign can be bad because it's singling people out. In another way, it makes the world what it is. Differences in cultures."

**Carly** had the last word: "How can there be normal if difference exists? How can you get an average between the world?"

Donald asked his students to consider a given category, "foreign," from a different angle of vision. These students shifted easily into this new perspective. As young adolescents, several moved quickly to moments when they had felt foreign—out of place in a new city or among peers. At the same time, the discussion pushed beyond the immediacy of their own lives to implicitly articulate two crucial insights about difference. First, as Harry pointed out, relativism is not a moral philosophy to live by: "[T]here is racism." As Carly noted, there is no "normal" ground against which difference stands out. For Donald, the point of multicultural education was "to put a concept in the center and see it from all angles" (see Banks, 1997). This discussion represented one of those moments when it became clear that the team's curriculum had realized this goal to some degree. By explicitly engaging race, gender, and ethnicity, Cynthia, Eugene, and Donald taught directly against the current of universalism that pervaded much of the City Friends curriculum. The curriculum they developed reflected the idea that recognition through representation of collective identities is fundamental for creating more equitable school environments.

### Recognition and Whiteness

As City Friends shifted more consciously toward explicit recognition of oppressed racial/ethnic groups in curriculum and public spaces, many white students and practitioners struggled to understand how they fit in to conversations about race and ethnicity—conversations many of them were confronting for the first time. In interviews with seventh grade students about their school experiences in general, white students often spoke spontaneously about their confusion about race. For example, in response to a question about how he might describe City Friends to a friend who was considering enrolling, Justin replied:

> Sometimes I feel, like not comfortable because assemblies—a lot of assemblies and things we talk about in English and history have to do with racism. And like one of my best friends is black—um, African-American, and um, I'm real good friends with him. But I don't understand when we go into history or something. It's, it's *their* heritage. I mean my history teacher is African-American and so is my English. But all we—most of what we talk about is about like oppression and like race, racism. And these days, I see more racism against whites than blacks. And sometimes, I just don't understand how everything is based on racism in this society.

Justin was struggling with his place in the conversation about racism, which had from his perspective dominated the English and history curriculum. He stumbled over the language of race; is his friend "black" or "African-American"? He did not understand the contemporary relevance of these history and English lessons because he believed that "these days I see more racism against whites than blacks." Justin's feelings of discomfort with and confusion about race and racism are not atypical for white adolescents confronting issues of racialized power and privilege (Tatum, 1997). A critical component of this confusion, even perhaps bitterness, might have evolved from the fact that Justin saw only African-American teachers raising these issues and questions. Eugene, Cynthia, and Donald had made what was, for City Friends, a radical shift in the curriculum, devoting a significant portion of the year to the study of the experiences of people of color. The focus on the experiences of "Others" by African-American teachers, however, struck Justin as irrelevant to himself as a white person and as "their" history. Whereas students of color felt strongly that City

Friends needed more educators of color to teach courses on race, ethnicity, and oppression, lessons from the seventh grade suggest it was also important for white adults to be visibly engaged in conversation and teaching about these issues (Tatum, 1997).

During a conversation in which I asked two white girls, "How do you like City Friends?," Alice immediately volunteered, "I'm not a racist, but I feel Cynthia and Donald try and relate everything to African-Americans. Sometimes English is just about English." Alice's final statement exposed a critical assumption that certain texts are unmarked by race, gender, class, and so on (see, for example, Pinar, 1993): "sometimes English is just about English." Her teachers' explicit focus on race and ethnicity, by contrast, was marked territory. Alice viewed them as working to impose their identity frameworks on texts that could otherwise be read as "color-blind." The product of an education that had previously promoted a color-blind stance, Alice could not yet see how race related to her, and she sought a return to a safer place where differences seemed not to exist. The response of many white students to a curriculum that for the first time focused intensively on race and oppression points to a key problem with organizing a curriculum along the lines of the racial/ethnic group identities traditionally excluded from the canon. This framework can fail to develop an understanding of the intimate connections between oppressor and oppressed, between dominant and subordinate groups, and so leave students from dominant groups without a sense that they belong in this conversation or that they can work for racial/ethnic justice.

Peter, another white seventh grader, expressed his desire to withdraw from confronting issues of race and racism: "I don't feel comfortable talking to people about racism 'cause I feel somehow I'll say something that's offensive. … There's other stuff to talk about. Race doesn't matter at all. I don't see the point in talking about it." Peter found talk about racism uncomfortable and frightening. He worried that he would unconsciously offend others. Peter argued "race doesn't matter at all" and proposed a retreat from such talk that he viewed as pointless. Peter's and his white peers' responses to a curriculum that confronted them with the experiences of people of color fits the trajectory of white racial identity development, which initially denies the significance of race (Tatum, 1997). However, their responses must also be understood to reflect their experiences in the wider context of City Friends. Confronted for the first time with a systematic study of the history and literature of oppressed groups in the United States, white students struggled to fit this new knowledge together with the dominant narrative they had until that time encountered.

Additionally, these students did not have enough opportunities to see white adults in the community model ways to think about their racial identities and their relationships to racism. This left many white students fearful of discussing or confronting difficult, scary questions about race and racism. As Donald put it, "What does it mean to be a white person in the world, let alone at City Friends? We've [African-American teachers] been saying white people have to put themselves in the place to fight racism so that students can see that it does matter in ways we need to engage, as opposed to it doesn't matter and we can back off from dealing with it, talking about it, until the next bomb goes off in the classroom, on the playing field. It's someone else's problem and concern."

From the beginning of my research at City Friends, some of the white teachers and administrators were actively exploring racism and examining their relationship as white people to racial oppression. The numbers of white teachers and administrators committed to fighting racism grew over the years. Several white practitioners described to me how over time they had developed more nuanced understandings of racial oppression and as a result had learned important strategies for advocating for educational justice in their classrooms and in their administrative roles. Faculty of color described these white colleagues as key allies in the fight to build a more equitable school community. However, faculty of color and white antiracist educators alike recognized the persistent problem that a majority of white practitioners, parents, and students simply did not view race and racism as their issue or responsibility to address.

Reflecting on how far the school had come in the six years between my initial fieldwork and the follow-up study, Tom Whitman argued, "We're much clearer that diversity enhances the academic mission, rather than competes with the academic mission." He, however, also articulated a perception that white male students had come to see themselves as a disenfranchised group. Tom stated:

> I think the white male in the upper school still feels disenfranchised or just not appreciated, bashed. On a bad day, they feel bashed. The seniors always bring that up. And that's particularly in the English curriculum where there's a lot more gender issues than even racial issues. The addition of female authors sometimes feels heavy-handed. The rap is we got so into that, that we sort of lost perspective. This is the intellectual adolescent saying, "I understand why you're doing it. It makes sense to me, but it's a little overboard. You need to right the ship."

At this point in the interview, I asked Tom if he really thought that the English curriculum included more female than male authors. He argued that in recent years there had been a shift in the high school curriculum indeed to include more female than male authors. Although the English department chair assured me that books by white male authors still constituted the majority of works that were read, it is important to attend to the perception of some white people that the balance had shifted. Thus, it is not only that some white people in the school felt little connection or responsibility to undo racism (or sexism); they experienced the public recognition of historically marginalized groups as a displacement and advocated more a "balanced" approach.

Describing the rationale he saw behind curricular diversification (and echoing the call for recognition), Tom Whitman argued a different perspective from that which he heard from white boys:

> My take on it is that every adolescent wants to see him or herself in the education process. And for 155 years, we weren't very good at having African-Americans see themselves anywhere in the curriculum. So now, when you do that, it's at somebody's expense. So the white person is not as central to everything a kid studies as they used to be. It's all a matter of what you focus on. I always pooh, pooh it. I just say. Don't you worry. You have plenty of time. White males still tend to win. Don't worry. And if this is shaking you up, you need to have a broader perspective. You need to get in somebody else's shoes.

Tom argued that one critical purpose of a multicultural approach is to support the individual adolescent to recognize herself or himself in the curriculum. Tom's words resonated with a key claim of the politics of recognition or identity: the public nonrecognition or misrecognition of our collective identities constitutes a wrong that must be redressed by the public acknowledgment of group identity or culture (see especially Taylor, 1992). He also suggested that white adolescent males, and by implication other groups, had much to learn from this revised curriculum.

Although Tom clearly addressed the ways that decentering the traditional curriculum benefited all students, what interests me is that rectifying the historical canon can be viewed in terms of winners and losers and a potential loss of balance. Curricular diversification offered historically marginalized groups a mirror in which to see their collective identities reflected, and it pushed white students to "get in somebody else's shoes" and develop broader perspectives. However, while it is certainly the case that, as Tom pointed out, the "white person is not as central to everything" as s/he was in the past, the language through which he ironically cajoled the boys—"white males still tend to win"—hints at the limitations of organizing justice claims around recognition. When social and cultural groups are treated as distinct and certain histories or literatures are awarded to different groups, there is a risk that the relationship between groups—the very relationship that produces inequality—will be left unexamined (Fine, 1997; McLaren, 1994). It is for this reason that I pointed earlier to the subtle ways that seventh grade students learned much rich detail about Indigenous nations in the United States, but often failed to reference their relations with European and early American conquest and colonization. The struggle becomes one over whose stories or histories will or should be told; the implication is that these narratives are unconnected.

The demand for representation or recognition of group identities often rests on a deeply problematic view of difference as fundamentally bounded and separate rather than multiply constituted and inextricably linked (see Appiah, 1996; Erickson, 2001; McCarthy, 1990; McCarthy and Crichlow, 1993). The discourse of recognition in schools often positions race, ethnicity, gender, and culture as a kind of static possession of distinct groups. Moreover, this view of difference fails to question whether, in fact, all people identified with a particular group walk in the same shoes. There is little acknowledgment of the ways individuals experience multiple group affiliations (Appiah, 1996; Benhabib, 2002).

This situation is not only harmful to people from historically oppressed groups who already suffer the effects of monolithic, misrepresentative discourse about them; it also does not offer people from dominant groups a vision for crossing boundaries and fighting against oppression. The white boys might be expected to take a different perspective for a short while, by walking in another group's shoes; however, ultimately they can feel reassured they will continue to win. This framework of recognition fails to make visible the ways all narratives are co-produced and the fact that their production constitutes power relations. If we treat the traditional literary canon or historical record as simply one among multiple bodies of knowledge, we never ask students to understand the relationship between domination and oppression. These narratives cannot simply coexist; rather, they challenge each other.

While I do not dismiss the critical import of the public cry for recognition, I want to consider the ways that organizing for educational justice around this claim risks framing difference in problematic ways that do not address how power and privilege are produced continually through the institutional arrangements of schooling and society (Fine, 1997; McCarthy, 1993a; McLaren, 1994). In the next section of this chapter, I narrate the story of some City Friends high school girls who fought to transform their mathematics education by grounding their demands for change in the recognition of gender differences. I focus my analysis explicitly on discourses about difference that were invoked in the face of this cry for recognition, to show why, as educators, we need to pay careful attention to where we locate the "problem" of difference. Although this story addresses how students framed their demands for equity, not how teachers organized for change, it offers key insights for building just educational practices.

## Gender as Difference

In the spring of their junior year at City Friends, a group of six white girls approached members of the administration to demand that something be done about their pre-calculus math course. The girls argued that a hostile and competitive environment fostered by their male teacher and a small cadre of their male peers denied them equal educational opportunity. Furthermore, they insisted that such a setting could not accommodate girls' preferred learning styles and desire for connected ways of knowing (see, for example, Belenky et al., 1997/1986).

As these girls articulated a critique of their mathematics class, they interpreted their experiences primarily through a lens that emphasized perceived differences between females and males. For example, one student, Meredith, said:

> I don't know if guys feel the same way about having it be such an important thing to give right answers. It seems to do with testosterone. There's a really big difference between men's and women's brains. I'm not saying I don't have the capacity. I'm not saying I'm not able to. I'm just saying my brain has a different—is not the same as these boys' brains. I'm not saying it's less good. I'm not saying it's better. I'm saying it's different. And I can be expected to learn things in different ways.

Meredith argued that gender-inflected learning styles, which she related to differences in brains and hormones, implied a need for a different pedagogical approach that would accommodate her female ways of knowing. Speaking of gender differences in terms of "testosterone" and "brains" may be eerily reminiscent of early 20th-century science repackaged for a contemporary audience. However, it should come as no surprise that these young women framed their criticisms of their math class by focusing primarily on the differences between males and females. We are living at a moment in which educational as well as public discourse about gender is saturated with talk about differences between men and women, boys and girls. A spate of popular books champion the cause of males strait-jacketed by culture and feminists and behaviorally driven by testosterone (see, for example, Gurian, 1996; Sommers; 2000).

From a different angle, academic research in mathematics education debates, for example, the origins and meanings of gender differences in problem-solving (see, for example, Fennema et al., 1998; Hyde and Jaffee, 1998; Noddings, 1998; Sowder, 1998). Within this broader cultural context, it was almost inevitable that the young women at City Friends drew on the language of gender differences to understand their experiences with math education. This discourse offered the women a collective language for critiquing their math education and provided them with a new way of thinking about gender equity in terms of a need for recognition.

In what follows, I focus on the discourses through which the girls framed their demands for gender equity and the language through which some of their male peers resisted their interpretation. Through this careful attention to discourse, I explore how our conceptualizations of difference create and limit possibilities for building equitable practices.

## Reforming Mathematics

The girls who articulated a strong critique of their pre-calculus course were enrolled in the City Friends advanced mathematics track. This course was unusual in several ways. Mathematics was the only curriculum area at City Friends that was tracked. Furthermore, the calculus course was the only class that explicitly followed the curriculum of the College Board's Advanced Placement (AP) examinations.

The advanced math track had an interesting history. A few years before I arrived at the school, a small group of vocal parents demanded that the mathematics department change its newly reformed curriculum. In the recent past, the department had engaged in developing a broader, more holistic approach to teaching mathematics that integrated, for example, reflective writing, and more problem-based learning into the curriculum. This reform effort had drawn on the National Council of Teachers of Mathematics (1989) new standards for math education. A small group of parents concerned that their children would not be adequately prepared for college level mathematics formed an independent committee, wrote a curriculum, and presented it to the math department. As one administrator explained to me, the mathematics department, in the midst of a transitional leadership, had responded to "the parents' command 'jump' with 'how high?'"

Since that time, a new department chair had sought to build a curriculum that would satisfy the demands of families that wanted an accelerated math program that prepared students directly for the AP examinations and, simultaneously, would lessen the burden of academic tracking for students who had been designated less proficient in math. The white department chair, Alex Worth, explained to me that when he arrived, he had found a school with three math tracks; many students had dubbed the lowest track "retardo math." Over the first three years of Alex's tenure, the math department had phased out the lowest track, but it had retained a two-tiered differentiation between regular and advanced math.

## The Classroom Context

It was in the context of the advanced track that girls raised questions about and critiques of the pedagogy and practices of mathematics. During their junior year pre-calculus class, all the girls in the advanced track had become severely disgruntled with the program due to what they perceived to be a hostile environment created by both the teacher and a number of their male peers. The girls expressed concern and anger that they were not being taken seriously as math students, that they were unable to participate in a context they experienced as competitive and anxiety provoking, and that they had therefore been generally denied an equal math education. As a group, they wrote about their experiences, lobbied for administrative intervention, and organized a school assembly on the topic of girls in math and science.

Journals, which the girls initiated to keep a record of their concerns, articulated eloquently the depth of their feelings of alienation and anger. Hannah wrote about a specific incident:

[The teacher] announced some optional problems. "To those of you heavily into theoretical math, these are very challenging and you should look into them. But they're not for everybody. Some of you should do them and some of you shouldn't." He was facing Carl, Andy, George, and Rob. Jessica protested about his demarcation of "some" people. "I'm not saying who the some people are," he replied. "But it feels like you do have them in mind," Jessica repeated. I said, "It doesn't feel right because it feels like you're setting up a special club." "I am!" he said, "There is a club. This class tends to divide in two areas and some people were very bored yesterday. I'm trying to address that." Well, unbeknownst to [the teacher] I was one of yesterday's very bored students, and yet I was definitely not invited into "The Club." Until we start thinking as a class and valuing each other's thought processes and *struggle* ... then the class will never be a comfortable place for me to learn. ... These issues are so subtle and slippery. (emphasis in the original)

Hannah and her peers felt that in implicit ways a certain group of male students had been invited to participate more deeply in an exclusive initiation process. Even without directly naming the boys, Hannah felt that the teacher had explicitly designated a male club from which she and her female peers were shut out.

As a result of their experiences, at the end of their junior year, the girls proposed an alternative format for their math course for the following year. Drawing on an established tradition at City Friends, the girls sought to learn mathematics in the context of a peer-led independent study. They detailed clear criteria for how students would be invited to join the group that included a strong interest in mathematics and a commitment to peer learning and peer teaching. The students planned to use the school's established curriculum and to be subject to the same midterm and final examinations as the regular advanced class. The math department faculty members, however, were concerned that the course material was too difficult for an independent study and rejected this proposal. The department chair and the director of curriculum felt that Marilyn Davis, a recently hired African-American teacher viewed by her colleagues as a brilliant mathematician, would be able to make a connection with these girls and rebuild their confidence and relationship with mathematics. Therefore, they assigned her to teach the advanced track calculus course the following year when the girls were seniors.

When the junior girls raised critiques of their advanced math course, several teachers and administrators became deeply concerned about these accusations, even as they were puzzled by them. To the practitioners' knowledge, there had never before been any questions of gender inequity in the advanced math track. They acknowledged that these girls' math section was unusual in that male students outnumbered females by 15 to 6.[5] In general, however, the school's advanced math track enrolled girls and boys in equal numbers or had girls outnumbering boys. Furthermore, teachers and administrators reported no prior accusations of gender inequity from female students. Moreover, despite their critiques, all but one of the girls in this section were performing well as measured by their grades and confirmed by reports of their teachers and the mathematics department chair.[6]

Two months into the girls' senior year, Marilyn Davis first invited me to speak with the female students and to attend her course. She wanted help understanding the troublesome atmosphere that pervaded the course. At the beginning of the year, Marilyn and several administrative colleagues had hoped to create a more positive learning environment by having students consciously examine the variety of agendas and learning styles they brought to the group. However, according to both Marilyn Davis and the school's curriculum director Mike Knight, after an initial class meeting during which the students each shared hopes and goals for the course, this attention to group process had fallen victim to the overpowering demands of the AP calculus curriculum. As the course proceeded, the previous year's struggles resurfaced. Marilyn and the administrators noticed that the class tone was contentious and students seemed frustrated and apathetic. Finally, in November Alex Worth (the department chair), Marilyn Davis, and Mike Knight decided to split the course in two, with one section preparing for the AB section of the Advanced Placement exam and the other for the more advanced BC section. They hoped that this division would improve the classroom climate as each section could serve the different needs and demands of the students. The tracking placed most of the girls (four out of six) in the lower section. One female student dropped the course.[7] The classroom climate in both sections remained contentious.

At this point, Marilyn Davis asked me to interview the girls and to begin attending her class. I conducted focus group interviews with the girls in November and February, and in March I invited them to speak in a multicultural education course I was teaching. Finally, in May, Marilyn, Alex, Mike, and I conducted single-gender focus group interviews with all the students in the class. We made the decision to divide these focus group interviews along gender lines because our experiences with the group suggested that the atmosphere in mixed gender groups was likely to be unproductive or painfully disrespectful of dissenting perspectives. I draw my analysis of the discourses about gender and equity from these multiple focus groups.

My observations of both sections of the class served to confirm the girls' descriptions of their math class. In the observations, I attended to the classroom dynamics and pedagogy, as these had been the areas of concern for the girls. Since the primary focus of this study was *discourse*, these observations were aimed to provide a context in which to understand the students' talk about gender and math, rather than to offer an analysis of practice. The classroom climate, created primarily by a small number of the male students, was often combative. For example, during one observation two male students were relating the calculus problem to an area of physics. Meredith, the girl quoted above, stated that she did not know what they were talking about since she was not taking physics. One boy quipped, "That's because you're too stupid," while the other simultaneously said, "You couldn't hack the physics." My field notes reflected numerous examples of students (mostly female, but including a few males) referring to themselves or their questions as stupid.

A small cadre of seven boys (four in the BC section and three in the AB section) expressed their intolerance of their peers' questions by, for example, referring to others' questions as "stupid," stating that the questioner should "know that," or rolling their eyes and sighing. Furthermore, these seven boys repeatedly challenged Marilyn Davis—for example, critiquing the techniques she used to solve a problem or the marks she had given them on a test—in tones that were remarkably dismissive and patronizing. Marilyn was deeply troubled by the tone of both sections of the class; however, she found it extremely difficult to interrupt. As an African-American woman, she perceived her authority to be challenged in ways that felt intimately interwoven with the dynamics of race as well as gender.[8]

Marilyn Davis felt an overarching pressure to prepare her students adequately for the AP examinations. The classes were driven at high speed to prepare for a series of examinations, all mini-steps building toward the AP exam. Using more traditional pedagogical approaches, during most of the class periods I observed, Marilyn either reviewed the homework and solved the equations at the board, or called on individual students (both male and female) to demonstrate solutions for their peers. I only once saw small groups of students in the AB section working together on calculus problems, as Marilyn circulated helping each group. This occurred late in the year as students prepared to take a test the next day. During this class period, however, all but two students seemed distracted, paid little attention to the task at hand, and generally engaged in conversation about other topics (for example, the upcoming prom). By the middle of the school year, most of the students (male and female) appeared apathetic and distracted in class, and by the end of the year many described themselves as frustrated and unsure of their knowledge of math.

In the end, of the remaining 21 students, only 5 boys (and none of the girls) chose to take the AP exam. The female students felt their concerns had been ignored at the peril of their sense of themselves as mathematically capable. As a woman and a person of color, Marilyn Davis had also worked hard to make a place for herself in the field of mathematics. She ended the year feeling frustrated and demoralized at not having been able to have the girls see her as an ally.

## Interpreting Experience

I offer this broader story of the girls' critique of their math education to set a context in which to explore three discursive frameworks that emerged as students sought to interpret their experiences. Drawing on interview and focus group data, in what follows, I examine first how the girls invoked the justice claim for recognition in order to make sense of their experiences and to argue for equal educational opportunity. I call this discourse of recognition "difference-talk" because the girls focused on differences between the genders as an explanatory framework. This difference-talk articulated clearly the justice claim that recognition of difference should serve as the foundation for building equitable practices. Next, I step away from this "justice as recognition" claim to analyze the response that the majority of the male students in the class had to difference-talk. Their discourse represented a backlash against a gendered analysis and called on a belief that education was a meritocracy rewarding those who worked hard. I pay attention to this discourse because it echoes the arguments made by detractors of multicultural education. I then turn to a third discursive strand through which students articulated (if in muted tones) a more far-reaching critique of education. This critique explored differences as a product of particular pedagogical practices and offered a different grounding on which justice claims might be based—one that emphasizes difference as relational.

*Difference-Talk and Its Discontents* Initially, as they sought to understand their experiences, the girls turned to popular research on gender and education, reading and drawing on feminist critiques of gender discrimination in schooling, such as Sadker and Sadker's book *Failing at Fairness: How Our Schools Cheat Girls* (1994). In large part, they came to think about their experiences in terms of a mismatch between girls' learning styles and those valued in their classrooms (see, for example, Belenky et al., 1997/1986; Gilligan, Lyons, and Hanmer, 1990). Thus, the girls made a claim for educational justice based on the need for group recognition and analyzed their education to date as a kind of nonrecognition of their gendered learning styles (Bingham, 2001; Taylor, 1992). A fair education was one that would take gender difference into account, tailoring curriculum and pedagogy to the needs and values of different groups of students.

What did girls' differences demand of their curriculum and pedagogy? What would recognizing difference entail? The girls demanded that understanding be central to their math education (see also Boaler, 1997). Moreover, they made their argument for the centrality of understanding on gendered terms. They proposed that, *as girls*, they desired less competitive and more collaborative opportunities to learn with their peers. They suggested that, given their verbal strengths, writing might be used in math courses as an important medium for making important connections and building deep understandings of mathematical concepts. Moreover, the girls described a need for more concrete and meaningful explanations of mathematical concepts. For example, Meredith spoke of her need to "understand a concept from the bottom part where it starts. I understand this is a circle and then you build on that. ... It's a verbal explanation. You know why you're doing this." Meredith desired to understand the relationship between each foundational concept and the purpose of the work. For Meredith, talk—"a verbal explanation"—supported learning and understanding. Mara continued:

> Yeah, and the connection to something physical. Some kind of tangible. Using real world examples. ... My brain can picture a rocket and completely understand everything going on. But my brain won't look at a tangent line and see exactly the same thing. It's easier for me to do it through something that I can picture and envision. To use common sense.

"Common sense," concrete and real-world uses, and pictorial examples marked many of the female students' ideas of necessary components for successful learning of mathematical concepts. In these and other examples, the women called for a curriculum that would draw on their strengths as females, emphasizing relationships between conceptual and applied knowledge.[9]

The idea that gender differences should be recognized and valued through a differentiated curriculum and pedagogy rests on two related (at times overlapping) claims about the origin and nature of these differences. Biological and socialization explanations for gender differences implicitly buoyed the arguments advocating pedagogy and curriculum that were responsive to girls. Students at times proposed that girls had been socialized to have a particular relationship with mathematics. However, most often, explanations for gender differences slid inexorably toward biological essentialism—a slippage that echoes some contemporary popular literature on gender and education (see especially, Gurian, 1996, 2002).

Treating gender as dichotomous, difference-talk often located it in the materiality—the very body and brains—of male and female students. The focus on girls' versus boys' learning styles glided all too easily into talk of "brains," "testosterone," and "nature." Recall Mara's previous words that her "brain can picture a rocket … but won't look at a tangent line." Her brain embodies a difference that is simply not of her making. Returning to the quote at the beginning of this section, Meredith stated that boys are more willing to experiment publicly with wrong answers and argued:

> It seems to do with testosterone. I'm dead serious … this comes from my dad (a scientist)—there's really a big difference between men and women's brains. And I've just accepted that my brain doesn't—I'm not saying I don't have the capacity. … I'm not saying it's less good. I'm not saying it's better. I'm saying it's different. And I can be expected to learn things in different ways. My brain works differently, I mean my verbal capacity is higher than my spatial capacity. … That doesn't mean I shouldn't be able to do well. It just means I need to be taught differently. That I need a little more time. I need to have it acknowledged that my brain is different. It can't just look at the board and see the connection and make it. I need to have it explained. I'm a teacher-oriented student … I can't teach it to myself. I don't have that capacity.

The notion that educational equity demands recognition of difference is partially premised on the assumption that *biology* explains the differences in female and male academic performance. Testosterone was responsible for boys' willingness to take public risks. Like Mara, Meredith described her brain as an independently acting entity: "It can't just look at the board. … It needs to have it explained." Her difference was out of her control, located in the body. This difference must be recognized and accommodated. Moreover, Meredith voiced a key premise of justice claims based around recognition: that differences demand not only to be recognized, but also to be respected. It is the failure to recognize *and* respect differences, rather than any inherent relative value of these differences, that leads to oppressive educational practices.

Despite Meredith's insistence that different does not equate with better or worse, smarter or less capable, she flagged some areas of difference that were viewed in the context of the math course as signs of deficit. Needing more time and being more dependent on the teacher for explanations became markers, not of difference but of deficiency in a context in which speed, independence, risk-taking and capacity for abstract thought were of the highest value.

Whether the origins of gender are taken to be biological or social, as long as these differences are located in particular bodies rather than in the invisible values and assumptions structuring curriculum and pedagogy, difference doubles as deficit (Walkerdine, 1990, 1998; Willis, 1995, 1996). In a discipline that dichotomizes and then hierarchically organizes "concrete" and "abstract" (see, for example, Walkerdine, 1990), these girls' demands for a curriculum more focused on understanding related to the "real world" was reinterpreted by some of their male peers as "the problem of girls in math." One overarching theme that emerged from the focus group interviews with the male students at the end of the year reflected a positioning of the girls as less capable. As one example of how this positioning occurred, several of the male students misread the girls' desire to gain a more holistic understanding of mathematics as a cry for a cookbook approach to the discipline. One student, George, discussed the "problems" of girls in math and science classes:

> Most of the females who have problems—most of the people who've had problems with the math and science courses have been females. And most of the people, most of the girls have wanted to just have things spelled out for them, told exactly how to do it and not have to really think for themselves. They want to do the old type of problems, like this is how it works, just change the numbers around and do the same exact thing. I've heard students comment, "we weren't told how to do this." You're supposed to figure out how to do this. That's the whole point. I definitely don't think all the girls are like that, but that is a trend that I've noticed.

George, echoing similar beliefs expressed by several of his male peers, argued that girls had "problems" with math and science because, especially in the face of increasingly difficult and abstract material, most females sought simple, patterned solutions rather than attempting to "figure it out for themselves." Thus, Mara's call for a "connection to something physical" and Meredith's demand to "understand a concept from the bottom part where it starts [through] a verbal explanation" were reinterpreted and denigrated as a plea for received recipes.

Furthermore, in an environment where maverick independence was of highest value, the girls' desires for cooperative learning fueled the idea that they were less capable math students. In the all-male focus groups boys repeatedly spoke about female students as dependent rote-learners in comparison to males, who were perceived as independent problem-solvers. When talk focused on gender differences, it was the girls, rather than the curriculum or pedagogy of math courses, who were scrutinized and identified as lacking.

Within the discourse of difference, girls' learning styles (see Belenky et al., 1997/1986)—whether attributed to biological or social origins—were positioned as antithetical to those of males. As girls identified female ways of knowing that needed to be recognized, a set of opposing tendencies was attributed to male students. If girls sought connectedness and cooperation, boys were drawn to risk-taking, individualism, and competition. Describing his peers, Andy stated:

> There's a guy's group that has an edge because of whatever—whether it's because they're trained to be that way or because they're really good in math, they spend more time studying it or because they're such a tight knit group that they have an edge. They really, I think, enjoy the edge. Nobody's trying to sabotage anyone. We're not ripping off people's homework or destroying people's calculators. I don't think it's competitive in that anyone's trying to defeat anyone else. It's just they like being one up. They like that energy. I like being better than people at something. It's natural.

Living on the edge and being better than others—all in good spirit, of course—are described as natural proclivities of a "guy's group." Competition is the unstated norm. By claiming no material injury (to calculators or homework) and positioning the desire to be "one up" as a natural or socialized tendency of guys, Andy obscured the interaction between the competitive atmosphere of the "edge" and a classroom environment that the female students did not find conducive to learning. For the girls, the "energy" that Andy described as driving his male peers created an environment in which they felt silenced and edged out of the opportunity to learn.

If competitiveness was intimately bound up with masculinity, so too was "natural talent" for mathematics. Although I heard both students and practitioners speak of the girls as capable math students, it was only a select group of boys who were described as *being* mathematical geniuses (see also Hyde and Jaffee, 1998; Walkerdine, 1990, 1998; Willis, 1995). Furthermore, because being a "genius" and competitive interactional styles were viewed as independent qualities endowed to certain boys in the group, the inextricable link between the two was missed. For example, Janie described her classmate, Rob, as follows:

> This one kid was like a math genius, got in early to [an elite math and science university], whatever. He would yell at us if he felt that he was right. And someone would ask a question and he'd be like, "Well, if you don't understand that!" The one problem with him—I mean it's horrible to condone what he did, but the problem was he totally knew everything and he did understand it all.

In this description, being a math genius was uncoupled from, rather than intimately bound up with, behavior. It is likely that, by participating in and policing a competitive classroom environment in which questioning was not tolerated, a small group of students had secured knowledge, confidence, and academic success for themselves at the expense of many of their peers. Thinking about gender and its consequent modes of interaction in terms of dichotomous group differences obscured the dynamic relationships within classrooms that produce inequality.

Seeing difference in terms of specific preferences and learning styles belonging to particular gendered bodies failed to focus attention on the dominant values and assumptions guiding the practices of the AP calculus class—values that privileged speed, competition, abstraction, and individualism over all else. Rather, the move to *recognize* girls' differences, while awarding them the realm of the concrete and the cooperative, ceded to boys speed, competition, and, most important, brilliance. Difference-talk obscured the ways that dominant values were not simply different from, but incompatible with the kinds of values the girls articulated. Inequities (in opportunities to learn, gain confidence as mathematicians, etc.) were not simply unfortunate accidents caused by the failure to recognize and respect gender differences; they were necessary outcomes of the gendered processes of that classroom.

### Denial: The Discourse of Meritocracy

Difference-talk engendered a strong backlash from many of the boys in the class, a backlash that echoed the resentment expressed by white students asked to confront race and racism. This backlash offers a space from which to analyze the arguments against the claim for *recognition*. With three exceptions, the boys in the class completely denied the girls' charge that gender was intimately bound up with students' experiences of math curriculum and pedagogy. Rather, they employed a discourse that placed responsibility for mathematical success on each individual student's willingness to engage in hard work, be responsible, and work independently. Most of the boys defended a notion of meritocracy upholding a strong conviction that academic success was achieved according to a just system of rewards. It is critical to pay attention to this discourse because it reflects the ways the call to make education more responsive to difference has been met with the counterclaim that schools offer neutral playing fields. This defense of the apparent neutrality of educational institutions reverberates throughout public debates that decry educational policies and practices that would recognize group difference through, for example, multicultural curricula or affirmative action (for example, Lasch-Quinn, 2001; Ravitch, 1990; Thernstrom and Thernstrom, 2002).

Some of the male students argued that the girls had employed gender as an excuse for either mathematical incompetence or insufficient effort. Describing himself as "enormously agitated" about the girls' charges, Joe stated:

> This could be kind of snotty or whatever, I don't care. But what I saw there was just an opportunity for people who could not learn at the pace in the advanced class to create an excuse to slow down and to basically blame that on somebody else. I personally think that well, these are the terms of the advanced class. You go in and you do it at the pace the teacher sets. If you can't handle it all, obviously there should be some help. And the help was given last year. But all these accusations I just find particularly groundless and there's no meaning whatsoever.

For Joe, the girls' attempts to describe their experiences in terms of gender dynamics was a diversionary tactic from the truth that they were not able to "learn at the pace in the advanced class." By focusing on the girls' lack and accusing them of trying to "slow down" the class, Joe froze the "terms of the advanced class" as axiomatic. In Joe's universe, the teacher sets the law—speed being the essence of this law—and students must follow suit. Recognizing that this hard-line attitude might make it difficult for some students who "can't handle it," Joe supported a limited welfare model—"there should be some help." The existence of help alleviated any need to consider further the fundamental principles invisibly guiding the curriculum and pedagogy. Like many of his male peers, Joe positioned the practices of mathematics as a given, thus maintaining the belief that success was awarded to deserving students. Many male students defended the axiomatic "terms" embedded in the practices of this calculus class, which privileged speed, competition, and self-reliance over the collaborative, holistic approaches to teaching and learning advocated by the girls (see also Boaler, 1997).

For many boys, there seemed to be ample evidence that their female peers had not earned the right to success. Some argued that it was not a matter of capability, but that the girls were not acting in responsible ways that would have guaranteed doing well in the course. Caleb stated:

> One thing that I think is extremely amusing. Last year, there were a whole bunch of times in class when Hannah and Emma would like turn over to me and say, "All the boys are on that side of the class and all the girls are on this side." And they'd make a big deal out of that. But then, couldn't they make a big deal out of the fact that they weren't listening at all? They were just sitting there. Emma, every day would write a letter to one of her friends. No wonder she wasn't doing well in math. I mean did they hand in their homework? No, I don't think they did. This seems sort of awkward to me that people are having trouble and saying that this trouble is based on this [gender]. That we should look at male-female relationships like we're doing now. In math, maybe. Or in the whole school. But we also have to look at the fact that some people that are not doing well are not doing well because they're lazy. They're not doing the work.

In fact, according to both the girls and their teachers, all but one of the female students were successfully completing the course work and receiving good grades; it was not failure or underachievement that drove the girls' demands for gender equity. However, in concert with Joe's interpretation, Caleb also claimed that gender was an excuse that female students employed to shirk responsibility for their actions. From Caleb's vantage point, the girls were inattentive during class and unproductive at home; the latter was a claim for which he had no definite knowledge, only a suspicion—he "thinks" they did not do their homework. Caleb characterized the girls as "lazy" and as not doing necessary work. In doing so, Caleb reiterated and staunchly defended the belief that hard work is inevitably rewarded.

In the very moments that male students claimed girls were not acting in appropriate, conscientious ways, they were positioning themselves as self-reliant parties whose academic success or failure was directly correlated with their effort. Continuing from what was previously quoted, Caleb said:

> I mean I didn't do well in math this year. Why did I not do well in math this year? Because I didn't do all of the homework when I should have done all the homework. Not because gender issues were screwing me up.

In pointing to his behavior as an explanation for his poor academic performance, Caleb saw himself as firmly in control of his educational outcome in the math class. Another student, Mark, contrasted his willingness to admit fault for failing to understand a concept with the approach of his female peers. The girls, he argued, blamed their teachers for teaching poorly or for failing to spend time in class reviewing homework. Of himself, Mark stated, "I said, 'I didn't know how to do this because it was my fault that I didn't pay attention.'" Like Caleb, Mark considered himself fully in control of his academic predicament. Thus, Mark and Caleb turned their academic underperformance into a virtue by eagerly resting blame on themselves. By contrast, they dismissed the female students as complainers who erroneously perceived gender inequality in the classroom to evade responsibility.[10] Caleb, Mark, and many of their male peers came to understand the dynamics and experiences of students in the advanced class within a meritocratic framework which proposed that individual students could guarantee academic success by acting responsibly: paying attention, doing homework, and seeking extra help all constituted such action.

The depths of what was being defended through this discourse of meritocracy was reflected in the tone and particular language these male students used when talking about their class. It is important to note again that there were three boys in the advanced class who, along with their female peers, proposed the need for rethinking the way math was structured as a discipline and the pedagogical approaches employed. This is described in the next section. It is equally remarkable, however, that only boys and no girls took up the discourse of meritocracy, and that they did so with a vengeance. The tone of their talk was often vituperative. In the focus groups, boys raised their voices, and their anger fed increasing fury. In one focus group interview, some male students who initially took a more sympathetic stance toward the girls' analyses completely turned around and dismissed gender as an excuse the minute one student, Joe, heatedly argued that point. It was as if Joe had opened up the possibility for them to lash out. In addition to anger, male students used patronizing, dismissive language, such as "ridiculous" and "amusing" in reference to the girls' claims.

The strong emotional currents running through many of the male students' talk moved alongside a stream of language that appropriated reasoned scientific discourse to support their case. For example, after rejecting the girls' propositions about gender dynamics and referring to them as "lazy," Caleb argued:

Now maybe gender issues are screwing them up. I'm not trying to disprove that. But maybe they're not doing well because they're not working. Because the evidence I'm seeing is they're not working.

There are girls like Janie who are working who do get good grades.
So, I don't see the correlation between the two.

In this passage, Caleb opposed the girls' interpretative framework by
carefully laying claim to the logic of empiricism. Beginning by stating that
he was not trying to "disprove" their theory, Caleb then cited the "proof" that
the girls were misguided in pointing to gender. He appealed to "evidence"
to show a lack of "correlation" between gender and academic outcome.

With reasoned proof squarely on their side, many of the boys sought
to discredit girls' claims as emotional overreaction. Daniel argued, "Once
they found this thing that could take the blame—that is that there were
gender problems—they sort of gave up. They just got frustrated and gave
up." Mark contrasted the response of a male peer who had missed a class
to that of a female peer. Asking for help, Mark argued that his male peer
responded "by saying, 'Okay, can you give me the example, take me
through it and see if I can understand it.' Whereas, the girl called me, had
a fit on the phone, was completely confused." Mark painted an image of his
male peer as a person who took a logical, efficacious approach to solving
two problems: the problem of having missed a class and the mathematical
problem. He portrayed his female peer in terms that suggested hysteria ("a
fit") and fuzzy-minded thinking ("completely confused").

In employing a discourse of meritocracy, many boys built a case against
the girls' objections to the pedagogy and curriculum of the advanced class.
They assumed that the girls were performing poorly, an assumption that
was not, according to both teachers and female students, the case. They
then dismissed the girls' critiques as a reflection of diversionary tactics
aimed at focusing blame on others rather than on their behavior. Many
of the boys characterized the girls' behavior in terms of laziness, incompetence, and an unwillingness to pay attention, do work, or ask for help.
Rather than examine the competitive environment of the class as a possible
cause for female students' increasing frustration and in some cases their
retreat from active participation during class time (see also Boaler, 1997),
these boys positioned girls as actively and without reason deciding not to
participate fully in the goals of the course. These boys' accusations diverted
attention away from any systematic analysis of curriculum and pedagogy
to blame individual girls for their disenchantment or disengagement.

By focusing on their *perceptions* of the girls' behavior and ignoring the
context of the class itself and their own behavior, these boys ended the
year with their belief in meritocracy untouched and their suspicions that
female students were unwilling or unable to master advanced math confirmed. Given that City Friends's mission is largely built on meritocratic
beliefs and that there were few opportunities for students to confront those

assumptions, it comes as no surprise that the boys' faith in the system was unshaken by their female peers' critiques. What the boys' defense against difference-talk offers is a window into two very different understandings of educational equity: they defended a view that looks to individual merit as the basis for academic success, while the girls demanded consideration of the ways that schools, by failing to recognize group differences, privilege some groups of students at the expense of others.

*Critiquing the Foundations: Imagining Transformation*
Although it was often difficult to hear above the omnipresent difference-talk and the defensive meritocratic discourse, a fainter discursive current articulated by the girls and some of their male colleagues suggested viewing the source of educational inequality in their math class from a different angle. Shifting away from a focus on gender differences, some students concentrated on the relationship between pedagogy and academic success. Thus, at times, students called into question three critical premises of the curriculum and pedagogy: the value put on individualism, the nature of assessment, and the relationship between the learner and the curriculum. By relocating the problem in specific classroom pedagogies and practices, these students offered some important ideas for creating another framework for educational justice.

At the end of their junior year, the girls had asked the administration to allow them to pursue their senior calculus course as a cooperative peer-run independent study—part of a well-established tradition in their school. Although their plan was rejected, their idea for the course reflected a critique of dominant ways of teaching and learning math. Rather than continue in a class premised on a more individualistic model of teaching and learning, these girls, along with some of their male peers, argued that the type of mathematical thinking required by advanced calculus was more conducive to group problem solving. For example, Gary stated that in the last two years the curriculum had taken a conceptual shift, one that demanded that students understand mathematics at a more theoretical problem-solving level. Gary argued:

> These are the kinds of problems I should be working on in small groups—problems that are new and unfamiliar. You know sometimes it's great to work on it by myself and I feel good when I figure something out like that ... But when I was actually using it at such an advanced level that I was sort of conjuring things up that might have been helpful if I could have asked Rob what he thought about it. And maybe he saw something that I didn't see and I'd see something he didn't see.

Gary suggested that collaborative learning held possibilities for a deeper understanding of mathematics through sharing a variety of perspectives to solve problems. This is not a radical proposal for many educational contexts, especially in mathematics reform efforts (Boaler, 1997; National Council of Teachers of Mathematics, 1989), but it represented a serious departure from the norm in the students' math class. The course's agenda—to plough through a broad field of calculus at a rapid pace in preparation for the AP exams—in combination with an environment supporting some students' individualistic, competitive styles, had made questioning, deep exploration and collaboration next to impossible.

Janie, making a similar argument to Gary, went even further to call into question the premise of individual evaluation. Speaking of times when her needs were met in the math course, Janie recalled:

> I remember one class we had a test that I think people answered one out of four problems. That was sort of the average was that no one got any of it. We decided to just do it in class. Marilyn [the teacher] didn't give us back the test; we just did the problems. And I remember coming away from that thinking, "God, why can't I take every test as a collaborative effort" because it just—when I came away I just really understood the problems because I had contributed what I knew and this person next to me contributed what they knew and we had our combined learning. And I think learning in small groups is always helpful for me.

As each person contributed her perspective, each individual was valued and knowledge became a possession of the entire group. Thus, underneath Janie's plea to take all her tests as a collaborative effort lies a radical, though unarticulated, idea to destroy the keystone of educational architecture built on individual achievement. Janie's idea suggests a different educational goal: that every student, as part of a community, develop an understanding of the material. This goal is fundamentally at odds with goals of the norm-referenced AP examinations that, by definition, rank students individually and hierarchically.

In addition to proposing that collaboration rather than competition might serve as the basis for a successful math class, some students offered a significant re-conceptualization of the relationship between curriculum and learner. Students suggested that to develop a math curriculum and pedagogy that could meet the needs of a diverse group of students, teachers must develop relationships with them that reflected deep knowledge of who they were as learners. Hannah spoke of feeling invisible and unknown by her math teachers:

I have never really felt that my math teachers had a sense of who I am as a student at all, and could describe me the way, say, an English teacher could. I understand there's a difference 'cause I'm continually writing for an English teacher or a history teacher. But there shouldn't be that huge of a chasm between the way a math teacher knows me and the way every other one of my teachers knows me.

Underneath this desire to be known is a certain view of curriculum that suggests there is an important connection between who one is as a learner and the material to be learned. This differs significantly from a more traditional perspective that conceptualizes mathematics as a body of knowledge existing "out there" which can be acquired by students without attention to any variety in preferred approaches to learning or particular interests (see, for example, Chapman, 1993).

In listening below the surface of the call for recognition, we can hear another framework for imagining more equitable classrooms, one through which some students challenged the pedagogy and practices of math classes to become more inclusive of a range of learners. Furthermore, this framework argued for classes that would support and reward collaboration, questioning, and curiosity rather than competition and right answers. Attending to the types of interactions between student and teacher, student and student, and student and curriculum, this discursive undercurrent began to unveil the dominant values and assumptions that had drawn the boundaries of practice, thereby opening those practices to the possibility of renegotiation. Focusing their initial claims for educational equity on a need for recognition of group differences, students' critiques led them to a deeper interrogation of the relationship between particular pedagogical practices and inequitable academic outcomes. They began to locate the problem of inequality, not in embodied group differences, but in the relationships of power produced by specific educational practices.

## The Power and Pitfalls of Recognition as a Justice Claim

In June 2005, the school district of Philadelphia announced a new requirement for high school students: a yearlong course in African and African-American history. The decision provoked an array of public responses, local and national. Supporters viewed the course as a welcome corrective to a long-neglected area of study. They argued that, given the history of race in the United States and the particular and extensive influences African and African-American cultures have had on the nation, this course was important for all citizens and was a particularly significant decision for a school district with a student population that is nearly two-thirds

African-American. Some advocates suggested that the course would benefit African-American students by improving their self-awareness and self-esteem.

Detractors argued that the course was unfair, representing special attention to one group of citizens. The decision drew political fire from conservative politicians and commentators. The Republican state assembly speaker asked the school district to remove the new requirement. He argued that the course was "unnecessary" and suggested that the school district focus on having students "master basic reading, writing and arithmetic" (Snyder, 2005) Scholars debated the merits and limitations of teaching African-American history as a separate course or integrating the history of African-Americans more fully into the general U.S. history curriculum. That one course—implemented nearly four decades after a group of students demonstrated to demand African and African-African American studies courses—should provoke this level of contention speaks to the disruptive power inherent in the claim for recognition.

The demand for recognition in the curriculum and the debates that have ensued have a long history in U.S. education. The controversy over one required course in Philadelphia public schools represents the ongoing struggles in U.S. education to have schools reflect the diversity of society. From the early battles over German language education and the Catholic objection to the use of the King James Bible in public schools, to contemporary debates about single-sex schools, deaf education, bilingual education, Afrocentric curriculum, or the inclusion of gay/lesbian/bisexual/transgender issues in the curriculum, educational institutions continue to confront recognition as an organizing principle for justice. Moreover, standardized curricula and textbooks can lead to heightened demands for recognition because they tend to ignore the histories and experiences of particular local groups. For example, at the same time that the school district of Philadelphia was implementing its new history requirement, it was facing criticism from an array of local community groups angered by the fact that the new core curriculum and the textbooks adopted by the city did not accurately or adequately reflect their constituencies (Davis, 2004). In diverse societies across the world, educational institutions are being challenged to recognize and attend to—to focus on, rather than gloss over—differences of race, ethnicity, gender, sexuality, and disability.

Questions about how to practice from this stance of recognition are critically important to contemporary debates about educational equity. The lessons from City Friends hold broad implications for schools building equitable practices around the claim for recognition. At City Friends, framing justice claims around group recognition offered practitioners and students an important discursive space within which to challenge the assimilationist approaches—represented in the justice claim for integration—that ignored rather than focused on difference. From a stance of recognition, practitioners and students advocated equitable practices that were responsive, rather than indifferent, to difference. These students and practitioners insisted that education that remained focused on individual achievement obscured the vested interests embedded in the school's curriculum, pedagogy, and social organization. Organizing justice claims around recognition made visible the ways the dominant institutional practices reflected particular interests and, as such, were exclusionary. Group identity offered practitioners and students a powerful site for resistance.

The road from resistance to institutional changes was slow and uneven. For the girls, little changed in their math education, but they developed new interpretive frames through which to give voice to their experiences. They were ultimately unable to effect necessary changes, but they were able to refuse to view their education through the lens of meritocracy and were able to name the inequities inherent in their mathematics education. Moreover, their story, together with the results of the gender survey the school had conducted in which a majority of girls reported that math was their least favorite subject, made gender inequalities in mathematics education more visible to the school's practitioners. Anti-racist, activist teachers and administrators clearly expressed that City Friends was a long way from being the equitable environment they sought. Recognizing the race and class interests of the school, they doubted that it would ever truly get there; however, they also marked important institutional changes they had implemented in administration, hiring, curriculum, and social support for students of color. They insisted on the importance of continually working for racial justice.

Resistance framed around recognition and identity had a critical impact at City Friends, making audible a discourse beyond the assimilationist stance that had evolved from integration. At the same time, in this chapter, I have tried to point to some of the limitations inherent in focusing claims for equity around group identities. In exploring the challenges to pedagogy and curriculum at City Friends, I have put flesh to theoretical arguments about the limitations of focusing on group differences as the starting point for developing equitable educational practices (McCarthy, 1993a; McCarthy and Crichlow, 1993; McLaren, 1994; Minow, 1990; Sleeter, 1996). If, for example, we begin from the position that girls learn differently from boys, what are the implications for building equitable practice? One obvious implication is that we separate girls and boys, and teach them accordingly. In both independent and public school settings, single-sex schools or classrooms (particularly in math and science) offer one strategy for remedying gender inequalities (see American Association of University

Women, 1998; Datnow and Hubbard, 2002; Phillips, 1998; Riordan, 2002). Single-sex schools may, as supporters argue, address a number of issues that contribute to the reduction of gender inequalities, including increased resources, higher curricular standards, leadership opportunities, and improved school climate (for an overview of arguments on both sides, see Campbell and Sanders, 2002).

However, there are also multiple arguments to be made against single-sex classrooms as a remedy for educational inequality. (Is segregation inherently unequal? Are all girls or all boys truly alike?) The most important of these arguments, I believe, addresses the question of the cultural production of gender and power. The problem for the female students in their calculus class was not simply that girls learn differently from boys. It was that the norms, values, and assumptions of that classroom produced inequitable opportunities and outcomes that were structured along the lines of gender. The girls' "difference" left unexamined the boys' accrual of mathematical skills and knowledge.

In an analogous way, focusing curriculum on the literature and history of marginalized racial and ethnic groups did little to shift the dominant base of white power at City Friends. There are two key problems inherent in organizing resistance to domination around subordinated group identities. First, notions of race/ethnicity are positioned in particular bodies and not others. Race/ethnicity is viewed, not as social processes in which we all participate, but as the sole property and province of people of color (Dominguez, 1992; McCarthy, 1990; McCarthy and Crichlow, 1993; Omi and Winant, 1986). Many white students and practitioners did not perceive a role for themselves in the discussions of race/ethnicity because they did not see whiteness (Fine, 1997; Frankenberg, 1993; McLaren, 1994). There is a dialogic process to racial/ethnic oppression that is obfuscated by a focus on subordinated groups.

Second, educational theorists have, rightly I would say, cautioned against multicultural discourse that positions certain bodies within the academy (bodies of individuals and texts) to suggest that racial subordination is no longer an obstacle to equity (Carby, 1992; Dominguez, 1992; McCarthy, 1990, 1993b; McLaren, 1994; Mohanty, 1989–90). This dynamic was at work in the charges of the white senior boys and the white seventh grade students that the school had gone "overboard" with diversity. From their perspective, representation may have signaled that racial/ethnic oppression no longer exists. Moreover, this visible recognition of traditionally marginalized groups did not push many white students or practitioners to examine the ways they continued to accrue power from the dominant institutional arrangements of schooling (Fine, 1997). My question, then, is how do we, as practitioners, develop resistance strategies that focus our gaze squarely on the dynamic *production* of power and privilege—on the *politics of difference* rather than on the bodies of those defined as different.

In no way do I want to imply that it is the responsibility of subordinated and marginalized groups to adopt a discourse or political strategies that bring dominant groups along in the process of debunking power. Recognition, I suggest, can offer a powerful grounding from which to practice for equity because it entails making visible the ways the hidden norms and assumptions guiding existing educational curricula and pedagogy represent the particular, situated knowledge and experiences of dominant societal groups. However, the power of this justice claim can be limited by its assumptions about difference. I want to challenge discourse that focuses on differences between groups without making visible the permeable and interrelated nature of these group boundaries. Rather than organizing justice claims around the differences between girls and boys, or students of color and white students, if we are to confront inequities, we must ask how the dominant values and assumptions of our educational system produce and perpetuate the success of some at the expense of others. We must reframe the debate to interrupt the tendency to think about difference in dichotomous terms. We must look at the ways that power and privilege are negotiated in the interaction—the relationship—*between* groups (Fine, 1997; Minow, 1990; Varenne and McDermott, 1998; Young, 1990).

Taking a relational view of difference in education does not answer the deeply contentious questions of how schools can and should "recognize" groups. It does not, for example, resolve the debates for and against single-sex schools. It is most certainly not an argument against curriculum that focuses on the histories, literatures, and experiences of oppressed and marginalized social groups. A relational view of difference, however, takes us out of the zero sum game implied when differences are treated as dichotomous. It asks us, as educators, to focus firmly on the production of power and privilege wherever it occurs and to ask ourselves continually how it is that schools are deeply political, fundamentally implicated in creating the differences that make a difference.

# CHAPTER 5

# The Difference Is in the Relationship: A Framework for Justice

When my daughter was five, she was diagnosed with Type 1 diabetes. Type 1 diabetes results from an autoimmune process in which the insulin-producing cells of the pancreas are destroyed. As a result, people with Type 1 diabetes do not produce the life-sustaining hormone insulin, which regulates blood glucose. From a medical standpoint, managing Type 1 diabetes is viewed primarily as a matter of regulating the ratio of carbohydrate intake to insulin and managing low blood sugars that result from taking insulin. On a social level, it is much more complex, for it demands addressing my daughter's difference in relationship to the human environments in which she lives—environments in which meals are a communal activity and concentrated sweets are ubiquitous.

It was clear to me from the first moment that my daughter returned to kindergarten after her diagnosis that, as a parent advocating for a child with a medical disability, the stance I took toward difference would matter greatly. One approach, perhaps the most obvious one, would have been to focus on her physiological disability and to understand the "problem of difference" as an individual one, making the fewest possible demands on the school community. The simplest way to manage her diabetes would be to pack her snacks and lunch daily and to provide special treats that she could eat when the classroom had birthdays or holiday celebrations.

This solution would make it reasonably easy to calculate my daughter's insulin requirements; however, it would also burden her with the sole responsibility for the challenge her difference posed. She would be constantly marked as different, excluded from routine classroom activities such as the sharing of daily snacks and lunches and the pleasure of special foods on festive occasions. Framing difference as a relational issue offered an alternate solution—one that, while more difficult to implement, privileged substantive inclusion in the community as the reigning value. I asked my daughter's teachers to reconsider their classroom practices—how they served snacks to children, how they supervised the playground,[1] and what kinds of snacks parents sent in for special celebrations—to ensure that my daughter could participate in the normal routine activities of kindergarten. Essentially, they had to consider how the normative practices of the classroom were structured for people without diabetes.

Taking a relational stance toward difference means shifting from thinking about diabetes only in terms of the difference my daughter brings to the classroom, to thinking about how the classroom is structured without diabetic children in mind. Thinking about difference from a relational standpoint not only demands that teachers unmask assumptive frameworks that exclude some individuals or groups; it also requires that the community make the substantive inclusion of all its members a primary value, whatever that takes in terms of reconfiguring practice. This is no small task.

I do not tell this story to suggest that the problems of educational inequality would be simple to solve if we would only take a relational stance toward difference. Nor do I wish to imply that being left out of the routines of classroom meals and special celebrations represents an inequality of comparable weight or consequence to the educational inequalities that are the effects of the systematic oppression of people on the basis of race/ethnicity, gender, class, disability, and sexuality. Although the risks of getting it wrong when dealing with the difference of diabetes are extremely serious because of the health consequences, it is obviously easier to change classroom practices to accommodate dietary needs than it is to fundamentally transform curriculum, pedagogy, and policy to address the more complex issues of educational injustice that follow from the seemingly intractable social inequalities that constrain the economic, social, cultural, and political opportunities of so many people. However, my story of advocating for a child with a medical disability illuminates four key observations about educational justice that cut across the argument I make in this book.

First, inclusion in an educational community must be substantive. The teachers need not have made any changes to include my daughter as a student in their classroom, but she would not then have been a full member of the community, able to participate in all the routine and special activities of the group. Substantive inclusion depends on my second and third observations: that we must simultaneously focus on the equality of all members in the community and recognize their differences. This focus certainly drove the advocacy position I took. The stance that my daughter must be valued as an equal member of the classroom community led me to the conclusion that there would be no acceptable reason for excluding her from any of the routine activities of the classroom. However, being an equal member of the classroom required focusing on, rather than ignoring her difference, and doing so from a relational perspective. In the case of a child with diabetes, the dangers of refusing to acknowledge difference are direct and obvious. More important for my advocacy position, recognizing difference in a way that achieves substantive inclusion requires taking a relational stance toward difference, recognizing the ways that her exclusion follows from setting up the classroom without diabetic children in mind.

Finally, my fourth observation is that when we take a relational stance toward difference, everyone is included in the process of change, often with clear benefits for all. In the case of my daughter, the changes required to include her in the routines of the community led to a healthier diet for everyone and fostered a climate in which other children felt equally involved in creating an inclusive environment, without either ignoring or stigmatizing her difference.

In what follows, I bring these four observations back to Parks and City Friends and suggest how we, as educators, can think about difference in ways that move us toward real possibilities for enacting justice in everyday practice.

## Substantive Inclusion: The Ethical Cornerstone of Practicing for Educational Equity

Substantive inclusion in the school community—the capacity to participate fully, and to contribute meaningfully to all its activities—should be the aim of educational justice. The presumption of substantive inclusion requires a broad definition of justice, one that ultimately aims at substantive inclusion into society at large. This definition encompasses the essential goals of equal educational opportunities and outcomes—the most common ways that public discourse frames educational equity (see, for overviews, Coleman, 1968; Howe, 1997). However, it also suggests that other aspects of our humanity are important in classrooms, schools, and, by extension, society. Recognition—having one's group affiliations fully acknowledged and included—and being equally valued as an active member of the community are components of a fair and just education. A narrower definition of educational equity—one that focuses on academic opportunities or outcomes alone—is not sufficiently encompassing. A broader framework—one based on inclusion with its sense of valuing each individual learner and each group and acknowledging their particular needs, values, and perspectives—must be at the center of practicing for equity.

The question of substantive inclusion—of how to create opportunities for all students to be active, contributing members of the educational community—troubled practitioners at both Parks and City Friends. All three of the justice claims discussed in this book were driven by a commitment to expanding inclusion in the educational community, and each raised questions about what constituted real (substantive) inclusion. Of the three, integration is most directly about including students who had previously been excluded by policy or neglect. The justice claim for equal standards is also about inclusion; it is about guaranteeing that all students, rather than just a few, receive an education of high quality. Recognition is about inclusion effected through the acknowledgment of difference. Recognition acts as a corrective to the exclusion wrought by refusing to see differences—differences that entail values, norms, knowledge, and experiences.

Inclusion must be substantive to serve the purposes of equity. As the examples from City Friends and Parks make clear, integration, defined in terms of expanding educational access but without a concomitant institutional transformation, makes it difficult, if not impossible, for people to be included as full participants in the educational community: They may sit in classrooms from which they were formerly excluded, but they find themselves unable to learn or contribute as equals. As a justice claim, equal standards aims to set high academic standards for all students, regardless of race/ethnicity, socioeconomic status, language community, gender, or disability. However, as Parks's experience demonstrates, for students to experience fully the power of academic achievement and be truly included in the educational community, we must interrogate the values, norms, and assumptions embedded in academic standards and pedagogical approaches. As a justice claim, recognition offers a much stronger foundation for substantive inclusion. Acknowledging multiple perspectives, knowledge, values, and norms represented in the community allows people to participate in substantive, meaningful ways—to be full members of the community.

Thinking about educational justice in terms of substantive inclusion supports the goal of creating classrooms that are diverse *and* just; however, it also leaves open the possibility that, at times, equity might in fact be served through programs created by and for groups that have faced oppression in the broader society. Examples include math and science courses designed for girls and women, African and African-American centered schools, bilingual/bicultural education programs that give equal status to students' home language, and schools for deaf children. Given a society saturated with inequalities, these kinds of programs are intended to eliminate the conditions of domination and oppression (see Young, 1990) that limit some students' opportunities to exercise their full capacities as active, contributing members of the learning community.

This is not to say that educational equity should be, or is always, realized through these kinds of programs. As an educator, I am committed to figuring out how we can build classrooms and schools that are diverse and equitable; however, at times, the conditions of social inequality may make this dream a difficult one to realize. Substantive inclusion sets a standard for equity that requires us to think broadly about what participation as a fully valued, equal, contributing member of a society entails. Thinking about substantive inclusion suggests that constructing strategies for educational justice requires attending to young people's fundamental equality and their differences simultaneously. This brings me to my second and third points.

## Equality of Each Member of the Community

The assumption that every child is entitled to full participation in the educational community entails focusing on the equal moral value of all people. It may seem absurd to have to make this premise explicit, yet many educational and by extension social inequalities can be understood to derive, at least in part, from a fundamental failure to focus on the moral equivalence of all people. The history of de jure racial segregation in the United States was based on a refusal to accord all children equal status as human beings. If de jure segregation reflected an egregious violation of the commitment to the equivalence of all people, it exposed the fundamental injustices of all policies that lead to practices of exclusion. In opposing legal segregation, civil rights activists created a language through which, for example, social activists could fight against discrimination on the basis of gender and disability from the premise of universal equality. I would argue, too, that the failure in the United States to commit equal resources to the education of all children (Kozol, 1991, 2005) is another manifestation of this refusal to accord each child equal moral value. The rhetoric of local control and the language of some economic analysis suggesting that "money doesn't matter" (see, for example, Hanushek, 1997, 2003) are often used to justify these disparities; however, the refusal in most states to fund the education of all children on an equal basis indicates a social policy that does not accord all children equal moral weight.

Disparities in the quality of education that different communities receive—disparities that coincide with structural inequalities of race/ethnicity, socioeconomic class, gender, and disability—are also suggestive of this problem. There has been a well-documented, widespread, and persistent failure to provide a majority of students from low-income families, students from oppressed racial/ethnic groups, and students labeled with disabilities with opportunities reflective of the best educational practices (see, for a few examples, Anyon, 1980; Gartner and Lipsky, 1987; Lipman, 1998, 2004; Oakes, 1985; Olsen, 1997). These differences in educational opportunities, which serve to perpetuate the inequalities of our society, are supported ideologically through a denial of the moral equivalence of all learners, of all humans. There is a failure to acknowledge that all people are deserving of a liberating education: one that acknowledges our most basic desire and shared human capacity to make and re-make, in our own distinctive ways, a life's story/work.

Here, I draw on the work of Patricia Carini, who writes of "humanness and the valuing of humanness as the starting point for education" (2001, p. 1).[2] For Carini, this humanness entails a shared capacity of all people, found in the works of young people everywhere. She writes:

> It is in just this sense that the works that children make are both ordinary—and extraordinary. They reflect a widely distributed capacity to be makers and doers, active agents in the world and their lives; to be, as Jay Featherstone said, poets of their lives. (2001, p. 20)

An education that begins from the premise of this "widely distributed capacity to be makers and doers" is one that does not tolerate narrow, deadening, limited, and limiting curriculum and pedagogy for any child. If we start from the premise of the universal equivalence of all humans as makers and doers, recognizing the desire in all people to make meaning of, and take action in, the world, then all children deserve an education that fosters each child's passions and interests and develops the knowledge, skills, and competencies for her full participation in society. Focusing on the fundamental equality of all persons, then, is not a denial of difference; rather, it entails an observation about what we all share as human beings— this impulse to make and make sense of our world through myriad different expressions. This stance holds profound implications for educational practice. Importantly, it offers a way to speak back to the discourses about difference that frame some students as deficient. Discourses about difference that have a tenacious hold on educational thinking—those that view some children as "low ability" or point to disabilities as "deficits" or perceive some groups as "culturally deprived"—all serve to deny the equal moral value of persons.

A commitment, then, to the fundamental equality of all persons is critical to notions of educational equity and carries various implications for educational policies and practices. It rested at the heart of many of the decisions implemented at City Friends and Parks. The Quaker spiritual belief that "there is that of God in everyone"—a commitment to the universal equality of all humans—challenged City Friends to confront its exclusionary practices and work toward creating a racially diverse community. Parks's decision to dismantle special education classes and build inclusive educational practices for all children led practitioners to focus on the moral equivalence of all learners, and by doing so, to speak out against the practice of segregating and separating students labeled with disabilities. At Parks, standards-based reforms also signaled a belief in the equal capacity of all learners in the sense of which Carini speaks. Beginning from this premise of equality, practitioners focused their efforts on developing a set of equal standards aimed at providing a rich, challenging, and meaningful education for all students. However, as I have shown throughout the chapters on integration and equal standards, one risk in focusing on equality is that it is equated with sameness and a denial of difference.

As a justice claim, recognition avoids this pitfall. Recognition also entails a belief in the equal value of all persons and by extension the social groups to which they belong. In the case of recognition, however, acknowledging the moral equality of all persons implies a need to value the different norms, perspectives, experiences, and so on, that individuals bring by virtue of their membership in social groups. Recognition suggests that a commitment to valuing each person equally does not always imply that justice is best served by treating everyone the same. In fact, recognition indicates that according each person equal moral value may require different treatment to create the kind of liberatory education of which Carini speaks: "an education that recognizes each as an ordinary person, a self-in-the-making, a maker of work." (2001, p. 52)

## Framing Difference from a Relational Perspective

My third point, then, is that to be able to act upon our commitments to this fundamental equality of all humans we must focus on, rather than ignore, difference, and we must do so from a relational perspective. As activists for racial, ethnic, gender, sexuality and disability equity have argued, refusing to *recognize* difference—to acknowledge varied perspectives, experiences, knowledge, values, ways of learning, and so forth—does irreparable harm to students who are excluded from meaningful participation in learning environments as a consequence of the failure on the part of those institutions to own up to ways that educational curriculum, practices, and policies reflect the particular vested interests of dominant social groups. Of the three justice claims I have examined, recognition is the only one that begins from the premise that educational equity requires that we, as educators, attend carefully to difference.

I agree that this attention to difference is one critical component of educational equity. However, I caution us to think carefully about how we frame our understandings of how differences come to make the difference that they do in educational settings. Parks and City Friends offer concrete examples of how educational discourse about difference tends toward a view of difference as located in the biology of the body or the "culture" of particular groups. It usually seeks to remedy the inequalities that accrue along the lines of difference by focusing attention primarily on those marked as different—on those people marginalized by the existing social order. Despite plentiful cogent critiques (see, for a few examples, Fine, 1997; Erickson, 1987; Varenne and McDermott, 1998), this essentialized view of difference has a tenacious hold on educational discourses. It offers an explanation for apparent learning "deficits" as exemplified by the medical discourse of disability we heard expressed at Parks. At the same time, it is employed to advocate that, for equity to be achieved, different groups of students should be educated in different ways to accommodate these cultural/biological differences, as we saw most clearly in the case of the girls at City Friends. These examples from Parks and City Friends reflect a much broader tendency in educational discourse to focus attention primarily on those individuals and groups that stand outside the assumed norm and to reify differences as properties of individual people or groups. Examples abound. There is an economy built around testing, identifying, and labeling children with learning disabilities; popular and research literature continues to search for gender differences in learning; some approaches to multicultural education seek to identify differences in learning styles and values attributed to various cultural communities.

This discourse of difference, I suggest, severely constrains the possibilities for educational equity. Focusing on differences that make a difference in education as if they were located in particular bodies/groups, rather than in the relationships of difference created by the arrangement of institutions—relationships that are political in the most fundamental sense that they produce distributions of power—is dangerous. It tends to lead us to wonder about either the "deficits" or the particular needs of some groups of people and not see the power afforded, by the reigning practices of schools and society, to people who are not marked as different. I suggest it is critical not only that we attend to difference, but that we interrogate our discourses about difference. It is only by viewing difference in relational terms that we can illuminate how particular arrangements of schooling and society make certain differences significant and not others (Minow, 1990; Varenne and McDermott, 1998). Difference is best understood as a marker of a political relationships set up through everyday institutional practices (Erickson, 1987; Fine, 1997).

Understanding difference from a relational perspective requires interrogating and reimagining our most basic assumptions about educational practice and policy. A relational view of difference does not mean denying the existence of differences (those that are truly biological like medical disabilities or those biologically arbitrary markers that come to hold significance through historical and contemporary regimes of power, like racial classifications). It does mean examining how differences become differences that matter only in relation to institutional norms and practices that often remain unexamined. Asking how the routine practices of schools and classrooms preclude the full participation of some children (and guarantee that of others) makes it possible to take the full weight of difference off those who are burdened by oppression and ensure their real inclusion in the community. Focusing on the ways that individual and group differences become a "problem" only in relationship to existing routines, norms and values opens up the possibility for creating classrooms and schools that are just.

## A Relational View of Difference: Including Everyone in the Process of Change

My fourth point is that taking a relational view of difference as the founding premise for building equitable educational practices demands reorganizing institutional practices and redistributing power in ways that involve the entire community in the process of change. It means interrogating the hidden values and norms buried in taken-for-granted educational practices and exploring how these most basic assumptions allow some students to accrue knowledge, skills, credentials, and power at the expense of others. The examples from both schools suggest that what we teach and how we teach reflect important decisions of the schools and society in which we live, and of the schools and society that educators committed to social justice hope to create.

At times, there are obvious benefits for everyone in the community when educators take a relational stance toward difference. All students benefit educationally from a more accurate, encompassing account of, for example, U.S. history—the kind of account that Donald, Eugene, and Cynthia implemented at City Friends. Certainly, as we saw in Martha Silverman's classroom at Parks, all students, not only those labeled with disabilities, can benefit from educational practices that allow for a broad range of expression and diverse paths for inquiry.

However, taking a relational stance toward difference often results in conflict and struggle as those who benefit from the existing relations of power resist the threat to their supremacy. We should understand, for example, the resentment on the part of white students and male students at City Friends to the attempts to change the Eurocentric curriculum or the AP calculus course as, at least in part, a defensive response to this threat of power redistribution. Across the nation, clashes over educational policies—from desegregation plans to detracking efforts to the introduction of multicultural curricula—reflect the challenges these changes pose to the status quo. Conflict is an inevitable part of the process of transforming education and building truly equitable school communities because those who benefit from the existing social order are unlikely to give up their power without a struggle. Taking a relational stance toward difference does not erase the contentious nature of the process of change. However, it creates a framework within which it is at least possible for everyone to be a part of the solution to educational inequality. When we shift to viewing race, gender, disability, and so forth as markers of relationships between groups of people—relationships that are created within a particular social order—then those relationships must be scrutinized and changed in the quest for justice. Transforming those relationships includes everyone (willingly or unwillingly) in the process of change.

## A Relational Stance in Education: A Framework for Doing Difference Differently

Our framework for understanding difference has concrete consequences for developing policies and practices aimed at realizing educational equity. Taking a relational stance toward difference demands our careful and continual reexamination of the ways that practices and policies, at the level of classrooms, schools, and educational systems, create or limit possibilities for substantive inclusion in particular, local contexts. This stance offers new perspectives on the three justice claims explored in this book. It opens up possibilities for action.

The ideal of building integrated classrooms and schools does not track inevitably into assimilative strategies if, rather than focusing primarily on access as the criterion for inclusion, we interrogate the exclusionary norms, values, and standards of our classrooms and schools. We can hold firmly to the commitment to equal standards in terms of our broadest aims for education—we can construct powerful and empowering learning experiences for all students—if we examine how particular educational practices (curriculum, pedagogies, assessments) invite or, alternately, preclude the full participation of diverse (and by this I mean all) learners. We can heed the call for recognition while avoiding the trap of treating differences as static and essentialized, if we focus on the relationship between groups as the locus for transformative work.

Understanding difference as a relationship challenges our tendency to define the problem of educational inequality as primarily a distributional one (Howe, 1997; see also Galston, 1980; Rawls, 1971; Young, 1990) as one of the unfair distribution of "educational goods" across the lines of social demarcation. Integration and equal standards are justice claims that reflect a call for the fair distribution of educational access, opportunities, and, to different degrees, outcomes. Within this distributive paradigm for justice, educational goods are usually understood to include the processes necessary for students to be empowered to participate fruitfully in their education (see, for critical discussion of distributive paradigms in political theory, Young, 1990). At Parks, for example, educators knew that for all students to be able to benefit from the curriculum they sought to implement—a curriculum based around the accepted standards of disciplinary practices—they would have to figure out how to design pedagogies that would reach youth with diverse skills, knowledge, and experience. City Friends's work to become a more racially and socio-economically diverse school reflected an attempt, albeit one limited by its independent school status, to distribute access to elite education more equitably. Practicing for educational equity demands attention to the fair distribution of educational goods, for without powerful academic tools, the lives of young people are severely circumscribed.

There are, however, serious limitations to thinking about educational equity in terms of distribution alone (see Fraser, 1997). Recognition suggests there are other important goals of a just educational community and challenges the apparent neutrality of the educational goods that are being distributed. Recognition makes visible the ways that curriculum and pedagogies represent the knowledge, values, and experiences of particular social groups. As the stories from City Friends illustrate, justice claims organized around recognition are not seeking a more just distribution of existing educational goods; rather, recognition calls for *different* educational goods that reflect the knowledge, values, and experiences of the group making the demands. Recognition, then, confronts the problematic nature of the distributive paradigm, which risks reproducing inequality because of the loaded nature of the goods to be distributed.

I have argued that recognition is important to educational equity precisely because of the challenge it poses to existing curriculum and pedagogy. However, its capacity to effect educational justice is often limited by its tendency to focus on subordinated groups and ignore the relationships that educational practices set up between dominant and subordinated groups. As Chapter 5 illustrates, we cannot, for example, reconstruct historical narratives to be inclusive of subordinated social groups without simultaneously deconstructing dominant perspectives on the development of the United States. We cannot focus our attention on girls' ways of learning in the math classroom, without attending to how boys silently accrue knowledge and power through the existing arrangements. Thinking about difference as a relationship offers a way to focus our attention on relations of power.

Taking a relational stance insists on examining educational practices in terms of the relationships they produce between groups—relationships that create or limit possibilities for building more equitable schools. This stance does not make distribution irrelevant to justice claims. However, it means looking critically at what is being distributed. Within this framework, it is never enough to focus on increasing access or opportunities without simultaneously asking how the existing arrangements of classrooms and schools preclude or promote the full participation of all students.

As the portraits of City Friends and Parks demonstrate, building just educational communities across the lines of difference is messy, uneven and, given the existing structural inequalities of society, not likely to be fully realized without dramatic changes in the social, political, and economic spheres. There are no easy remedies for persistent educational inequalities; these inequalities are interwoven with the injustices of our society (Anyon, 2005; Varenne and McDermott, 1998). Although schools cannot solve the problems of injustice in our society, they continue to be important sites for social activism—places where a range of justice claims are deliberated and negotiated in and through everyday practices. For educators, students, parents, and activists, local schools remain communities of possibility from which to imagine and work toward a world in which differences do not continue to make the difference they do in our society. Our hope for educational justice depends on understanding that the differences that make a difference in education are markers of relationships that we have created, and as such, can and must undo.

# Appendix: The Research Process

## A Research Stance

My interest in investigating discourses about difference undergirding the work of educators who were actively seeking to build more equitable educational practices led me to Parks Middle School and City Friends. Each school had been recommended to me as a place where interesting inquiry was taking shape around "difference." Within these contexts, I positioned myself in "parallel play" with practitioner inquiry teams that were in the process of researching questions about difference. That is, as practitioners examined particular issues about difference in relationship to building fair educational practices, I investigated the discourses about difference that implicitly and explicitly drove their talk and practices, as well as those that guided institutional policies. Committed to research that supports social change, this project developed out of an affinity for the growing tradition of collaborative, action-oriented, and feminist research (see for example, Erickson, 1994–5; Fine, 1992; Lather, 1992; Schultz, 1991). Fine perhaps best describes the research stance that I took in this study with her analysis of "activist feminist research." This is research that is:

> [C]ommitted to positioning researchers as self-conscious, critical, and participatory analysts, engaged with but still distinct from our informants. Such research commits to the study of change, the move toward change and/or is provocative of change. (1992, 220)

The questions this book addresses grew from my interests and concerns about processes of social change. These questions ran parallel to ones which teachers and administrators in each school were asking about transformative practice in relation to difference. I designed this research to be shaped and informed by, but not restricted to, the questions that practitioners were asking. By perching outside of their processes and looking across sites of social change, I sought to describe the undergirding beliefs and assumptions that influenced that process. Acknowledging that my perspective as an outsider necessarily precludes having the same knowledge as insiders, I hoped that the partial, but different perspective from which I viewed the schools would be informed by, and in turn inform, the work of practitioners. Throughout my research and writing process I shared what I was learning with each school, albeit, as I will describe below, to different extents and in different contexts.

I conducted research for this book over a long time period. I initially did intensive ethnographic research in both schools during the 1995–96 school year and engaged in more focused interviewing from 1996–1998 as I was analyzing and writing up my findings from this stage of the research process. In the spring of 2001, I returned to Parks for six months, conducting focused ethnographic research around the school district's new promotion policy. During the 2002–03 school year, I returned to City Friends, working with the school's committee on racial concerns and conducting follow-up interviews with practitioners.

Over the course of years of research, the data pointed me in a different direction for analysis than the one that first guided my work. In my initial study, which resulted in a dissertation, my analysis focused primarily on the discourses about difference that were in play in the processes of educational reform. It was toward the end of that study that I came to see that these discourses entailed ideas about justice; however, my analysis was a limited one, focusing on the dilemmas of whether equal or different treatment was just. The observation that there were ideas about justice embedded in the practitioners' work led me to consider this issue, analytically in relationship to theoretical literature and public ideas about justice. I conducted more research and re-analyzed my data, teasing apart the three implicit justice claims that guided educators' work. These became the subject of this book.

In what follows, I describe the trajectory of the research process for each setting.

## Parks Middle School

In the spring of 1995, I contacted Melanie Post to discuss the work the school had been doing with the Coalition of Essential Schools as well as their policy of full inclusion of children labeled disabilities. At that time Melanie told me about a grant the school had just received from The Annenberg Institute for School Reform to form Critical Friends Groups

(CFGs) to support practitioners' mutual examination and development of innovative classroom practices. Melanie discussed the faculty's concern that they needed to develop practices that better addressed the learning diversity of their students, a concern that had been heightened with the full inclusion program. Further, she expressed her interest (one she felt would be shared by faculty members) in having an ethnographer present to document and reflect upon the school's work. Having recently completed a collaborative research project with outside ethnographers, parents, teachers and students, Melanie was committed to furthering mutual research relationships between insiders and outsiders. Melanie introduced me to some of the teachers who had been members of the research team. Given everyone's expressed interest in pursuing a relationship, I applied to the school district for permission to enter Parks the following fall as an ethnographic researcher.

In the fall of 1995, I introduced my project and described confidentiality procedures to all of Parks's teachers and administrators during an early faculty meeting. Most practitioners expressed an interest in the project and welcomed me to observe in their classrooms. (Only two teachers, out of a total of 14, were not interested in classroom observations, although they did participate in focus group interviews.) After the faculty had consented to my presence, I began my fieldwork observing at least two days a week at the school. In the first months, I observed broadly in various school contexts: classrooms, faculty meetings, library/lunchroom, hallways, governance council meetings, and so forth. I also shadowed three students from each team throughout a school day. In addition, I had many informal conversations with faculty and administrators about the differences that were salient for them, as well as conversations with students about their experiences at the school. As such, I spent the first several months of my stay absorbing a general, textured feeling for the school culture to generate questions for more focused observation.

What emerged from these observations and conversations confirmed Melanie's perspective that learning diversity was the most explicit concern of teachers in relationship to difference. This issue was particularly heightened for the Stage 2 team where teachers were trying to understand by what criteria to evaluate students for their graduation. Beginning in January, I decided to focus my fieldwork intensively on the work of this team. I concentrated my observations on the classrooms of graduating students and on the Stage 2 team meetings. I spent two full days at Parks each week, and went to the weekly team meeting. During classroom observations, where appropriate, I spoke with students and supported their work on assignments. As often as possible, I would speak at least briefly with teachers following these observations. However, tight time schedules made this more difficult than all of us would have liked. Therefore, at several points during the project, I planned times to meet with the team to discuss general themes I was observing across classrooms and to elicit their feedback.

I interviewed almost every teacher and administrator at Parks.[1] In addition to the feedback meetings I had with the Stage 2 team, I scheduled individual interviews with each team member, as well as with the counselor, principal, and librarian. I conducted focus group interviews with the other two teams of teachers. These individual and group interviews explored practitioners' perspectives on several questions: What types of differences among students seemed salient in the context of school? What did not? How did the interviewee understand the reasons these differences made a difference in educational contexts? What types of institutional and classroom practices supported or constrained the work to create more equitable educational environments for different groups of students? (Interviews at City Friends were focused in the same way.)

I conducted these interviews in a semi-structured manner. I came to the interviews with a set of questions that I wanted to be sure we might address. For example, if participants did not mention the role they believed certain dimensions of difference (for example, gender, or class) played in their school, I would ask them about it. However, these interviews were usually wide ranging conversations in which practitioners pushed the boundaries of the questions in rich and unexpected directions.

At the same time, I began conducting focus group interviews with graduating students to hear their perspectives on the school environment. I interviewed just over 50% of the graduating students (a total of 47 students interviewed). I was interested in how they experienced Parks, and particularly wanted to hear students' perspectives on the conflict and tensions (pervasively apparent throughout my classroom observations) between themselves and their teachers over graduation standards and expectations. These focus groups touched on issues of school reform, academic standards and expectations, peer-peer and peer-teacher social interactions, and racism. I began these groups with very general questions about what students might relay to a friend who was considering coming to Parks. Their answers guided more specific questions. My aim in doing these interviews was to understand how students viewed what was working and not working in terms of the educational reform efforts in which practitioners were engaged.

The CFGs offered another important site for data collection. Over the course of two years, I attended almost every CFG meeting as well as a week-long institute in the summer of 1996. CFGs were new to the school the year I began my fieldwork. The idea behind (as well as the funding for) CFGs came from external sources. CFGs were intended to help practitioners critically and collaboratively examine their practices; the groups were to use specific processes to become "critical friends" to each other. The question of how educational practices might best address a diverse group of learners rested implicitly at the core of the CFG processes. My role in the CFGs was primarily observational. (This was different, as will be discussed subsequently from my role on the Gender Audit Committee.) That is not to say that I was simply an observer in the groups. I was expected and was happy to participate in discussions and specific group processes for examining teachers' work (for example, tuning protocols). At times, I acted as recorder for the group. However, the nature of the work (examining classroom practices), and the fact that these groups had a difficult time working up their momentum, in part due to numerous cancellations of professional development days because of weather-related emergencies, meant that I did not play the role initially anticipated. I had hoped to engage with practitioners in collaborative data analysis about their process.

In addition to observations and interviews, site documents were another important data source for understanding discourse about difference. I collected Parks's statements of philosophy, written material that the faculty had developed to define curriculum, content and performance standards, samples of narrative reports on student progress, newsletters, etc. These documents helped me understand how for example, "fair" educational practices were being defined (for example, equal standards for all students); they held implicit discourses about difference (for example, narrative reports indicating theories about choice, see Chapter 4).

From 1996–1998, as I was analyzing and writing up the initial study, I continued to observe CFGs (that first year) and I met with teachers and administrators to share my developing analyses and conduct follow-up interviews with them. The nature of the demands on the faculty's professional development time precluded me from having the opportunity to make a presentation of the research to the full faculty.

Funded by a School Reform Planning Grant from the Spencer Foundation, Jolley Christman, Ellen Foley (colleagues of mine at the time), and I returned to Parks in the 2000–01 school year to conduct a focused study to examine, from students' perspectives, a new mandate from the school district that made eighth grade graduation dependent on two high-stakes requirements: meeting proficiency requirements on a multidisciplinary project and a standardized test. During the spring semester, we conducted intensive participant observation at the school, and interviewed teachers, administrators and students about their experiences with the graduation requirements. For this study, we brought together Parks's principal and four of the teachers with whom I had worked closely during my dissertation research to help us design the study and analyze the data. In this study,

Parks's practitioners were, as ever, concerned with questions about how to address students' learning diversity, especially in a reform context that was narrowing the measures for assessment. Moreover, as we all discovered through the process of data analysis, the students felt the assessments, especially the standardized tests, were poor measures of their learning.

At the time of this second study, I was beginning to tease apart my analysis of the justice claims undergirding practitioners' work. I was able to share some initial thoughts about the contradictions of equal standards with the practitioners who joined our team in our analysis. They resonated with the problematic nature of trying to acknowledge and attend to students' learning diversity and create an environment that provided rich and empowering educational experiences for all. Unfortunately, by the time I had finished my analysis of the three claims and completed a full draft of this book, the teachers and the principal with whom I had worked intensively at Parks had retired or moved on and I was unable to contact them again.

## City Friends

In the spring of 1995, a research colleague of mine proposed that I meet with City Friends's director of curriculum, Mike Knight. Aware that the school was grappling with questions about race and ethnicity, and in addition had recently launched a Gender Audit Committee to research gender issues, she suggested I might find City Friends interested in building a collaborative research relationship. I met with Mike Knight who was at the time completing his first year at City friends; this was also his first year as an administrator. Mike's philosophical orientation and his growing understanding of the professional culture at City Friends left him committed to fostering practitioner inquiry as the foundation for educational change. Mike was therefore interested in my presence in the school as a way to support the climate of inquiry that he was seeking to develop.

In August, Mike set up a time for us to meet with the head of school and the middle school principal to discuss the proposed research project. With their approval to proceed, I was introduced briefly to the entire faculty on the first day of the school year. I then scheduled times to discuss the project in more detail with members of the upper, middle, and lower school faculties, as well as with the Gender Audit Committee. At these meetings, I described the project, solicited interested faculty members to seek me out, and described confidentiality agreements.

The Gender Audit Committee was, from the start, one critical site for this research. I attended and documented all of their meetings from the fall of 1995 through the spring of 1997. The following year, the committee was writing its report, and I returned in the spring of 1998 to collaborate in planning and presenting their work to the faculty at large. The Gender Audit Committee at City Friends was charged with the task of doing research about students' experiences in relation to gender, with attention to potential differences across racial groups. During the year before the beginning of my fieldwork, the committee had discussed some of the larger troubling questions about gender and education, and had developed a plan to begin their study. I entered the process at the point where two subcommittees were designing research protocols. Therefore, the committee members asked me to help them think through aspects of the research design. Although never fully "of" the committee, over the course of my work at City Friends, I suggested approaches to the research design, helped with data analysis, and participated in planning and presenting at a school-wide in-service day about the report. I also shared with the committee some of the work I had been doing around gender and math in the upper school. Thus, in contrast to my role at Parks with the CFGs, I was engaged on the Gender Audit Committee in a more collaborative research relationship.

At City Friends, I initially spent a few days in each of the three divisions to gain a general feeling for the climate of the school. I decided quickly, however, to focus my observations primarily on the middle school for two reasons. First, in a study that was broad in scope, it created points of similarity with Parks. At the same time, the middle school was both a site of experimentation (as teachers had recently been organized into teams) and an important place where questions about race and gender were coming into focus for faculty and administrators. By early January, I had decided to focus my work further on the seventh grade team as the teachers were both interested in my presence and were actively pursuing questions about difference, most specifically race and ethnicity. In addition, as described in Chapter 5, the English and history teachers had designed an interdisciplinary multicultural study of the United States. I spent two days a week observing in the classrooms of the Core 7 teachers (English, History, Math, and Science); however, because I structured some of my observations around shadowing specific students, I also attended the rich range of classes in which they were enrolled (art, Quakerism, group process, Spanish, etc.). As was true at Parks, I often spoke with students or helped them with their work, where appropriate; I had conversations with teachers about the observations when time allowed for such discussions.

Although the middle school was the primary site for my classroom observations, from the beginning of my fieldwork, I was involved with the 12th-grade advanced calculus course. As described in Chapter 5, questions about gender had become salient for that group. Mike Knight and Marilyn Davis (the calculus teacher) had expressed an interest in having me observe the class as a possible means to help understand the dynamics of that group. Therefore, I began attending the calculus course early in the fall of 1995. In the winter, Cheryl Andrews, another math teacher, approached me about her ninth grade algebra class. She was concerned about the dynamics of the course in relation to questions about race and class. Although it was highly unusual for City Friends, half of the students in this class were white, and the other half were students of color. Almost every white student in the course had, in their eighth grade year, been in the lower track that did a pre-algebra curriculum; nearly every student of color was new to the school and had come from institutions that did not offer algebra to eighth graders. Most of the students of color in that class were Community Scholars. Cheryl felt that there were many unspoken tensions in the class between white students and their new peers (around self-esteem as well as cultural styles, race, and racism), as well as conflicts between white students and herself as an African-American woman. At Cheryl's request, I began attending her class and discussing with her the dynamics I observed. It was through these observations that I was introduced to high school students of color and began discussions with them that later led to the formal interviews I conducted with students of color in grades 9–12.

At the same time that I was documenting classroom practices and the meetings of the Gender Audit Committee, I began interviewing practitioners. I interviewed members of the Gender Audit Committee (eight out of ten), all four members of the Core 7 team, ten upper school teachers, the head of school, director of curriculum, the middle school principal, and four other key administrators. These interviews were focused in the same fashion as those at Parks to gain a better understanding of how these practitioners viewed the issue of "difference" in their school setting.

I also conducted focus group interviews with seventh grade students, with high school students of color, and with the entire senior calculus class (a total of 68 students). Focus groups with seventh graders were structured in a similar manner to those at Parks and were aimed at soliciting their perspectives on the curriculum, pedagogy, and general environment at City Friends. Group and individual interviews with students of color were also wide-ranging, but we mostly focused on their experiences as students of color. With the senior calculus class, I interviewed all the girls early in the year to hear their ideas about what had occurred during the previous school year and what they were currently experiencing in their class. Their perspectives proved interesting and insightful, and I invited them to speak to a graduate class in multicultural education that I was teaching at the time. Toward the end of their senior year, Mike Knight, Marilyn Davis, Alex Worth (the math department chair), and I conducted single-gender focus group interviews with all of the students in the course. We then brought the whole class together to reflect upon the perspectives we had heard in each group.

As was the case at Parks, I collected many documents at City Friends that provided critical data on how difference was framed at the institution. Documents from the multicultural assessment plan (MAP), the long-range planning committee, the Community Scholars program, the school's statement of philosophy, harassment policies, newsletter, faculty meeting notes, etc., were all sources for analyzing discourses about difference and approaches to building fair practices.

As I had at Parks, from 1996–1998, I returned to City Friends to share observations and conduct follow-up interviews. I also worked with the Gender Audit Committee on a presentation and workshops for the entire faculty about the research we had conducted. My research with the senior class also informed that process.

In the 2002–03 school year, I returned to City Friends to work with the school's Committee on Racial Concerns and to conduct key interviews with faculty and administrators. By that point in time, I had written an early draft of this book organized around the theme of the justice claims. The racial concerns committee, a subcommittee of the School Committee (the Quaker school equivalent of a school board), was interested in reading through and reflecting upon that draft. Over the course of the year, they read the draft chapters and we met each month to discuss their perspectives on this analysis. Their analysis informed further thinking and re-drafting of this book. Working off those meetings, I also conducted further interviews with key administrators, department chairs, and teachers to track how the dialogue about gender and race had evolved in the years since my initial study.

# References

Abu El-Haj, T. (2003a). Challenging the inevitability of difference: Young women and discourses about gender equity in the classroom. *Curriculum Inquiry 33* (4), 401–426.

Abu El-Haj, T. (2003b). Practicing for equity from the standpoint of the particular: Exploring the work of one urban teacher network. *Teachers College Record 105* (5), 817–845.

Alcoff, L. (1988) Cultural feminism versus post-structuralism. *Signs 13*(3), 295–306.

American Association of University Women (AAUW). (1992). *How schools shortchange girls: A study of major findings on girls and education.* Washington, DC: AAUW.

AAUW. (1998). *Gender gaps: Where schools still fail our children.* Washington, DC: AAUW.

Anyon, J. (1980). Social class and the hidden curriculum of work. *Journal of Education 162*, 67–92.

Anyon, J. (2005). *Radical possibilities: Public policy, urban education and a new social movement.* New York: Routledge.

Appiah, K. (1996). Race, culture, identity: Misunderstood connections. In K. A. Appiah & A. Gutmann (Eds.), *Color conscious: The political morality of race* (pp. 30–105). Princeton, NJ: Princeton University Press.

Artiles, A. J. (2003). Special education's changing identity: Paradoxes and dilemmas in views of culture and space. *Harvard Educational Review 73* (2), 164–202.

Balkin, J. M. (2001). *Brown v. Board of Education* — A critical introduction. In J. M. Balkin (Ed.), *What* Brown v. Board of Education *should have said* (pp. 3–74). New York: New York University Press.

Baker, B. (2002). The hunt for disability: The new eugenics and the normalization of school children. *Teachers College Record 104* (4), 663–703.

Banks, J. A. (1997). *Teaching strategies for ethnic studies* (6th ed.). Boston: Allyn and Bacon.

Banks, J. A. (2004a). Introduction: Democratic citizenship education in multicultural societies. In J. A. Banks (Ed.), *Diversity and Citizenship Education: Global Perspectives* (pp. 3–15). San Francisco: Jossey-Bass.

Banks, J. A. (2004b). Multicultural education: Historical development, dimensions and practice. In J. A. Banks, & C. A. McGee Banks (Eds.), *Handbook of research on multicultural education* (2nd ed., pp. 3–29). San Francisco: Jossey-Bass.

Barth, P., Haycock, K., Jackson, H., Mora, K., Ruiz, R., Robinson, S., & Willis, A. (1999). *Dispelling the myth: High Poverty schools exceeding expectations.* Washington, DC: Education Trust.

Belenky, M. F., Clinchy, B. M., Goldberger, N. R., & Tarule, J. M. (1997/1986). *Women's ways of knowing: The development of self, voice and mind* (2nd ed.). New York: Basic Books.

Bell, D. (1987). *And we are not saved: The elusive quest for justice.* New York: Basic Books.

Bell, D. (1995). Serving two masters: Integration ideals and client interests in school desegregation litigation. In K. Crenshaw, N. Gotanda, & K. Thomas (Eds.), *Critical race theory: The key writings that formed the movement* (pp. 5–19). New York: New Press.

211

Bell, D. (2004). *Silent covenants: Brown v. Board of Education and the unfulfilled hopes for racial reform*. New York: Oxford University Press.

Benhabib, S. (2002). *The claims of culture: Equality and diversity in the global era*. Princeton, NJ: Princeton University Press.

Biklen, D. (1992). *Schooling without labels: Parents, educators, and inclusive education*. Philadelphia: Temple University Press.

Bingham, C. (2001). *Schools of recognition: Identity politics and classroom practices*. Lanham, MD: Rowman & Littlefield Publishers, Inc.

Boaler, J. (1997). *Experiencing school mathematics: Teaching styles, sex and setting*. Buckingham, UK: Open University Press.

Booher-Jennings, J. (2005). Below the bubble: "Educational triage" and the Texas Accountability System. *American Educational Research Journal 42* (2), 231–268.

Bourdieu, P. (1984). *Distinction: A social critique of the judgment of taste*. Cambridge, MA: Harvard University Press.

Brayboy, B. (2004). Hiding in the Ivy: American Indian students and visibility in elite educational settings. *Harvard Educational Review 74* (2), 125–152.

*Brown v. Board of Education*, 347 U.S. 483 (1954).

*Brown v. Board of Education II, 349* U.S. 294 (1955).

Campbell, P. B., & Sanders, J. (2002). Challenging the system: Assumptions and data behind the push for single-sex schooling. In A. Datnow, & L. Hubbard (Eds.), *Gender in policy and practice: Perspectives on single-sex and coeducational schooling* (pp. 31–46). New York: Routledge-Falmer.

Carby, H. V. (1992). The multicultural wars. *Radical History Review 54 (Winter)*, 7–18.

Carini, P. (2001). *Starting strong: A different look at children, schools and standards*. New York: Teachers College Record.

Carrier, J. G. (1986). *Learning disability: Social class and the construction of inequality in American education*. New York: Greenwood Press.

Cary, L. (1991). *Black ice*. New York: Vintage books.

Castenell, L. A., & Pinar, W. F. (1993). Introduction. In L. A. Castenall & W. F. Pinar (Eds.), *Understanding curriculum as racial texts: Representations of identity and difference in education* (pp. 1–30). Albany: State University of New York Press.

Center on Educational Policy (March 2006). *From the capital to the classroom: Year 4 of the No Child Left Behind Act*. Washington, D. C.

Chapman, O. (1993). Women's voice and the learning of mathematics. *Journal of Gender Studies 2* (2), 206–231.

Chase, B. (2000). Making a difference. In J. Cohen, & J. Rogers (Eds.), *Will standards save public education?* (pp. 40–43). Boston: Beacon.

Christensen, C. (1996). Disabled, handicapped or disordered: "What's in a name?" In C. Christensen, & F. Rizvi (Eds.), *Disability and the dilemmas of education and justice* (pp. 63–78). Buckingham, UK: Open University Press.

Coleman, J. (1968). The concept of equal educational opportunity. *Harvard Educational Review 38* (1), 7–22.

Connell, R. W., Ashenden, D. J., Kessler, G. W. & Dowsett, G. W. (1982). *Making the difference: Schools, families and social division*. Sydney: George Allen and Unwin.

Crenshaw, K., Gotanda, N., & Thomas, K. (1995). Introduction. In K. Crenshaw, N. Gotanda, & K. Thomas (Eds.), *Critical race theory: The key writings that formed the movement* (pp. xiii–xxxiii). New York: New Press.

Crosby, F. J., & Blake-Beard, S. (2004). Affirmative action: Diversity, merit and the benefit of white people. In M. Fine, L. Weis, L. C. Powell, & L. M. Wong (Eds.), *Off white: Readings on race, power and society* (2nd ed., pp. 145–159). New York: Routledge.

Darling-Hammond, L. (1997). *The right to learn: A blueprint for creating schools that work*. San Francisco: Jossey-Bass.

Datnow, A., & Hubbard, L. (2002). Introduction. In A. Datnow, & L. Hubbard (Eds.), *Gender in policy and practice: Perspectives on single-sex and coeducational schooling* (pp. 2–9). New York: Routledge-Falmer.

Davis, B. (2004). Group charges curriculum falls short of addressing diversity. *Public School Notebook 12* (1).

Dehyle, D. (1995). Navajo youth and Anglo racism: Cultural integrity and resistance. *Harvard Educational Review 65* (3), 403–444.

Delpit, L., (1986). Skills and other dilemmas of a progressive black educator. *Harvard Educational Review 56* (4), 379–385.

Delpit, L. (1995). *Other people's children: Cultural conflict in the classroom.* New York: The New Press.

Dewey, J. (1922/1966). Individuality, equality and superiority. In J. Ratner (Ed.), *Education today* (pp. 171–177). New York: Macmillan.

Dominguez, V. R. (1992). Is multiculturalism postracism? Chronicles of and for the U.S. in 1992. Paper delivered at the Scripps/Claremont conference, "Writing the Post-Colonial." La Jolla, CA.

Donovan, S., & Cross, C. (Eds.). (2002). *Minority students in special and gifted education.* Washington, DC: National Academy Press.

Du Bois, W. E. B. (1903/1989). *The souls of black folk.* New York: Penguin Books.

Duncan, G. A. (2002). Beyond love: A critical race ethnography of the schooling of adolescent black males. *Equity and Excellence in Education 35* (2), 131–143.

Dyson, A. (1999). Inclusion and inclusions: theories and discourses in inclusive education. In H. Daniels, & P. Garner (Eds.), *Inclusive education: World yearbook of education* (pp. 36–53). London: Kogan Page.

Education of All Handicapped Children Act, Pub. L. 94-142, 89 Stat. 773 (1975).

Eitle, T. M. (2002). Special education or racial segregation: Understanding variation in the representation of black students in educable mentally handicapped programs. *Sociological Quarterly 43* (3), 575–605.

Elmore, R. F., Abelmann, C. H., & Fuhrman, S. H. (1996). The new accountability in state education reforms. In H. F. Ladd (Ed.), *Holding schools accountable: Performance-based reform in education* (pp. 65–98). Washington, DC: The Brookings Institute.

Erickson, F. (1987). Transformation and school success: The politics and culture of educational achievement. *Anthropology and Education Quarterly 18* (4), 336–355.

Erickson, F. (1994–5). Where the action is: On collaborative action research in education. *Bulletin of the Council for Research in Music Education. 123* (Winter), 10–25.

Erickson, F. (1996a). Discourse analysis as a communication channel: How feasible is a linkage between continental and Anglo-American approaches? Keynote address at Georgetown University.

Erickson, F. (1996b). Inclusion into what: Thoughts on the construction of learning, identity and affiliation in the general education classroom. In D. L. Speece, & B. K. Keogh (Eds.), *Research on classroom ecologies: Implications for inclusion of children with learning disabilities (pp. 91–105).* Mahwah, NJ: Lawrence Erlbaum Associates.

Erickson, F. (2001). Culture in society and in educational practices. In J. A. Banks & C. A. McGee Banks (Eds.), *Multicultural education: Issues and perspectives* (pp. 31–58). New York: John Wiley and Sons, Inc.

Erickson, F. (2004). *Talk and social theory.* Cambridge, UK: Polity Press.

Fairclough, N. (1995). *Discourse and social change.* Cambridge, UK: Polity Press.

Falk, B. (2002). Standards-based reforms: Problems and possibilities. *Phi Delta Kappan 83* (8), 612–620.

Fennema, E., Carpenter, T. P., Jacobs, V. R., Franke, M. L., & Levi, L. W. (1998). New perspectives on gender differences in mathematics: A reprise. *Educational Researcher 27* (5), 19–21.

Fine, M. (1991). *Framing dropouts: Notes on the politics of an urban public high school.* Albany: State University of New York Press.

Fine, M. (1992). Passion, politics and power. In M. Fine (Ed.), *Disruptive voices: The possibilities of feminist research stances (pp. 205–231).* Ann Arbor: University of Michigan Press.

Fine, M. (1997). Witnessing whiteness. In M. Fine, L. Weis, L.C. Powell, & L.M. Wong (Eds.), *Off white: Readings on race, power and society* (pp. 57–65). New York: Routledge.

Fine, M., Anand, B., Jordan, C., & Sherman, D. (2000). Before the bleach gets us all. In L. Weis, & M. Fine (Eds.), *Construction sites: Excavating race, class and gender among urban youth* (pp. 161–179). New York: Teachers College Press.

Fine, M., Bloom, J., Burns, A., Chajet, L., Guishard, M., Paye, Y., et al. (2005). Dear Zora: A letter to Zora Neale Hurston 50 years after *Brown. Teachers College Record 107* (3), 496–528.

Flinspach, S. L., & Banks, K. E. (2005). Moving beyond race: Socioeconomic diversity as a race-neutral approach to desegregation in Wake County Schools. In J. C. Boger, & G. Orfield (Eds.), *School resegregation: Must the South turn back?* (pp. 261–280). Chapel Hill: University of North Carolina Press.

Fordham, S. (1991). Racelessness in private schools: Should we deconstruct the racial and cultural identity of African-American adolescents? *Teachers College Record 92* (3), 470–484.

Fordham, S. (1996). *Blacked out: Dilemmas of race, identity and success at Capitol High.* Chicago: University of Chicago Press.

Foucault, M. (1972). *The archaeology of knowledge and the discourse on language.* New York: Pantheon Books.

Frankenberg, E., & Lee, C. (2002). *Race in American public schools: Rapidly resegregating school districts.* Cambridge, MA: The Civil Rights Project, Harvard University.

Frankenberg, R. (1993). *White women, race matters: The social construction of whiteness.* Minneapolis: University of Minnesota Press.

Fraser, N. (1997). *Justice interruptus: Critical reflections of the "postsocialist" condition.* New York: Routledge.

Freeman, A. D. (1995). Legitimizing racial discrimination through antidiscrimination law: A critical review of Supreme Court doctrine. In K. Crenshaw, N. Gotanda, & K. Thomas (Eds.), *Critical race theory: The key writings that formed the movement* (pp. 29–45). New York: New Press.

Friend, R. (1993). Choice not closets: Heterosexism and homophobia. In L. Weiss, & M. Fine (Eds.), *Beyond silenced voices: Class, race, and gender in United States schools* (pp. 209–236). Albany: State University of New York Press.

Fuhrman, S. (1993). The politics of coherence. In S. Fuhrman (Ed.), *Designing coherent educational policy: Improving the system* (pp. 1–34). San Francisco: Jossey-Bass.

Galston, W. (1980). *Justice and the human good.* Chicago: University of Chicago Press.

Gartner, A., & Lipsky, D. K. (1987). Beyond special education: toward a quality system for all students. *Harvard Educational Review 57* (4), 367–395.

*Gaskin v. Pennsylvania Department of Education* (2004). No. 94-CV-4048. Ed. Pa. 21 Dec. 2004.

Gay, G. (2004). Curriculum theory and multicultural education. In J. A. Banks, & C. A. McGee Banks (Eds.), *Handbook of research on multicultural education* (2nd ed., pp. 30–49). San Francisco: Jossey-Bass.

Gee, J. P. (1999). *An introduction to discourse analysis: Theory and method.* New York: Routledge.

Gilligan, C. (1993). Joining the resistance: Psychology, politics, girls and women. In L. Weiss, & M. Fine (Eds.), *Beyond silenced voices: Class, race, and gender in United States Schools* (pp. 143–168). Albany: State University of New York Press.

Gilligan, C., Lyons, N. P., & Hanmer, T. J. (1990). *Making connections: The relational worlds of adolescent girls at Emma Willard School.* Cambridge, MA: Harvard University Press.

Goals 2000: Educate America Act of 1994. Pub. L. 103-227. 108 Stat. 125. 31 March 1994.

Gordon, B. (1993). Toward emancipation in citizenship education: The case of African American cultural knowledge. In L. A. Castenall, & W. F. Pinar (Eds.), *Understanding curriculum as racial texts: Representations of identity and difference in education* (pp. 263–284). Albany: State University of New York Press.

*Gratz v. Bollinger,* 539 U.S. 306 (2003).

Groce, N. (1985). *Everyone here spoke sign language.* Cambridge, MA: Harvard University Press.

*Grutter v. Bollinger,* 123 S. Ct., 2325, 2342 (2003).

*Grutter v. Bollinger,* 539 U.S. 306 (2003).

Gurian, M. (1996). *The wonder of boys: What parents, mentors and educators can do to shape boys into exceptional men.* New York: Putnam Books.

Gurian, M. (2002). *The wonder of girls: Understanding the hidden nature of our girls.* New York: Atria.

Gutmann, A. (1992). Introduction. In C. Taylor, *Multiculturalism and the "politics of recognition."* Princeton, NJ: Princeton University Press.

Gutmann, A. (1996). Responding to racial injustice. In K. A. Appiah, & A. Gutmann, *Color-conscious: The political morality of race* (pp. 106–178). Princeton, NJ: Princeton University Press.

Gutmann, A. (2003). *Identity in democracy.* Princeton, NJ: Princeton University Press.

Haberman, M. (1991). The pedagogy of poverty versus good teaching. *Phi Delta Kappan 73,* 290–294.

Hale, J. E. (2001). *Learning while black: Creating excellence for African American children*. Baltimore: John Hopkins University Press.

Hanushek, E. A. (1997). Assessing the effects of school resources on student performance: An update. *Educational Evaluation and Policy Analysis 17* (2), 141–164.

Hanushek, E. A. (2003). The failure of input-based schooling policies. *The Economic Journal 113* (February), F64–F98.

Hauser, R. M. (2001). Should we end social promotion? Truth and consequences. In G. Orfield, & M. L. Kornhaber (Eds.), *Raising standards or raising barriers? Inequality and high-stakes testing in public education* (pp. 151–178). New York: The Century Foundation.

Hare-Mustin, R. T., & Maracek, J. (1990). Gender and the meaning of difference: Postmodernism and Psychology. In R. T. Hare-Mustin, & J. Maracek (Eds.), *Making a difference: Psychology and the construction of gender* (pp. 22–64). New Haven: Yale University Press.

Haycock, K. (2001). Closing the achievement gap. *Educational Leadership* 6–11.

Hehir, T. (2002). Eliminating ableism in education. *Harvard Educational Review 72* (1), 1–32.

Heubert, J. (2001). High-stakes testing and civil rights: Standards of appropriate test use as a strategy for enforcing them. In G. Orfield, & M. L. Kornhaber (Eds.), *Raising standards or raising barriers? Inequality and high-stakes testing in public education* (pp. 179–194). New York: The Century Foundation.

Highwater, J. (1977). *Anpao: An American Indian odyssey*. New York: Harper-Collins Children's Books.

Hilliard, A. (1998). The standards movement: Quality control or decoy? *Rethinking Schools 12* (4), 4–5.

Hirshman, N. J. (2003). *The subject of liberty: Toward a feminist theory of freedom*. Princeton, NJ: Princeton University Press.

Holme, J. J. (2002). Buying homes, buying schools: School choice and the construction of school quality. *Harvard Educational Review 72* (2), 177–205.

Hopkins, R. (1997). *Educating black males: Critical lessons in schooling, community and power*. Albany: State University of New York Press.

Horton, M. (1990). *The long haul: An autobiography of Myles Horton*. New York: Doubleday.

Howe, K. R. (1997). *Understanding equal educational opportunity: Social justice, democracy and schooling*. New York: Teachers College Press.

Hyde, J., & Jaffee, S. (1998). Perspectives from social and feminist psychology. *Educational Researcher 27* (5), 14–16.

Individuals with Disabilities Education Act Amendments of 1990. Pub L. 101-476. 30 Oct. 1990. Stat. 1824. (1990).

Individuals with Disabilities Education Act Amendments of 1997. Pub L. 105-17. 4 June 1997. 111 Stat. 37. (1997).

Individuals with Disabilities Education Improvement Act. Pub. L. 108-446. 3 Dec. 2004. 118 Stat. 2647. (2004).

Irvine, J. J., and York, D. E. (1995). Learning styles and culturally diverse students: A literature review. In J. Banks and C. A. Banks, (Eds.), *Handbook of research on multicultural education* (pp. 484–497). New York: Macmillan Publishing.

Isaacs, P. (1996). Disability and the education of persons. In C. Christensen, & F. Rizvi (Eds.), *Disability and the dilemmas of education and justice* (pp. 27–45). Buckingham, UK: Open University Press.

Jaggar, A. (1983). *Feminist politics and human nature*. Totowa, NJ: Rowman & Littlefield Publishers, Inc.

Jennings, J. (2001). From the White House to the schoolhouse: Greater demands and new roles. In *From the Capitol to the classroom* (Vol. 2, pp. 291–309). Chicago: National Society for the Study of Education.

Jones, M., Yonezawa, S., Ballesteros, E., & Mehan, H. (2002). Shaping pathways to higher education. *Educational Researcher 31* (2), 3–11.

King, M. L. Jr., (1986). The ethical demands for integration. In J. M. Washington (Ed.), *A testament of hope: The essential writings of Martin Luther King, Jr*. San Francisco: Harper & Row.

Kluth, P., Straut, D. M., & Biklen, D. P. (Eds.) (2003). *Access to academics for all students: Critical approaches to inclusive curriculum, instruction, and policy*. Mahwah, N.J.: Lawrence Erlbaum Associates.

Korhhaber, M. L., & Orfield, G. (2001). High-stakes testing policies: Examining their assumptions and consequences. In G. Orfield, & M. L. Kornhaber (Eds.), *Raising standards or raising barriers? Inequality and high-stakes testing in public education* (pp. 1–18). New York: The Century Foundation.

Kozol, J. (1991). *Savage inequalities.* New York: Crown Publishers.

Kozol, J. (2005). *The shame of the nation: The restoration of apartheid schooling in America.* New York: Crown Publishers.

Kymlicka, W. (1995). *Multicultural citizenship: A liberal theory of minority rights.* Oxford: Clarendon Press.

Ladson-Billings , G. (1994). *The dreamkeepers: Successful teachers of African American children.* San Francisco: Jossey-Bass.

Ladson-Billings, G. (2004). Landing on the wrong note: The price we paid for *Brown. Educational Researcher 33* (7), 3–13.

Ladson-Billings, G., & Tate, W. F. (1995). Toward a critical race theory of education. *Teachers College Record 97* (1), 47–68.

Lasch-Quinn, E. (2001). *Race experts.* New York: W. W. Norton and Company.

Lather, P. (1992). Critical frames in educational research: Feminist and post-structural perspectives. *Theory into Practice 31* (2), 87–99.

Lee, S. J. (1996). *Unraveling the "model minority" stereotype: Listening to Asian-American youth.* New York: Teachers College Press.

Linn, R. L. (2000). Assessments and accountability. *Educational Researcher 29* (2), 4–16.

Lipman, P. (1998). *Race, class and power in school restructuring.* Albany: State University of New York Press.

Lipman, P. (2002). Making the global city, making inequality: The political economy and cultural politics of Chicago school policy. *American Educational Research Journal 39* (2), 379–419.

Lipman, P. (2004). *High stakes education: Inequality, globalization and urban school reform.* New York: Routledge.

Lipsky, D. K., & Gartner, A. (1996). Inclusion, school restructuring, and the remaking of American society. *Harvard Educational Review 66* (4), 762–796.

Lipsky, D. K., & Gartner, A. (1997). *Inclusion and school reform: Transforming America's classrooms.* Baltimore: Paul H. Brooks.

Lipsky, D. K., & Gartner, A. (1999). Inclusive education: a requirement of a democratic society. In H. Daniels, & P. Garner (Eds.), *Inclusive education: World yearbook of education* (pp. 12–23). London: Kogan Page.

Losen, D. J. & Orfield, G. (2002). *Racial inequality in special education.* Cambridge, MA: Harvard Education Press.

Lucas, S. (1999). *Tracking inequality: Stratification and mobility in American high schools.* New York: Teachers College Press.

Luna, C. (1997). "Otherwise qualified": An action-oriented study of the experiences of learning disabled-labeled undergraduates at an Ivy League university. (Doctoral dissertation, University of Pennsylvania, Philadelphia.) *Dissertation Abstracts International.*

Massey, D. S., & Denton, N. (1993). *American apartheid: Segregation and the making of the underclass.* Cambridge, MA: Harvard University Press.

McCarthy, C. (1990). *Race and curriculum: Social inequality and the theories and politics of difference in contemporary research on schooling.* London: Falmer Press.

McCarthy, C. (1993a). After the canon: Knowledge and ideological representation in the multicultural discourse on curriculum reform. In C. McCarthy, & W. Crichlow (Eds.), *Race, identity and representation in education* (pp. 289–305). New York: Routledge.

McCarthy, C. (1993b) Multicultural approaches to racial inequality in the United States. In L. A. Castenell Jr., & W. F. Pinar (Eds.), *Understanding curriculum as racial text: representations of identity and difference in education* (pp. 225–246). Albany: State University of New York Press.

McCarthy, C., & Crichlow, W. (1993). Introduction: Theories of identity, theories of representation, theories of race. In C. McCarthy, & W. Crichlow (Eds.), *Race, identity and representation in education* (pp. xiii–xxix). New York: Routledge.

McLaren, P. (1994). White terror and oppositional agency: Toward a critical multiculturalism. In D. T. Goldberg (Ed.), *Multiculturalism: A critical reader* (pp. 45–74). Cambridge, MA: Basil Blackwell Ltd.

McDermott, R., & Varenne, H. (1995). Culture as disability. *Anthropology and Education Quarterly 26* (3), 324–348.

McNeil, L. (2000). Creating new inequalities: Contradictions of reform. *Phil Delta Kappan 81* (10), 728–734.

McNeil, L., & Valenzuela, A. (2001). The harmful impact of the TAAS system of testing in Texas. In G. Orfield, & M. L. Kornhaber (Eds.), *Raising standards or raising barriers? Inequality and high-stakes testing in public education* (pp. 127–150). New York: The Century Foundation.

Mehan, H. (2000). Beneath the skin and between the ears: A case study in the politics of representation. In B. A. U. Levinson., K. M. Borman, M. Eisenhart, M. Foster, A. E. Fox, & M. Sutton. (Eds.), *Schooling the symbolic animal: Social and cultural dimensions of education* (pp. 259–279). Lanham, MD: Rowman & Littlefield, Inc.

Mehan, H., Hertweck, A., & Meihls, J. L. (1986). *Handicapping the handicapped: Decision making in students' educational careers*. Stanford, CA: Standard University Press.

Mehan, H., Villenueva, I., Hubbard, L., & Lintz, A. (1996). *Constructing school success: The consequences of untracking low-achieving students*. Cambridge, UK: Cambridge University Press.

Meier, D. (2000). Educating a democracy. In J. Cohen, & J. Rogers (Eds.), *Will standards save public education?* (pp. 3–31). Boston: Beacon Press.

Mickelson, R. A. (2005). The incomplete desegregation of the Charlotte-Mecklenburg schools and its consequences. In J. C. Boger, & G. Orfield (Eds.), *School resegregation: Must the South turn back?* (pp. 87–110). Chapel Hill: University of North Carolina Press.

Minow, M. (1990). *Making all the difference: Inclusion, exclusion and American law*. Ithaca, NY: Cornell University Press.

Mohanty, C. T. (1989–90). On race and voice: challenges for liberal education in the 1990s. *Cultural Critique* 14 (Winter), 179–208.

Murnane, R. J. (2000). The case for standards. In J. Cohen & J. Rogers (Eds.), *Will standards save public education* (pp. 57–63). Boston: Beacon Press.

Murrell, P. (1993). Afrocentric immersion: Academic and personal development of African-American males in public schools. In T. Perry, & J. W. Fraser (Eds.), *Freedom's plow: Teaching in the multicultural classroom* (pp. 231–260). New York: Routledge.

Nash, G. (2000). Expert opinion. In J. Cohen, & J. Rogers (Eds.), *Will standards save public education?* (pp. 44–49). Boston: Beacon Press.

National Commission on Excellence in Education (1983). *A nation at risk*. Washington, DC: Government Printing Office.

National Council of Teachers of Mathematics (NCTM) (1989). *Curriculum and evaluation standards for school mathematics*. Reston, VA: Author.

NCTM (1991). *Professional standards for teaching mathematics*. Reston, VA: Author.

NCTM (1995). *Assessment standards for school mathematics*. Reston, VA: Author.

National Research Council, Committee on Appropriate Test Use (1999). *High stakes: Testing for tracking, promotion and graduation*. J. P. Heubert, & R. M. Hauser (Eds.). Washington, DC: National Academy Press.

National Research Council, Division of Behavioral and Social Sciences and Education (2002). *Achieving high standards for all: Conference summary*. T. Ready, C. Edley, & C. Snow (Eds.). Washington, DC: National Academy Press.

Natriello, G., & Pallas, A. M. (2001). The development and impact of high-stakes testing. In G. Orfield, & M. L. Kornhaber (Eds.), *Raising standards or raising barriers? Inequality and high-stakes testing in public education* (pp. 19–38). New York: The Century Foundation.

Neill, M. (2003). Leaving children behind: How No Child Left Behind will fail our children. *Phi Delta Kappan 85*(3), 225–228.

Nieto, S. (1996). *Affirming diversity: The sociopolitical context of multicultural education* (3rd ed.). Amherst, NY: Longman Publishers.

Nieto, S. (1999). *The Light in their eyes*. New York: Teachers College Press.

No Child Left Behind Act of 2001 (NCLB). Pub. L. 107-110. 8 Jan. 2002. 115 Stat. 1425. (2001).

Noddings, N. (1998). Perspectives from feminist philosophy. *Educational Researcher 27* (5), 17–18.

Noddings, N. (1999). Renewing democracy in schools. *Phi Delta Kappan 80* (8), 579–83.

Oakes, J. (1985). *Keeping track: How schools structure inequality*. New Haven, CT: Yale University Press.

Olsen, L. (1997). *Made in America: Immigrant students in our public schools*. New York: New Press.

Omi, M., & Winant, H. (1986). *Racial Formation in the U.S.: From the 1960s to 1980s*. New York: Routledge.

Orfield, G. (2005). The Southern dilemma: Losing *Brown*, fearing *Plessy*. In J. C. Boger, & G. Orfield (Eds.), *School resegregation: Must the South turn back?* (pp. 1–25). Chapel Hill: University of North Carolina Press.

Orfield, G., & Eaton, S. E. (1996). *Dismantling desegregation: The quiet reversal of Brown v. Board of Education*. New York: The New Press.

Orfield, G., & Yun, J. (1999). *Resegregation in American schools*. Cambridge, MA: The Civil Rights Project, Harvard University.

Perry, T., & Fraser, J. W. (1993). Reconstructing schools as multicultural/multiracial democracies: Toward a theoretical perspective. In T. Perry, & J. W. Fraser (Eds.), *Freedom's plow: Teaching in the multicultural classroom* (pp. 3–24). New York: Routledge.

Phillips, L. (1998). *The girls report: What we know and need to know about growing up female*. New York: National Council for Research on Women.

Pinar, W. F. (1993). Notes on understanding curriculum as racial text. In C. McCarthy, & W. Crichlow (Eds.), *Race, identity and representation in education* (pp. 60–70). New York: Routledge.

Pollock, M. (2004). *Colormute: Race talk dilemmas in an American school*. Princeton, NJ: Princeton University Press.

Porter, A. (1995). The uses and misuses of opportunity-to-learn standards. *Educational Researcher 24* (1), 21–27.

Powell, J. A. (2005). A new theory of integrated education: True integration. In J. C. Boger, & G. Orfield (Eds.), *School resegregation: Must the South turn back?* (pp. 281–304). Chapel Hill: University of North Carolina Press.

Ramos-Zayas, A. (1998). Nationalist ideologies, neighborhood-based activism and educational spaces in Puerto Rican Chicago. *Harvard Educational Review 68* (2), 164–193.

Rawls, J. (1971). *A theory of justice*. Cambridge, MA: Harvard University Press.

Ravitch, D. (1990). Multiculturalism: E Pluribus Plures. *The American Scholar 59*(3), 337–354.

Ravitch, D. (1995). *National standards in American education: A citizen's guide*. Washington, DC: Brookings Institute.

Reich, R. (2002). *Bridging liberalism and multiculturalism in American education*. Chicago: University of Chicago Press.

Rhode, D. L. (1990). Theoretical perspectives on sexual difference. In D. L. Rhode (Ed.), *Theoretical perspectives on sexual difference* (pp. 1—12). New Haven, CT: Yale University Press.

Riordan, C. (2002). What do we know about the effects of single-sex schools in the private sector? Implications for public school. In A. Datnow, & L. Hubbard (Eds.), *Gender in policy and practice: Perspectives on single-sex and coeducational schooling* (pp. 10–30). New York: Routledge-Falmer.

Rist, R. C. (1970). Student social class and teacher expectations: The self-fulfilling prophecy in ghetto education. *Harvard Educational Review 40*, 411–451.

Rizvi, F., & Lingard, B. (1996). Disability, education and the discourses of justice. In C. Christensen, & F. Rizvi (Eds.), *Disability and the dilemmas of education and justice* (pp. 9–26). Buckingham, UK: Open University Press.

Romberg, T. A. (1998). Comments: NCTM's curriculum and evaluation standards. *Teachers College Record 100* (1), 8–21.

Sadker, M., & Sadker, D. (1994). *Failing at fairness: How our schools cheat girls*. New York: Touchstone.

Salamone, R. (2002). The legality of single-sex education in the United States: Sometimes "equal" means "different." In A. Datnow, & L. Hubbard (Eds.), *Gender in policy and practice: Perspectives on single-sex and coeducational schooling* (pp. 47–72). New York: Routledge-Falmer.

Schultz, K. (1991). Do you want to be in my story?: The social nature of writing in an urban third- and fourth-grade classroom. (Doctoral dissertation, University of Pennsylvania, Philadelphia 1991). *Dissertation Abstracts International, 3058*.

Scott, J. (1988). Deconstructing equality-versus-difference: Or, the uses of poststructuralist theory for feminism. *Feminist Studies, 14* (1), 33–50.

Shange, N. (1977). *For colored girls who have considered suicide when the rainbow is enuf.* New York: Simon & Schuster.

Shepard, L. (2000). The role of assessment in a learning culture. *Educational Researcher 29* (7), 4-14.

Skrtic, T. M. (1991). The special education paradox: Equity as the way to excellence. *Harvard Educational Review, 61* (2), 148-206.

Sizer, T. R. (1992). *Horace's school: Redesigning the American high school.* Boston: Houghton Mifflin Company.

Slee, R. (1999). Policies and practices? Inclusive education and its effects on schooling. In H. Daniels, & P. Garner (Eds.), *Inclusive education: World yearbook of education* (pp. 195-206). London: Kogan Page.

Sleeter, C. E. (1996). *Multicultural education as social activism.* Albany: State University of New York Press.

Sleeter, C. E., & Grant, C. (1993). *Making choices for multicultural education: Five approaches to race, class and gender.* New York: MacMillan Publishing Company.

Snyder, S. (2005, June). Philadelphia school mandate: African history. *Philadelphia Inquirer* (p. A1).

Sommers, C. H. (2000). *War against boys: How misguided feminism is harming our young men.* New York: Simon & Schuster.

Sowder, J. T. (1998). Perspectives from mathematics education. *Educational Researcher 27* (5), 12-13.

Spring, J. (2004). *Deculturalization and the struggle for equality: A brief history of dominated cultures in the United States* (4th ed.). Boston: McGraw-Hill.

Staff (1998). California referendum mandates "English-Only." *Rethinking Schools* 12 (3), 1ff.

Tatum, B. D. (1997). *Why are all the Black kids sitting together in the cafeteria? And other conversations about race.* New York: Basic Books.

Taylor, C, (1992). *Multiculturalism and the "politics of recognition."* Princeton, NJ: Princeton University Press.

Thernstrom, A. (2000). No excuses. In J. Cohen, & J. Rogers (Eds.), *Will standards save public education?* (pp. 35-39). Boston: Beacon Press.

Thernstrom, A., & Thernstrom, S. (2002). Introduction. In A. Thernstrom, & S. Thernstrom (Eds.), *Beyond the color line: New perspectives on race and ethnicity in America* (pp. 1-12). Stanford, CA: Hoover Institution Press.

Thompson, S. (2001). As the standards turn: The evil twin of "authentic standards." *The Education Digest 66* (8), 12-19.

Tomlinson, C. A. (1999). *The differentiated classroom: Responding to the needs of all learners.* Alexandria, VA: Association for Supervision and Curriculum Development.

Tyack, D. B. (1974). *The one best system: A history of American urban education.* Cambridge, MA: Harvard University Press.

Unger, R. (1990). Imperfect reflections of reality: Psychology constructs gender. In R. T. Hare-Mustin, & J. Maracek (Eds.), *Making a difference: Psychology and the construction of gender* (pp. 102-149). New Haven, CT: Yale University Press.

Valenzuela, A. (1999). *Subtractive schooling: U.S.-Mexican youth and the politics of caring.* Albany: State University of New York Press.

Varenne, H., & McDermott, R. (1998). *Successful failure: The school America builds.* Boulder, CO: Westview.

*Virginia v. United States,* 518 U.S. 515 (1996).

Walkerdine, V. (1990). *School girl fictions.* London: Verso.

Walkerdine, V. (1998). *Counting girls out: Girls and mathematics.* London: Falmer Press.

Weedon, C. (1987). *Feminist practice and poststructuralist theory.* Cambridge, MA Blackwell Press.

Wells, A. S., & Holme, J. J. (2005). No accountability for diversity: Standardized tests and the demise of racially mixed schools. In J. C. Boger, & G. Orfield (Eds.), *School resegregation: Must the South turn back?* (pp. 187-211). Chapel Hill: University of North Carolina Press.

Wells, A. S., Holme, J. J., Revilla, A. T., & Atanda, A. K. (2004). How society failed school desegregation policy: Looking past the schools to understand them. *Review of Research in Education. 28,* 47-99.

Wells, A. S., & Serna, I. (1996). The politics of culture: Understanding local political resistance to detracking in racially mixed schools. *Harvard Educational Review 66* (1), 93-118.

Welner, K., & Oakes, J. (1996). (Li)ability grouping: The new susceptibility of school tracking systems to legal challenges. *Harvard Educational Review 66* (3), 451–470.

Wheelock, A. (1998). *Safe to be smart: Building a culture for standards-based reform in the middle grades.* Columbus, OH: National Middle Schools Association.

Willis, S. (1995). Mathematics: From constructing privilege to deconstructing myths. In J. Gaskell, & J. Willinsky (Eds.), *Gender in/forms curriculum: From enrichment to transformation* (pp. 262–284). New York: Teachers College Press.

Willis, S. (1996). Gender justice and the mathematics curriculum: Four perspectives. In L. H. Parker, L. J. Rennie, & B. J. Fraser (Eds.), *Gender, science and mathematics* (pp. 41–51). London: Kluwer Academic Press.

Woodall, M. (2006, January 18). All boys, all girls. *Philadelphia Inquirer* (p. A1).

Yep, L. (1991). *Star Fisher.* New York: Puffin Books.

Young, I. M. (1990). *Justice and the politics of difference.* Princeton, NJ: Princeton University Press.

# Notes

## Introduction

1. All names of places and people have been changed to protect the confidentiality of the participants in this research.
2. As a book that addresses how we "think" about difference, I am mindful of the power of language and its limitations. I have chosen to use the admittedly awkward phrases "children labeled with disabilities" and "children identified with disabilities" in this text, as I argue that we must reframe how we think about the location of disabilities. Speaking of "children with disabilities" or "disabled children" reinforces a view of disabilities as located solely within the bodies and minds of particular individuals.
3. Standards-based reform characterizes a vast array of policies and practices. Chapter 4 addresses in further detail the complexity of this movement.
4. The risk of slipping from this position back into biological essentialism always exists (for critiques, see Alcoff, 1988; Hare-Mustin and Maracek, 1990; Scott, 1988).
5. While sexuality is one significant dimension along which power and privilege are organized in society, it does not emerge as a salient category in my work here. This reflects the fact that it was not one of the dimensions of difference that practitioners were actively investigating at either school. There was a gay and lesbian students' group at City Friends. However, because my starting point was practitioners' active concerns, this group did not become part of my study. Although I recognize that this was an enormous project, and I could not attend to everything, I worry that this research has, once again, contributed to the near total silence in educational settings on the question of sexual orientation.

## Chapter 1

1. I recognize that symbolic representations of diversity often do not correspond with real attention to issues of systemic power and privilege in relation to differences, such as class, race, gender, and disability. At Parks, this was not the case, and practitioners routinely wrestled deeply with issues of race, class, and disability.
2. Admittedly, making choices about how and when to identify a person's race/ethnicity is fraught with complexity (see Pollock, 2004). As will be clear in this book, it is my perspective that race/ethnicity shapes our experiences on many levels, in much more complex ways than we have language to describe. I have chosen here to identify individuals by race/ethnicity the first time they are introduced in this book, yet not encumber the writing with repeated reminders to the reader.

3. A majority of the faculty and staff at Parks had been with the school since its earliest years. Of the 17 staff members who were either teachers or administrators, 11 had arrived within the first four years of the school's inception. Only one teacher was a new hire. The remaining four had been at Parks at least eight years.

4. Given that Parks subscribed to the school district's school-based management (SBM) program, the principal was not about to make this decision on her own. As the meeting progressed, several teachers commented on the travesty that SBM represented because in reality, and given the many contractual items that were not negotiable, the school personnel had little leeway in deciding how to spend their money.

5. The School Committee is the name some Quaker schools have for the group that serves as a Board of Trustees. Many Quaker schools, like City Friends, come under the care of one or more local Friends Meetings, which are responsible for running the school and appoint some members to the School Committee.

6. Before 1995, City Friends had no middle school division. Sixth grade had been part of the elementary school, and the seventh and eighth grades had been part of the high school.

7. By the 2002–2003 school year, when I conducted follow-up research, the athletic department had added soccer and softball as options for girls—options that appeared to attract more students of color.

## Chapter 2

1. In *Brown II*, the Supreme Court stepped back from demanding that equal and integrated schooling become a reality across the land (*Brown v. Board of Education II*, 1955; see Bell, 2004; Ladson-Billings, 2004).

2. Although Tom Whitman stated that this decision was made in 1961, other members of the community claimed it was made earlier. In fact, 1961 was the year a rival private school moved to the plot of land first offered City Friends.

3. It is critical to note here that in a classroom integrated across different types of differences, the Socratic seminar might not work to invite all students' participation. The centrality of text and analytic argument might, in turn, exclude some other children.

4. Integrationist ideals are not supported by all in the disability-rights community. For example, advocates for hearing-impaired often argue that integration amounts to cultural annihilation and does not serve the interests of the deaf community.

5. There were only two teachers whom I did not have a chance to interview.

## Chapter 3

1. This is a different standard for measuring educational equity from, for example, standards used in many court cases that determined whether districts had attained unitary status regarding racial integration. In court cases, equity was usually measured in terms of whether facilities had been racially integrated, rather than by assessing the quality of educational outcomes for students (Bell, 1995).

2. Note how this differs from the arguments that allowed for the rescission of desegregation orders, which relied on saying that it was only past discrimination that needed to have been ended, not that current inequalities had to be remedied.

3. According to school documents, content standards were defined as "information or skills specific to a particular discipline or content domain." Curriculum standards were defined as "the goals of classroom instruction, the means to achieve the content standards."

4. During the 1995–96 academic year, 41.8% of Parks's students scored at or above basic proficiency in reading, 17.5% in math, and 9.0% in science; 37.7% of students scored in the lowest quarter in math and 49.3% in reading. Even as many practitioners expressed a healthy dose of skepticism about the ecological validity of these standardized tests, they were troubled by these and other assessments of students' academic performances.

5. Many authors also caution about the danger of assimilationist stances toward education, calling into question dominant practices of schooling (Delpit, 1986; Ladson-Billings, 1994; Hale, 2001).

# Chapter 4

1. Bingham (2001) argues that multiple perspectives on recognition can be addressed in educational settings, of which public recognition of group identity is one.
2. Discussing the experiences of Indigenous students at Ivy League institutions, Brayboy (2004) has pointed out that visibility may not always be desirable because of the ways that dominant narratives about American Indians serve to marginalize and oppress; he argues that invisibility may be a fruitful resistance strategy.
3. In other interviews, Julia and at least one white female senior expressed similar concerns about the lack of curriculum that felt relevant to their lives as Puerto Ricans and girls, respectively.
4. These offerings included more traditional canon courses such as Shakespeare and Great British novels, a number of creative writing courses in different genres, and courses in contemporary fiction such as gay literature, African literature, and women immigrants' experiences.
5. During their junior year, the advanced section had six girls in a total of 21 students. At the beginning of their senior year, another female student joined the class. A few months into the year, one girl left the course.
6. This view would change, interestingly, as a result of the gender survey of all students in the school, which was conducted during this same year. The survey showed that the majority of young women who stuck with math throughout their high school tenure reported not liking the subject. By their junior and senior years, almost 70% of girls reported math to be their weakest subject.
7. In an interview, this young woman told me she was asked to leave the advanced course. Administrators told me she had chosen to drop it.
8. Across the school, African-American female faculty often felt their authority similarly challenged by white students. In many classrooms, I observed a marked difference between the ways some white students treated their African-American female teachers, displaying challenges to their authority that I did not see when I observed those same students in the classes of white teachers or male African-American teachers. Speaking of one of her challenging students, another African-American female teacher explained, "I wonder how many black teachers has [this student] had? Does she equate me with her housekeeper?"
9. Willis (1995), for example, discusses calculus reform efforts in Australia that reflect such an approach to transforming mathematics in relationship to gender equity.
10. In many ways, this argument echoes conservative commentators like Elisabeth Lasch-Quinn (2001), who uses the language of "black rage," "harangues," and "racial dogma" to dismiss the ongoing legacy of racism on schools and society.

# Chapter 5

1. Children who are insulin-dependent are at risk of low blood sugars with exercise and must be monitored carefully during activity. In a school with a strong commitment to having children learn to be unsupervised on the playground, this was a huge demand because teachers used the students' outdoor time as time to plan or set up for classroom activities.
2. John Dewey wrote in a similar vein of the moral equality of all humans being located in what he called the "incommensurability" of all human work (1922/1966).

# Appendix

1. At Parks, I was unable to interview the vice-principal and one social studies teacher who was absent the day that his team did a focus group. I interviewed 12 teachers, the librarian, the counselor, and the principal.

# Index